To Henry Stewart Fothringham,
published three years ago, this
true story of Sir William
Stewart's fabulous and lusty
life. I hope he does'nt
mind being so exposed.
Mae Reed Porter,
Nov. 9-'66

Scotsman in Buckskin

SCOTSMAN
IN BUCKSKIN

Sir William Drummond Stewart
and the Rocky Mountain Fur Trade

By MAE REED PORTER and ODESSA DAVENPORT

ॐ HASTINGS HOUSE, PUBLISHERS · *New York* 22

Contents

List of Illustrations

Dust Jacket:
Attack by Crow Indians—oil by Alfred Jacob Miller
 owned by Stewart Fothringham, Murthly

Between pages 148 and 149

William Drummond Stewart in dress uniform
   Courtesy Mae Reed Porter
Stewart armorial bearings
   Courtesy Mae Reed Porter
Sir William Drummond Stewart
   Courtesy Mae Reed Porter
Grandtully Castle
   Courtesy Mae Reed Porter
Lord Stewart
   Courtesy M. Knoedler Co., New York
Lady Stewart
   Courtesy Mae Reed Porter

Preface

§◆ The brief, tumultuous span of years between 1832 and 1844 saw the fur trade of the Far West reach its frenzied crest, then subside to a trickle that soon disappeared. It saw the beginning of the decimation of the thronging black herds of buffalo. It saw proud tribal chieftains of prairie and mountain sense the cruel truth that they, their people, and their way of life were doomed. It saw the first sheeted wagons of the emigrant trains roll across the continent to the valleys of California and Oregon.

These epic times were the back-drop for the flashing passage of a man who was the most colorful, and at the same time the most enigmatic, man the Far West ever saw. He came to America as Captain William Stewart, second son of one of the oldest and wealthiest noble families of Scotland. Twelve years later, when he left America for the last time, he had become, by right of succession, Sir William Drummond Stewart, owner of Grandtully and Murthly castles, twenty miles distant from each other on the River Tay in Perthshire, with their immense lands and vast revenues.

People who have happily fallen under the spell of the Old West often speculate as to what motivated Sir William's many contradictory acts, which of course sprang from equally contradictory facets of his complex character.

What manner of man was he? they ask. What is the real story of his adventures in America? What was the manner of his life before he deliberately subjected himself to the dangers and hardships of a land so alien to his native Perthshire? What did he do in the years that followed his final departure from our shores? Until now, no one has attempted to give more than a fragmentary answer to these questions.

The story of Sir William Drummond Stewart has not been an easy one to piece together. Its threads stretched through countries thousands of miles apart, and were entangled in cultures as far removed from each other as the courts of Europe, life in the capitals of Asia, and the councils of the Shoshone Indians in the Wind River Mountains.

It is an over-simplification to say that he was torn between three widely divergent worlds, all of which he loved and for short periods tried to combine: the world of military order and discipline, the world of luxury and high position, the world of adventure and danger. However, the thought may serve as a clue leading to some comprehension of the man and what he did.

The life Sir William led before going to America could be recreated in considerable detail from family letters, periodicals, legal documents, and the folk tales of today's Scottish countryside.

The story of his life on the prairies and among the mountains of the Far West appears as bright bits scattered through journals, diaries, newspaper articles, and books written by his companions on the trail. These narrative gems are like the bright stones embedded in the blue clay of the Kimberly mines. Dug out and assembled in orderly fashion, they make a spirited story, sparkling with lively color.

On his first expedition into the Far West with a fur caravan, he was limited in his expenditures, having at his disposal only the half-pay of a retired captain in the British Army, and a meager income from a small amount of money left to him by his father and doled out to him by his older brother, then holder of the title. Even under these cramping circumstances he managed to provide himself with blooded horses, London-made guns, and elegant clothing, all of which astonished beyond measure the rough trappers in their greasy buckskins.

Later, his situation improved. On his final trip, after he had succeeded to the title and estates of the family, he went into the wilderness with what very nearly amounted to the pomp and circumstance of an Eastern potentate.

But these trappings of luxury told less than half the story. He shared with the humblest packer the hardships imposed by the conditions of the life. He rode through hail, wind, cold, and drenching rain without complaint. He helped to provide meat for his fellow travelers by means of his superb marksmanship. He avoided no duty, no experience, regardless of how arduous or dangerous it might be. The directors of the fur companies' trains, the gay young blades who went along for fun, the packers, the camp cooks, all respected Sir William. They conferred on him their highest accolade when they said, "He has the hair of the b'ar in him."

Returning at last to his castles and the responsibilities of his position as 19th Lord of Grandtully and 7th Baronet of Murthly, he gathered there all of the Far West that he loved that it was possible to transport across the thousands of intervening miles.

There he entertained the noble families of Scotland and England in royal style. And often his mind must have strayed from those courtly and decorous scenes to the wild saturnalia of the rendezvous on Green River, or to hump ribs eaten by the campfire in the Wind River Mountains.

Storm and stress continued to surround him here in the peaceful valley of the Tay. Sir William Drummond Stewart would always be waging battles that ended now in victory, now in defeat. His life was a series of stirring campaigns conducted by a valiant warrior.

                                                                Odessa Davenport

CHAPTER I

Lieutenant Stewart at Waterloo

෫෨ Dawn came slowly, held back by thick clouds. Rain fell on sodden fields of recently planted corn and wheat, on grasslands and woods, as it had been doing all the previous night. The place, a broken, rolling plain between the Belgian cities of Dinant and Mons, not far from an insignificant village named Waterloo. The date, June 18, 1815.

Wellington's troops began to stir after miserable hours of darkness passed without shelter, standing in deep, soupy mud. They found dry wood in the near-by forest of Soignes, built campfires to warm themselves by, and were given a makeshift breakfast. Scottish pipers played stirring pibrochs. Sporadically there sounded the roll of drums, quickly broken off, the blare of an occasional trumpet. Napoleon's troops remained silent, without perceptible movement, having neither food nor access to firewood. Monotonously, the rain continued to fall.

Lieutenant William Stewart, of the 15th King's Hussars, cold and wet to the skin, was not depressed by the rigors of the situation; he was vastly impatient to begin the battle that was to be fought that day. Hardship was not new to him: he had served under Arthur Wellesley, recently made Duke of Wellington, through the final cold, starving, bloody struggle of the Peninsular War. He lacked six months of being twenty years old.

1

Lieutenant Stewart's military bearing made him appear taller than his five feet, eleven inches. His dark brown hair and blue eyes were well-suited to the ruddy English coloring of his face, which showed a maturity beyond his years. His straight, prominent nose gave him a faint resemblance to Wellington, one of the handsomest men in the British Isles. This fact, not unnoticed by his fellow-officers, brought embarrassingly waggish comments.

Due to Wellington's plan of waiting for the French forces to attack first, hours of inaction went by while Napoleon deployed his army. About nine o'clock the weather began to clear. At eleven-thirty French soldiers fired on British troops stationed around Hougoumont and the battle had begun.

Richard Ryder, William Stewart's servant since boyhood, brought the lieutenant's horse, a fine gray animal bred in Scotland. Colonel Sir Colquohoun Grant, commanding the 5th Light Cavalry Brigade, which included the 15th King's Hussars, gave the order to mount. Colonel Grant had been the lieutenant's superior officer in several battles of the Peninsular War, concluded only a few months before.

The soldiers under Colonel Grant moved off, but not into action, as Lieutenant Stewart had hoped. Instead, Colonel Grant led his men by a roundabout way to a spot near the conjunction of the Nivelles-Wavre roads and disposed them where they were hidden from the enemy behind steep banks. They waited, hearing the uproar of battle as it advanced and retreated, advanced again: the shouts of men and blaring of trumpets, cannon fire, the screams of wounded horses, fusillades of musketry. Tension mounted. Hours passed. The men of the 15th King's Hussars began to mutter among themselves. Lieutenant Stewart held himself rigidly erect on his horse, as became a veteran soldier, but the waiting grew almost intolerable.

Colonel Grant rode up and informed his young officer that orders had come from the command post in the rear. A French troop consisting of ten squadrons of Pire's Lancers was moving to attack an English regiment directly in front of where the 5th Light Cavalry was stationed. As soon as the Lancers appeared, he would give the order to charge.

Lieutenant Stewart alerted his men. They waited, holding

in check their restless horses, excited by the uproar of battle, the
smell of gun smoke. The French Lancers came in sight, moving
rapidly. Lieutenant Stewart raised his sword and led his Hussars
in a charge that wiped out the first wave of Lancers almost to a
man, with but few losses among the British. Lieutenant Stewart
and his men rode back to the commanding officer.

Colonel Grant met the lieutenant with a bleak look of displeasure. Why, he demanded, had his young officer charged without specific orders to do so? Only then did Stewart realize that
he had not received actual orders to take his men into action. The
offense was a serious one in Wellington's army, and he knew that,
if it was brought to the Duke's attention, his punishment would
be severe, regardless of the extenuating circumstances.

Another wave of Pire's Lancers appeared. Now Colonel Grant
shouted the order to charge. Lieutenant Stewart led foray after
foray until the opposing enemy forces at that point were virtually
wiped out.

The incident made a deep impression on Lieutenant Stewart.
Wellington was his hero, and the Duke held his troops under tight
discipline. Any infractions, either by officers or men, resulted in
swift and, some thought, unreasonably severe punishment. Stewart,
however, never questioned their justice; he agreed with Wellington
that an army without discipline was no army at all. His deep concern as to what his punishment would be was made sharper by
the anguished self-condemnation only youth can know.

As it turned out, the young lieutenant Stewart received no
punishment whatever—not even a reprimand, other than the
rebuke administered to him on the battlefield. There could have
been only one reason for this. His commanding officer did not report the incident to headquarters. Colonel Grant, while at Olite
during the Peninsular War, had found himself in serious trouble
with Wellington over some small irregularity of military conduct
and had been deeply humiliated by the Commander-in-Chief,
and the memory of this painful episode may have made Grant
reluctant to inflict an experience of similar nature on the young
officer whose only fault had been excessive zeal in the performance
of his duty.

The battle went on with increasing fury as the opposing com-

manders brought up their reserves. At last the French were driven
back. As twilight deepened into night the French gave way, retreated. Napoleon's last bid for power had ended in defeat.

Soon after Lieutenant Stewart's return home he was awarded
the Waterloo Medal, a decoration given only for exceptional bravery during this last stand against the threat of the Little Corporal.
The medal, made of silver, hung from a black and red ribbon. On
the obverse side appeared the head of the Prince Regent, who
afterward became George IV, and on the reverse side, the head of
Wellington and an eagle. Underneath that were the words: *Waterloo, June 18, 1815*; around the edge was inscribed, *Lieutenant W.
Stewart, 15th King's Hussars.*

Even this mark of grateful recognition bestowed on him by
the Prince Regent could not wipe from his mind the memory of
his one lapse from military duty, made even though it was in the
excitement and stress of battle. It influenced him throughout his
life, causing him to obey implicitly any order given him by recognized authority and to demand, with Wellingtonian harshness,
complete obedience to orders issued by him. This trait of attach-
ing great importance to obedience to orders, both given and received, also may have been to some extent an inheritance from the
long line of William Stewart's ancestors, extending back into the
13th century. These men were for the most part fiercely loyal and
obedient to their rulers, and in turn demanded unquestioning obedience from the people they ruled.

The facts concerning William Stewart's birth and early life
are available in existing records at Murthly Castle and Edinburgh,
and in the archives of the British War Office. Born at Murthly
Castle, Perthshire, Scotland, December 26, 1795, he was the second
son of Sir George Stewart, 17th Lord of Grandtully, Fifth Baronet
of Murthly, and of Catherine, eldest daughter of Sir John Drummond of Logiealmond, a cadet of the Earls of Perth.

William's older brother, John, also born at Murthly Castle,
entered this world October 25, 1794. There also were three younger
brothers, George, Thomas and Archibald. All played more or less
important roles in William Stewart's life.

There were also two sisters, Catherine and Clementina. After
a brief notation of Clementina's birth and a casual reference in

one of her mother's letters, her name does not appear in any family document. Catherine, the older sister, was an amiable child who grew up to be a nice young lady who, as far as can be ascertained, roused no antagonisms in this family that developed some really fierce ones as the years passed. She married a Frenchman and lived on the Continent. Beyond an occasional letter, of interest only to the family, no knowledge of her remains.

The two castles, Murthly and Grandtully, with their large estates, and the lands of Strathbraan extending to the south, formed the background of William Stewart's life. Even during the years he was absent in America they, along with the family, must have been a pervading presence, never entirely out of his mind. More than once he tried to break away, but each time he was drawn back, until at last he knew that the ancient pull would hold him there as long as his life should last.

Most of William's boyhood was spent at Murthly Castle, a beautiful example of 17th-century architecture. It was not built in the manner of the older castles, as fortresses against the robber barons of the Highlands, but as the home of a nobleman. It stood —and still stands—on the south bank of the lovely Tay River, with a mile-wide stretch of greensward between it and the placidly flowing stream. During William's boyhood and youth, this lawn was mowed to velvet smoothness every three days. As a youngster, he played on famous Birnam Hill, not far from the castle, and climbed the two great gnarled trees, all that remained of Shakespeare's Birnam Wood.

In the grounds of Murthly Castle stood an ancient chapel dedicated to St. Anthony the Eremite. A wide pathway, bordered by dense trees, led to one of its entrances. This path was called the Deadwalk, because only funeral processions marched along its somber length, human feet treading its carpet of brown pine needles at no other time.

In the early part of the 18th century, the then Lord of Murthly, a kindly disposed man, decided to build a hospital for the sick and aged of his estate. The structure, a pleasant two-story building, even today almost modern in appearance, stands not far from the castle. On its completion in 1711, Sir John Stewart, the donor, placed £20,000 in a trust fund to be used for its maintenance.

To Sir John's great disappointment, his tenants refused the comforts of the hospital, preferring to be ill, and even die if need be, in their own homes. The building was later remodeled to serve as a hunting lodge, and rented to wealthy sportsmen from London and Edinburgh. At this time it was named Dalpowie, though people sometimes referred to it as the Hospital, or the Cottage.

Four miles in a northerly direction from the castle, a long, gracefully arched bridge spanned the Tay. It was built of stones taken from the ruins of a structure dating back to Roman times. Across the bridge lay the ancient village of Dunkeld, with its thatched one-story cottages, a tracery of ivy clinging to their walls and tiny dooryards bright with flowers.

About eighteen miles farther up the winding Tay, grim old Grandtully Castle reared its nine-foot-thick stone walls with their small, irregularly placed windows. It offered safety, but little comfort, to those who occupied it during the danger days of long ago. Built in 1560, it was preceded by a castle erected in 1414, of which only scant ruins now remain. One of its narrow, winding stairways leads to a small room on the third floor where, legend has it, Bonnie Prince Charlie once sheltered. A quarter of a mile away stood Old St. Mary's Chapel, a long, low, barnlike ancient structure, built while the first Grandtully was occupied. Here, many of the Stewarts lie buried in narrow lead coffins. Grandtully, like Murthly, overlooked the Tay, but at Grandtully the river flowed in a northwesterly direction for a little while, then turned to pursue a more southerly course that led away from the craggy, forbidding scenery of the Highlands.

William's father had graduated from Oxford University, but the son was educated at home by tutors. His career was decided for him—he was to go into the army. William appears to have made no objection to this plan. In a letter written by his mother when he was about ten years old, she states that he is a good boy and doing well in fractions. When he was a little older, Richard Ryder, a young man-servant at Murthly who was to serve him throughout his military career, occasionally took William to Edinburgh to see the sights of that great city. He must have been deeply impressed by Edinburgh Castle, that massive fortress built on a huge up-thrust of solid rock. It dominated the city, standing

high and forbidding above the beautiful Princes Street Gardens
that bordered it on one side.

Once in a while, when illness disrupted family life at Murthly,
Catherine Stewart would send one or more of her brood to Logiealmond, not far away. There they would be cared for by Catherine's
two spinster sisters, Frances Marie and Elizabeth, and the housekeeper, Mrs. Gilchrist, until the emergency passed. Long after
William was grown, he remembered those visits with his aunts,
recalled walking along a frightening sunken corridor, smelling the
pleasant scent of burning peat and toasted oat cakes.

The religious affiliations of the Stewart family during the time
William was growing up are obscure. Apparently they were at
least nominal Catholics, though none of them seems to have taken
churchly matters with any great seriousness. Afterward, individual
members of the Stewart clan developed strong feelings for and
against the Catholic Church, which resulted in considerable conflict. The two chapels, Old St. Mary's at Grandtully and St. Anthony the Eremite's at Murthly, were more and more neglected
and eventually fell into serious disrepair.

William's mother, Catherine, took more interest in the details of running the three estates, with their aggregate of over
32,000 acres, and looking after its people than did his father. He
sometimes went off for long periods of time, spending months at
Grandtully, or in Edinburgh, or, rather oddly, at Logiealmond,
Catherine's home before she married him. William's parents seem
to have been on friendly enough terms, but there was something
less than a grand passion about their relationship.

His father sometimes took a hand in estate matters and issued
orders that displeased his mother. In one letter she scolded him
sternly for having removed an old woman from the cottage where
she had lived for many years and arranged for her to lodge else-
where. "I cannot bear cruelty to poor harmless people," she chided
him. It must have been from her that William inherited his deep
feeling of protectiveness toward people in his care.

A not unimportant member of the Stewart household at
Murthly Castle was a four-foot dwarf named James Anderson and
known as "the Fool of Murthly," one of whose duties was to act
in the role of a medieval jester. He seems to have been a man

of considerable intelligence, possessing only the usual eccentric-
ities to be expected of a person of his diminutive stature whose
position was that as a servant at one moment, an impudent,
privileged jester the next. The family, the servants at Murthly,
and the villagers of Dunkeld called him Jamie.

This strange, misshapen little man had short legs and large
feet, spraddled like those of a fowl. Yet he made love to the maids
and, if legends still told in Dunkeld be true, they were not averse
to his attentions. Besides being expected to entertain his betters
with exciting stories and clever quips, he made himself useful
opening gates with a flourish for titled visitors, of whom there were
many, collecting the eggs, and riding to Dunkeld on a white mule
to post letters. Members of the family, as well as visitors, sometimes gave him small sums of money.

Jamie held his position as an honored retainer of the Stewart
family for many years. When he finally died, banknotes totaling
more than £300 were found in his room, hidden under old candle
ends and aging newspapers; and the pockets of his clothes yielded
£126 more.

The irreconcilable hatred that was to develop between William and his brother John when they became adults no doubt
had its roots in their boyhood. They were both educated at home,
which forced them to be much together. William, proud and
fiercely independent, would hardly have been human had he not
violently resented his inferior position in relation to John, the
oldest son. John, arrogant, acutely conscious from his earliest years
of wealth and material possessions, probably overlooked few opportunities to lord it over William. The estate was entailed: John
would someday succeed to the titles, become owner of the two
castles, the recognized head of the family, and the recipient of a
rich revenue. The best William could reasonably look forward to
was a career in the army, with perhaps a pittance doled out to him
at his older brother's pleasure.

George, next in line after William for the title and its ap-
purtenances, cared nothing whatsoever about either money or position. Since he was a member of the Stewart family, his simple
needs would always be provided for in some fashion. He was good-
natured, kindly, not too bright; he always saw the best in every-

one, even an obvious rascal, and he wanted only peace—a commodity hard to come by in and around the Stewart clan.

Thomas, a dark, handsome lad, the fourth son and therefore with no reasonable hope of ever inheriting the title, early showed a leaning toward Catholicism—at least, toward what Catholicism had to offer in the way of power and prestige. Long before any member of his family was aware of it, he may have entertained dreams of becoming a Prince of the Church, a position for which his brilliant intellect and consuming ambition eminently fitted him.

Archibald, the youngest, was a sharp-featured, puny boy who hoarded the small coins that came his way, spending them reluctantly on items that would give him personal pleasure. He liked to play mean little practical jokes, to frighten the maids, and to trap young rabbits in the woods. The few times that members of the family, other than his mother, mentioned him in their letters to each other, it was always disparagingly. He seems to have been an extraordinarily unpleasant child who not surprisingly grew up to be an extraordinarily unpleasant man.

Taking everything into consideration, William's boyhood life at Murthly must have been a fairly unhappy and frustrated one. In his seventeenth year it became possible for him to escape from it, having then reached the age of military service.

Shortly after his birthday, which was the day after Christmas, 1812, he asked his father to buy him a cornetcy—the lowest military rank in a crack English regiment at that time—in the famous and fashionable 6th Dragoon Guards. His father did so, at a cost of £735.

Let no one be misled by the fact that membership in the finest English regiments could be had only by purchase, and at what seems today like a fancy price. Their personnel was of the highest quality and they were unexcelled as fighting units. William's appointment was confirmed on April 15, 1813. He immediately joined his regiment and began rigorous training.

The Peninsular War, which had been going on in Spain and Portugal since 1808, was being stepped up in intensity by popular demand. William hoped he would see service soon on the Iberian Peninsula. There was also a war going on between Britain and the United States, but William had no hope of taking part in that

conflict. After the first few months, during which American troops
had taken on the Canadian fighting men and come off second
best, the two countries had decided to let their navies do most of
the fighting, which at the time William started his military career
they were busily engaged in doing.

Almost a year went by. Then came news of the battle of
Vitoria. This engagement took place June 21, 1813, in the north-
eastern part of Spain, two or three days' march from the Pyrenees.
The English victory won there was considered so important, and
so brilliantly achieved that the Prince Regent gratefully presented
Wellington with the baton of a Field Marshal. The 15th King's
Hussars was also signally honored. This regiment, which had seen
service in Portugal and Spain since 1812 and was now commended
for its gallantry, already had a reputation for fine marksmanship
that was unexcelled in the British Army. These facts were doubtless
noted by the young cornet, impatient to see action.

However, almost six months passed after Vitoria before William could do anything about his situation. On the 22nd of December he made application to Colonel Dalrymple, the officer
commanding Dundalk Barracks, for an appointment to a lieutenancy in the 15th King's Hussars, regiment of Light Dragoons. No
records have come to light stating what his father paid for this
appointment, but the appointment was confirmed by the War
Office on January 6, 1814. It is safe to assume that Lieutenant
Stewart asked for immediate active service, and that shortly after
that date he was sent to Spain and joined Wellington's army.
This army was now pressing hard, through exceptionally bad
weather, toward Wellington's objective, that of forcing the French
troops out of Spain and to ultimate defeat on their own soil.

CHAPTER II

War, Peace and Marriage

Sir Wm was NOT in the Peninsular at all.

꧁ Losing no time joining his regiment in Spain, Lieutenant
Stewart probably arrived in late January 1814, disembarking at the
port of San Sebastian on the Bay of Biscay. Wellington's troops
were uncomfortably waiting out the harsh Iberian winter in barracks slightly east of Vitoria, the scene of their brilliant victory
the year before. Here Lieutenant Stewart, for the first time in his
life, experienced real hardship. Though Wellington was impatient
to start, alternate snow and rain made the roads impassable and
kept his army immobilized. The barracks that housed his soldiers
were unheated, ramshackle structures, infested with rats, bats and
even less pleasant members of the animal kingdom. Food was
poor, scarce, sometimes nonexistent.

Lieutenant Stewart left no account of the hardships of English
army life that winter, but others did. Quartermaster-General—also
Major-General in Wellington's army—Sir Benjamin D'Urban became quite specific on the subject in his journal. Sir Benjamin,
a dressy gentleman—in one portrait of him there hangs about his
thin neck and is pinned on his narrow chest an astonishing number
of large jeweled decorations—described the situation in which
Wellington's army found itself in these forthright words:

11

An advance into France will soon take place and the cavalry is accordingly brought up from the Valleys of the Ebro and the Agra. Mine has been so starved by the villainous arrangements of the Commissariat that I must go to it and get it in such order as may make it disposable. Troops are passing a very severe winter, not only in Barracks which for the better part, do not shelter them from the winter, but altogether (in many instances) destitute of Blankets, Matresses, or any article of Barrack furniture. My reiterated representations turned over to the Marshall, to the Minister of War, and Col. Fave, produced no results.

An elegant-looking German gentleman—as shown in a self-portrait—named August Ludwig Friedrich Schaumann, the Deputy Assistant Commissary General of the British Army, painted a water-color picture of his own quarters, which were no doubt very like those occupied by Lieutenant Stewart. It shows Schaumann huddled uncomfortably in a hammock slung between rough walls. A number of huge rats are scampering over the floor, while one rodent chews jauntily on one of August's boots. Bats flit about. A large owl and a yellow-green moon peer malevolently in through an unglazed window.

The conditions of life that surrounded Lieutenant Stewart on his arrival in Spain were a far cry from the stately luxury of Murthly Castle, and even from the comfortable English barracks of the 15th King's Hussars. However, since he said to a companion many years later that he liked something to contend against, he no doubt found some elements of pleasure in the situation.

About the middle of March an unusually cold spell froze the mud of the roads and Wellington was able to move his troops forward toward their next major objective, the French port of Bayonne, some fifteen or twenty miles beyond the Spanish border. To reach it, the army had to march inland through several Spanish provinces in order to avoid crossing the River Nive, which was short but unfordable for the greater part of its length. Lieutenant Stewart's commanding officer was Sir Colquhoun Grant, and his forces saw considerable action on the march, as the retreating French general, Soult, kept up a series of strong rear-guard delaying tactics with many casualties on both sides.

Rain began again and continued without cessation. At last they reached Bayonne, where the Adour pours its waters into the sea. At this point the river is 800 yards wide, with a strong, almost violent current. Wellington sent a contingent of troops to distract Soult, then dispatched the main body of his men about three miles upstream, where the river narrowed to 500 yards. There his engineers constructed a pontoon bridge of unusual design and by this means he got his troops across the river. Lieutenant Stewart fought in battle after battle as Wellington pushed forward. Soult retreated only when forced to do so. Casualties were shockingly heavy on both sides, but the British suffered far the heavier losses of the two. Wellington was pressing for victory and meant to have it quickly, no matter the cost. He urged his troops forward.

On April 10, Lieutenant Stewart found himself in the thick of the battle as Wellington attacked Toulouse. After two days of the fiercest fighting, Soult evacuated the city. On the 18th an agreement to lay down arms was signed. The Peninsular War was over.

Wellington returned to England almost immediately, leaving to his officers the task of getting the British Army out of Spain and France, a process that encountered long delays. Lieutenant Stewart was fortunate. His regiment was marched almost at once across France to the Channel and there shipped to England.

Arriving at London, he embarked with his men for the town of Dundalk, on the east coast of Ireland. Soon they were back in Dundalk Barracks, headquarters of the 15th King's Hussars, and at least the simple comforts of peace. Lieutenant Stewart had served three months of the hardest kind of military action, filled with almost continuous warfare, and had come through without even a minor wound. Since his regiment was noted for its marksmanship, the young lieutenant had plenty of training in accurate shooting, and competition as well, a circumstance that accounted for his outstanding prowess along that line when he reached the Far West.

Months went by. Peace seemed to have settled on England and the Continent. Napoleon had been a prisoner on the Island of Elba, believed to be escape-proof, for almost a year. Lieutenant Stewart was getting fed up with the monotony of life at Dundalk Barracks.

Then, on the first of March, news that Napoleon had landed

on the Continent spread like the reverberations of a vast explosion. On the 20th he was at the Tuileries. Soldiers flocked to his banner. The people of France loudly proclaimed their loyalty to him and to the national dream he symbolized.

The military might of Britain and Prussia was galvanized into action. Wellington resumed supreme command of the army. On April 8, 1815, the 15th King's Hussars, along with many other regiments, embarked for Ostend. At daybreak four days later, the harbor of that Belgian city was so crowded with ships bearing troops, horses, guns, and all sorts of supplies, that one or two ran ashore. Disembarking amid what seemed utter confusion, Wellington produced order out of the chaos. Lieutenant Stewart rode with his regiment across Belgium to Ghent, on to Brussels, then to the field of Waterloo, arriving there some time during the cold and rain-drenched night of June 17.

Waiting sleeplessly for the dawn, Lieutenant Stewart's thoughts must have been heavy with foreboding as to what the coming day might bring to him, to England, to the world. The stakes were beyond computation. What happened to him has already been told. The result for England and for the world is history.

After Waterloo, Lieutenant Stewart returned to his barracks at Dundalk. Life there went on as before, broken by an occasional leave of absence that enabled him to visit London, where the Stewart family kept a smart town house at 77 Eaton Place, to enjoy the social delights of Edinburgh, or—if nothing better offered —to stay for a while at Murthly.

His future as a soldier began to look very dull to him. Napoleon was safe on the Island of St. Helena, a lonely and helpless prisoner, suffering from an incurable disease. There was peace between England and the United States. Like many another young man who has fought in violent and bloody campaigns, Lieutenant Stewart became restless and discontented. No doubt he saw the handwriting on the wall which foretold the inevitable reduction in military forces that comes with peace. His mind turned to visions of travel. He longed to see strange countries, exotic peoples, bizarre customs.

In spite of his sometimes unconventional actions, Lieutenant Stewart had a practical side to his nature and to his way of thinking. He had been a lieutenant for six years. Before his retirement from the army came about, either voluntarily or involuntarily, he determined to improve his condition. Just how he managed it is not known, but on June 12, 1820, Lord Lyndoch, a powerful Scottish nobleman, wrote a letter to Major General Sir Hubert Taylor, K.C.B., etc., asking that Lieutenant William Stewart, the son of his neighbor, Sir George Stewart of Grandtully, be considered for promotion to the rank of captain.

Remarkably prompt action ensued, leaving the impression that the whole matter had already been arranged. The London War Office records show that on June 15 the promotion became official. A significant notation says that Lieutenant Stewart was traveling on a leave of absence at the time he was elevated to a captaincy. In October of the following year, the 15th King's Hussars was disbanded and Captain Stewart was retired at half-pay, which amounted to the undeniably meager sum, even by the standards of that time, of seven shillings, six farthings a day, or about one dollar and five cents by present values.

For several years following 1821, Captain Stewart's movements and activities can be traced only dimly and to some extent by inference, though the implication is almost inescapable. One valuable source of information is the collection of family letters preserved in the archives of Edinburgh. Others, just as tangible but less explicit, we shall come to later. He spent some time in London, leading the life of a fashionable young man, attending parties, balls, court functions, riding horseback in the park. Occasionally he was at Murthly, or making brief visits to his aunts at Logiealmond, living in their ancient castle, which they let fall into a ruinous state rather than change one of its—to them—sacred stones. He traveled and hunted extensively in Turkey, Russia and other countries of the East. There are indications that he spent considerable time in the major cities of Italy and of Portugal. What he did there we do not know, but on his return to England he brought with him four decorations presented to him in gratitude for his services. One was a Maltese Cross of red enamel, now lost, though a picture of it remains. Another was the Order of Christ of Portugal, red and white enamel, with a large pin so it could be worn on a coat or cape. Then there were two medals, resembling coins, in a velvet box, presented to him by the Pope. Since the families of both his father and mother had long records in the diplomatic service, it may be concluded that these decorations were awarded in recognition for achievements in that field.

In 1827 Captain Stewart's father, Sir George Stewart, died, and the title, castles and estates went, of course, to John, the property being entailed and therefore not subject to distribution by Sir George. From his private fortune, Captain Stewart's father left him the sum of £3,000, but with the provision that John should control and manage it, paying the interest to his younger brother. This disposition of the father's estate, in so far as William was concerned, shows how the family felt about Captain Stewart. They saw him as an erratic, unsettled seeker for adventure, and not to be trusted to act sensibly in financial matters, as steady, stay-at-home John would be sure to do. It was a serious miscalculation, as John was to prove later on.

Captain Stewart was, understandably, outraged at this action of his father's. Before this time, Sir George apparently had seen to it that William had enough money to do pretty much as he pleased, but now William was dependent on John's whims, even in regard to the money the younger brother considered rightfully his. The bitterness already existing between the two brothers increased. Nor did the people on Sir John's estates entertain any great feeling of cordiality for their lord. An observation made at the time of Sir George's death by Jamie, the Fool of Murthly, has come down to the present day. Sir John presented Jamie with a new black kilt to wear to Sir George's funeral and the dwarf declared it was the most sensible thing he had ever known John to do.

Later in that same year, Catherine Stewart's brother, for whom Captain Stewart had been named, Sir William Drummond, died in Italy, where he was the British ambassador. He left the large and valuable estate of Logiealmond to Captain Stewart's mother, she being the next eldest in the Drummond family. It made her a very wealthy woman. There is little doubt that she was the source of most of the money spent by Captain Stewart for the next few years. The interest on his father's legacy and his officer's half-pay would hardly have covered his basic expenses. However, he never had enough money to permit of any really gaudy expenditures. He felt these monetary restrictions keenly and blamed John for his inability to travel as much as, or in the style, he wanted to.

He appears to have spent a good deal of his time in London. When the boredom of society life became intolerable, as it appears to have done at intervals, he went to Murthly, or visited his friends, Lord and Lady Breadalbane, whose home, Taymouth Castle, stood near where the River Tay emerged from Loch Tay. There are also accounts of his staying sometimes with Lord George Glenlyon, whose seat was near the village of Blair-Atholl, farther north on the swift River Till that flowed into the Tay. He probably did not spend much time at Murthly, in the proximity of John, the solid, stable head of the Stewart clan.

It probably was sometime in 1829 that Captain Stewart visited a near-by farm house belonging to his friends, the Atholls, who were connections of Lord Glenlyon. Here in the courtyard he saw an extraordinarily beautiful girl, her skirts tucked up until they barely covered her knees, and immediately William lost his head, if not his heart. A contemporary said, "He fell in love with her nether limbs when he saw her tromping blankets in a tub." The girl's name was Christina Stewart—no relation to the Stewart family—and she was working on the Atholl farm as a maid. Legends are still told by the villagers of Dunkeld concerning the beauty of her face and character. That the handsome Captain Stewart roused in Christina a full measure of love and devotion no one who reads her story can doubt.

Sometime in 1830 Christina bore Captain Stewart's son. The child was given the name of George, that of William's father and also his brother. Though no marriage between him and Christina had taken place, Captain Stewart seems from the first to have acknowledged the boy as his offspring. Three months after the child's birth, Captain Stewart and Christina were married in Edinburgh. The record says that little George was present at the ceremony "for purposes of legitimization." This was, of course, according to Scottish law. The official record gives the date of George's birth as sometime in 1829. Years later, when William had succeeded to the title, he superintended the compilation of two large tomes, the Red Book of Murthly, filled with family history. In this record he shifted the date of George's birth to about a year after his marriage to Christina.

No secret seems to have been made of this marriage, but it does not appear that Captain Stewart and Christina ever occupied the same house together. He established her and George in a modest apartment in Edinburgh, acknowledged her as his wife, visited her occasionally. He made sure that she and little George had whatever they needed, but Christina's wants were simple. It is said that he engaged a private tutor for her, but after consideration, she decided against any plan he may have had of making her over into a fine lady, preferring to remain as she was, a charming, capable woman who won the respect and admiration of everyone who knew her. As long as she lived she asked nothing of him, whether of money or companionship, other than what he gave her of his own initiative. Lovely Christina Stewart and her relationship with the adventurous Scottish nobleman she had married hold a touch of tantalizing mystery and of pathos that can rouse only conjecture and regret. Though of humble birth, Christina Stewart was an extraordinary woman with sturdy traits of loyalty and faithfulness.

On January 14, 1832, Sir John Stewart married Lady Jane Steuart, eldest daughter of Francis, Earl of Moray, an entirely suitable and proper alliance for the 18th Lord of Grandtully and Sixth Baronet of Murthly. Sir John and his lady honeymooned briefly and economically at Logiealmond, as guest of the spinster aunts, Frances Marie and Elizabeth, then took up their life at Murthly. If Captain Stewart had ever, even briefly, dreamed that he might some day come into the Stewart title and estates, he must have definitely given up the thought now. There would certainly be children born of this union, if for no reason other than to spite him, of that he would have felt sure.

Shortly after this marriage Captain Stewart and John quarreled so violently that the ancient walls of Murthly must have trembled, as well as the hearts of all those within hearing distance. What they quarreled about is not known, but there were plenty of bones to be picked: William's appallingly unsuitable marriage to Christina, John's habitual procrastination when it came to paying William the sums due him from his father's legacy, William's extravagances and proclivity for roaming. Goaded to a high state of fury by some especially barbed castigation from John, William declared that he would never again, as long as he lived, sleep beneath the roof of Murthly Castle. And he never did, though adherence to that vow caused him considerable inconvenience after he became master of Murthly.

Following this climactic quarrel with John, Captain Stewart's mind turned more and more toward travel and adventure. The social round in London palled. The thought of the United States and its Far West returned insistently, holding as it did a promise of new scenes, struggle and danger. Then, too, traveling there would cost less than journeying about the capitals of Europe and Asia, where he had to keep up the standards of his class.

Finally Captain Stewart reached a decision. He did not know exactly where his interest might take him on the North American continent, but to be prepared for any contingency, he asked for and received an introduction to several head men of the Hudson's Bay Company in Canada. According to papers in the archives of the Hudson's Bay Records Society, these letters were addressed to John Allan, Esquire, York, Toronto; Samuel Gerrard, Montreal; Governor Simpson; and the Chief Factors and Chief Traders, Hudson's Bay Company—in other words, to anyone of consequence in this great and powerful organization. This blanket introduction was to serve him in good stead when the time came.

It called for plenty of tongue-clucking and head-shaking when Captain Stewart's plans were revealed to his family. His marriage to Christina had been hard to take—another example of his tendency to break with tradition. An affair with a girl of her station would have occasioned little more than a shrug—so why marry her, even though there was a son? Now he was going to a land of strange wild animals, murderous savages, mountains and rivers so vast that the people of Perthshire could not even envisage them. But Captain Stewart went ahead with his preparations, unheeding, encouraged only by his friend, Lord Breadalbane, who seems to have been enthralled by the prospect of the adventures on which Captain Stewart was embarking.

William took with him a wardrobe of elegant clothes for city

wear, for he intended to stay several months in New York, then
go on to New Orleans and St. Louis. Just how he would make his
way to the Far West, time would reveal. He took with him two
Manton rifles, handmade by the Manton Brothers of London,
the finest rifles in the world. They cost him forty guineas each.
Only the best would do for this, the greatest hunting adventure
he would ever know.

After negotiations carried on through an attorney, Captain
Stewart finally received from John part of the money currently due
him from his father's legacy. In the early part of April he sailed for
New York. He was in his thirty-seventh year but eagerness for new
scenes and new experiences, for danger and adventure, burned in
him with a clear, undiminished flame.

Face to the West

→ Captain Stewart left Perthshire without, so far as it is known, the approval of a single member of his family. Their unpredictable adventurer was setting forth again, this time to the wilds of America, where he would almost surely come to some peculiarly horrifying end.

The gentle "leddies o' Logie," his aunts, his mother, and his kindly brother George mourned as for a kinsman already lost. Thomas, away on the Continent studying for the position of Cardinal which he hoped someday to attain, appears to have dismissed the matter as the kind of foolishness to be expected of William. John unleashed his acrimonious tongue at the folly of William's course, but felt relieved that an ocean and half a continent would soon separate him from his troublesome brother. Archibald couldn't have cared less.

Captain Stewart's ship made good time, crossing the Atlantic well under the normal span of sixty days. His first view of New York was doubtless depressing. The skyline of the city was nothing to rouse admiring comment, none of the buildings being more than four stories high. Short wharfs fringed the shore in a straggling line. The United States was a little more than fifty years old.

Nevertheless, here was the gateway to the land of high ad-

venture that began on the western bank of the Missouri River
and extended all the way to the shore of the Pacific. Part of this
land had been acquired in 1803 through the Louisiana Purchase,
but with the exception of a vast tract known as the Oregon Territory, none of it lay beyond the Rocky Mountains. Boundaries were
extremely vague and much of the country was still waiting for
the advent of the first white man. Here lay one of the last large,
almost unexplored temperate areas of the world.

A duller mind and imagination than Captain Stewart's would
have lifted at the sight of this drab-looking city on the tip of
Manhattan Island because of the bright promise of adventure
that lay beyond. Landing on the dock, he was whisked away in a
hired carriage through cobblestone streets to the City Hotel, the
finest lodging place New York had to offer. The building was a
four-story brick structure furnished in the red-plush-and-mahogany
fashion of the day.

He had been in New York only a few days when, quite by
accident, he met J. Watson Webb, one of the most influential
men in the city. A lasting friendship sprang up between them.
Webb belonged to a wealthy and distinguished New York family,
his father being General S. B. Webb, a friend of Washington and
Lafayette. Webb was only thirty-one when he and Captain Stewart
met but he had behind him ten years of army experience on the
western frontier and three years as editor of the two foremost New
York newspapers. The army background and a mutual love of the
Far West, of adventure and danger, formed a strong bond between
the two men. Webb was much impressed by the fact that Captain
Stewart had fought at Waterloo, and by his five medals.

J. Watson Webb's illustrious army career in the West and
the many friends he had made there enabled him to smooth the
pathway of his friend, Captain Stewart. Webb gave him letters of
introduction to that famous St. Louis resident, William Clark,
of the Lewis and Clark Expedition, formerly governor of Missouri,
now Superintendent of Indian Affairs; also to General William
Ashley, king of the fur trade; and to William Sublette and Robert
Campbell, young men who at that time headed the outfitting and
carrying division of the Rocky Mountain Fur Company. They
also were the bankers for that powerful and far-reaching enterprise.

Stewart's intention had been to go directly from New York to New Orleans by boat, then up the Mississippi to St. Louis. However, dispatches to Webb's newspapers announced that New Orleans was suffering from one of its recurrent cholera epidemics and Stewart, heeding the earnest admonitions of J. Watson Webb, decided to postpone his visit to that stricken city.

Reserving a small amount of thick, warm clothing, one blanket and a Manton rifle, he shipped the rest of his baggage to St. Louis by boat. Setting out on horseback, he rode in a northeasterly direction across New York State to Niagara Falls. Pausing long enough to take a good look at the majestic cataract, he resumed his journey westward through the thinly settled states of Ohio, Indiana, Illinois and Missouri. This was a jaunt of major proportions and one not to be undertaken lightly. Here it was that Captain Stewart got his first taste of wilderness life.

Beyond the western boundary of New York, taverns—even of the poorest kind—were rare. Stewart tried seeking food and shelter at the rude log cabins of occasional settlers, but after several experiences of trying to eat the unappetizing, carelessly prepared food offered him and of sleeping on dirt floors surrounded by farmers' children, he hit on another plan.

During the day he would shoot a brace of squirrels, or a few pigeons. As evening approached he dressed the game, roasted it before his campfire. When darkness fell, he rolled himself in his blanket and slept, his only shelter the branches of some sturdy tree.

The journey was long and arduous, but endurable to a man who had gone through a winter and spring of the Peninsular War. Arriving at last in St. Louis, Captain Stewart established himself at the city's finest hotel, the Mansion House, on the corner of Vine and Third streets, where his baggage awaited, having preceded him by several weeks. According to an advertisement in the St. Louis *Republican* at the time, this "tavern" contained "thirty-six comfortable and spacious lodging rooms, one dining room sixty-five feet by twenty-five feet, a bar room, sitting rooms, two kitchens, one spacious smoke house, etc."

Within a few days Captain Stewart called on Sublette and Campbell, presenting his letters of introduction from J. Watson Webb. These two men had recently returned from their trip to the summer rendezvous in the Rocky Mountains, bringing back the previous season's catch of beaver, plus a few skins of marten, otter and mink. Robert Campbell, not yet thirty years old and unmarried, lived in the city. William Sublette, a few years Campbell's senior, took keen interest and delight in his farm just outside St. Louis, where he raised fine stock, especially blooded horses.

These three men, differing widely in background, heritage and experience, were drawn together by the many qualities they possessed in common, among them a love of adventure, courage of the highest order, and an unwavering integrity. So strong were the ties formed between them that during the more than ten years of their association, they not only trusted each other with considerable sums of money, but with their lives as well.

When Captain Stewart called on William Clark, he did so at that gentleman's office and museum, which Clark had built in order to have a suitable place to receive his Indian friends. The museum occupied one large room. Here William Clark had assembled a priceless collection of Indian artifacts, many of them presented to him by chiefs and head men, each one the finest of its kind. There were feathered headdresses, porcupine quill-embroidered skin shirts, moccasins beaded in elaborate designs, intricately carved and decorated peace pipes made from the traditional red sandstone, and almost numberless other items.

General Clark, gray-haired and crowned with honors, received Captain Stewart with his usual urbane cordiality. The Scotsman returned many times that winter, as he did also during his subsequent stays in St. Louis, to renew his friendship with the great man.

Although Captain Stewart enjoyed travel and new experiences, he was not intent only on pleasure. The more serious aspects of life in America interested him deeply. He had many opportunities to hear the rich, influential men of St. Louis talk of the expansionist plans of President Andrew Jackson and Thomas Hart Benton, the ebullient Missourian. A few of the wiser heads realized the part the fur trade was playing in these plans, as its partisans and trappers explored the mountains and followed rivers to their sources. There were long discussions of the shipping of pelts to the fur-hungry markets of England, the Continent, and most voracious of all,

China; of the fabulous cotton market at New Orleans, 600 miles down the Mississippi. From the port thousands of bales of the precious white fiber were shipped every year to the whirring looms of England and Scotland, where for more than a hundred years most of the cotton goods of the world had been manufactured. Captain Stewart was fully aware of the importance of cotton to Britain's economy, so its growth, processing, and shipping were of deep interest to him.

During that winter of 1832–33, Captain Stewart no doubt met Thomas Hart Benton, United States Senator from Missouri. Several years before his election to that office in 1820, Benton had moved from Tennessee, where he was already a respected political figure, to St. Louis and established his home in that fast-growing city. He was a firm believer in the expansionist doctrine, and worked wholeheartedly throughout his long career to establish the western boundary of the United States on the shore of the Pacific. That this boundary would some day be pushed across three thousand miles of ocean to include Hawaii exceeded even his far-sighted vision. Years later, Benton's son-in-law, John Charles Frémont, played a part, though admittedly a feeble one, in making the senator's dream come true.

At that time a transcontinental railroad was generally considered to be in the realm of fantasy—but Senator Benton was pointing out the possibilities of one, maybe two, with all the vigor of which he was capable, and that was a great deal. Two short lines, the first in the United States to be operated by locomotives, had been built four years before. One of these pocket-sized railroads was the Delaware and Hudson, in New York; the other was known as the Charleston and Hamburg, in Georgia.

Benton's astute mind saw the practical value of more and longer railroads, especially after the United States would have acquired the Mexican provinces of California and New Mexico, and established clear title to Oregon. Some men laughed at the senator's ideas, but not Captain Stewart. The daring of such far-reaching plans appealed to him.

Though the visitor from Perthshire spent many hours in serious conversation and the discussion of such important questions, his first winter in St. Louis was a gay one. He was received by the

élite of the city. They invited him to teas, to dinners, and to their
most elegant functions, called gumbo balls: between dances, there
was served delicious gumbo soup made from chicken and okra.
There were also distinguished theatrical performances brought up
from sophisticated New Orleans. On all these occasions Captain
Stewart cut a dashing figure with his military bearing, London
clothes, Continental manners and easy charm. He was one of
those rare men who attract women with no perceptible effort and
at the same time command the respect and admiration of men.
There were hints of a discreet amour or two that winter . . . the
ladies of St. Louis were very beautiful.

Between social engagements he spent hours on the broad
levee by the side of the mighty Mississippi. Here the keelboats
tied up, and occasionally a steamboat belonging to one of the fur
companies. Cargoes of staple goods, as well as almost fantastic
luxuries were unloaded, hustled into great horse-drawn drays by
Negro roustabouts, and hauled away to vast storehouses. Here the
busy traffic of the river swirled and rumbled about him. He felt
its throb and urgency. No city he had ever seen was like this one;
rough, raw and lusty on the levee; fortunes quietly made and lost
by suave, broadcloth-coated men in city offices; luxury and elegance in the homes on the outskirts of the town. It made a heady
draught and he drank deeply of it, at the same time impatient to
get on to still greater adventures. But that must wait for spring,
and for grass to grow on the prairies. No fur caravan could move
until there was food for pack animals along the way.

Living as a fashionable gentleman in St. Louis was expensive
and Captain Stewart's funds were becoming depleted. He was not
especially concerned about this. With the sums his attorney in
Perth could manage to collect from John, he would have, when
it came time to start, the wherewithal to carry out his purpose in
coming to America.

Early in February Sublette and Campbell began to make
preparations for their summer trip to the fur country, taking supplies for the trappers, presents and trade goods for the Indians.
The two partners did not have the same destination: Sublette
would head for the mouth of the Yellowstone, Campbell for the

site of the rendezvous on the Green River. Sublette would take two keelboats, towed by the steamer *Otto*, from St. Louis to Lexington. There, the cargo of one keelboat would be turned over to Campbell, and Sublette would proceed upstream on the *Otto*, the other keelboat trailing behind. From Fort Pierre to the mouth of the Yellowstone the keelboat would be cordelled by twenty men straining at the tow rope.

Campbell did not know exactly where the rendezvous was to be held in 1833, but he was confident he could pick up this information on the way. At these rendezvous, fur traders, trappers and Indians met each year for a prolonged session of business, drinking, gambling, horse racing and a generally wild and woolly time.

Not until preparatory activities began did Captain Stewart suggest to his friends, Sublette and Campbell, that he go with the caravan to the rendezvous. These experienced men were understandably doubtful of the wisdom of the idea. William was a fine fellow, but just the same they were something less than enthusiastic about making themselves responsible for a greenhorn on the long, hazardous journey ahead. How would he react to the dangers and hardships of prairie and mountain trails, to the tricks and treacheries of Indians? Finally, however, they consented to his accompanying Campbell. At Stewart's insistence, he did not go as a guest, but paid the partners $500 for a place in Campbell's train.

Sometime in March Captain Stewart set off on horseback, his destination North Bend, a small town in Ohio some 350 miles away. The reason for his taking this trip, necessarily filled with discomforts, occasioned by poor lodgings and inclement weather, can only be surmised, but the evidence indicates that he went as a favor to his friends, Sublette and Campbell. Immediately on arriving at North Bend, he sought out the home of General William Henry Harrison, the man he had come to see.

This gentleman was one of the most distinguished men in the United States at that time. His father was a signer of the Declaration of Independence. He himself could boast of a long and honorable military career, having been Major-General in the War of 1812. A varied political life followed, during which he held several important elective offices. His greatest honor was still to come, that of becoming the ninth President of the United States. At the time Stewart visited him, his health was not good and he was living in retirement.

Captain Stewart presented the letter he had brought from Campbell and Sublette. Its exact contents were never divulged, but they can be deduced with reasonable accuracy from what followed.

A son of General Harrison's, the sixth of ten children, Dr. Benjamin Harrison, was a young man of considerable attainments in the medical profession, but given to excessive indulgence in strong drink. At that time a trip to the Rocky Mountains was considered a practically sure cure for any deviation from the normal, either of health or character, from tuberculosis to alcoholism.

Captain Stewart no doubt added his persuasions to those Sublette must have penned in the letter, to the effect that Dr. Harrison, then at home with his father, would be materially benefited by a sojourn in the Far West. Both Harrisons finally agreed to this plan, but the father insisted on paying $1000 to defray the expenses of his son's trip. General Harrison was evidently more affluent than he was when Benjamin was born: at that time he had written to his friend President Andrew Jackson that his "nursery grew faster than his bank account." The details of the matter settled, Dr. Harrison returned to St. Louis with Captain Stewart.

No sooner was William back in his comfortable Mansion House quarters than there arrived in the city a wizened, chronically irritated little man of fifty or so who called himself Baron Braunsberg. It is likely that he, too, took lodgings at St. Louis's favorite hostelry and that he met Captain Stewart there.

The insignificant-looking little man soon let it be known that he was really Prince Maximilian of Wied-Neuwied, a traveler, a scientist, and almost every variety of "ologist" known to the learned world. Accompanying him was a servant with the improbable name of Driedoppel, and an artist of considerable fame, Charles Bodmer.

Prince Maximilian inquired, in barely understandable English, if there was a caravan forming to go to the Indian country. He had traveled, he said, among the Indians of South America and wished to compare them with the aborigines of western North America. Also, he desired to collect plant specimens. Probably through the good offices of Captain Stewart, Prince Maximilian was soon introduced to Robert Campbell.

This chance meeting between Stewart and Prince Maximilian, and the fact that the little scientist was taking a painter with him, may have planted a seed in the Scottish nobleman's mind that bore significant fruit four years later. For it was then that Stewart, leading his own party and in command of the American Fur Company's caravan, headed toward the Rocky Mountains, taking with him the already well known young painter, Alfred Jacob Miller.

While negotiations were pending in regard to Prince Maximilian's going to the mountains with the Campbell train, the prince and Captain Stewart, accompanied by William Clark, Superintendent of Indian Affairs, departed downriver by boat to Jefferson Barracks, a few miles south of town. The object of the jaunt was to visit Black Hawk, the Sauk chief and one of the most famous among the Indian leaders, who had recently been defeated in battle and captured by United States troops. This great man had his portrait painted a few weeks later by the artist, George Catlin, and shortly thereafter was taken on a tour of eastern cities. During their trip to Jefferson Barracks, Prince Maximilian found that he and Captain Stewart had much in common, both having fought in the Napoleonic Wars.

When the Prussian scientist was once more back in St. Louis, he had a long talk with Campbell, who must have spoken quite plainly about trail conditions to the fussy little man from Wied-Neuwied. Almost at once the prince announced his firm decision to go upriver by steamboat, that being the safest way to study Indians. If, he observed, he went across the prairies and into the mountains, he might have to fight them. Soon after that he boarded the *Yellowstone,* accompanied by his two companions.

Spring seemed very slow in coming—at least, it did to Captain Stewart. Each day that passed brought his impatience to a new high.

CHAPTER IV

The Fur Traders

⁂ Sublette and Campbell now set to work in earnest, for spring had come and a thin veil of green covered the prairies, promise of the luxuriant grass to follow. Months before, the partners had journeyed to New York and Philadelphia, where they bought most of their supplies. The list of purchases seemed endless, and was certainly bewildering in its variety. At the rendezvous, and at the trading posts Sublette proposed to establish, they would have two types of customers: trappers and Indians. So they bought, among other things, large knives that could be used for skinning, butchering, table ware, and for scalping the enemy. They laid in stocks of blankets, gunpowder, lead for bullets, guns, beaver traps to replace those lost or stolen during the preceding season, thick woolen capotes which were the standard jackets of the mountain men when they could be had, bacon, salt pork, vermilion, beads of many colors, small mirrors, hawk's bells, ribbons, awls, bright silk handkerchiefs—there was no end to the things that could be sold or traded, either to the white men or Indians, at a 400 per-cent advance on St. Louis prices.

Sublette's task of packing was comparatively easy. Once his goods were aboard the keelboat, they would not be disturbed until his arrival at the Yellowstone. Campbell, traveling overland across a thousand miles of prairie, would pack his stores on mules and horses, loads being taken off chafed backs at night, put on again each morning. However, both cordelling keelboats and packing on horses were appallingly laborious methods of transportation.

It is indicative of Stewart's persuasive powers that an experienced mountain man such as Robert Campbell allowed him to take along a bale of clothing that was, he stated, not to be opened until the rendezvous was reached. His two Manton rifles met with approval, of course, especially after the partners found that Captain Stewart's marksmanship was superb. The men of the caravans, usually numbering from forty to sixty, subsisted almost altogether on the game they could secure, and a good hunter was a real asset.

One of the most important items the fur companies had to transport, over enormous distances and difficult terrain, was a supply of straight alcohol. This commodity would be lavishly watered down and perhaps flavored on the spot where it was consumed. The year before, taking any form of alcohol into the Indian country, except under a system of licensing, had been forbidden by law, except small quantities for "medicinal purposes." The passing of this law was a completely futile gesture, since the Indians refused to trade until they were given, or sold, liquor.

The Hudson's Bay Company enforced a ban against liquor in their own territory, where no American trappers were allowed. But when they sent brigades into American territory, which they often did, more liquor—and at lower prices—was furnished any Indian whom they could thereby induce to trade with them. This situation being well known to all in the fur trade, no more than a token effort was ever made to stop the distribution of liquor to the Indians at the rendezvous held by the American fur traders. The only real restraint put on the Far West liquor business was that enforced by the American and English fur companies themselves. Sheer self-interest required them to keep the number of crazy-drunk trappers and Indians to a minimum.

England and the United States both looked with acquisitive eyes at the great expanses of the Far West, over most of which the fur companies operated freely and without much supervision from their governments. Far to the north in Alaska crouched the Russian Bear, with a foothold already well established in northern California near Bodega Bay. It was fairly well known that the *Californios* were too weak to do anything about the Russian paw pressing on their territory, and were heartily tired of the irresponsible remote control by which they were governed from Mexico City. But no one could be at all sure what they would do if an effort was made by another country to take over their potentially rich province.

Perhaps no one realized the situation with greater clarity than Senator Benton, but he had no first-hand facts to go on and such information as he needed was hard to come by. One of Benton's efforts to gain the important knowledge he needed regarding the topographical and political facts regarding this vast territory touches our story. We shall come to it in good time.

Captain Stewart made several modest purchases in St. Louis before his departure. He bought a thick woolen capote that cost twenty dollars, a pair of stout pantaloons and two heavy shirts to last him until they came to the Indian country. There, Campbell assured him, those fine seamstresses, the Crow women, would make him shirts of the finest tanned deerskins, properly smoked so that they would remain soft even after being wet. To this Stewart made no reply, having his own plans as to what he would wear at the rendezvous.

This was big business in which Robert Campbell and William Sublette were engaged—how big, it is difficult to realize fully now. The fur industry was at its height. Every man of any consequence, actual or imagined, in the States, in England, and on the continent of Europe owned at least one beaver hat. China's appetite for furs was insatiable, since her wealthy people preferred to wear their heating arrangements rather than install them in their homes. Captain Stewart was headed for the largest, wildest rendezvous ever held in the Rocky Mountains—or anywhere else.

There were treasures of fur and large investments of money at stake. Competition for the business and for the services of trappers was nothing short of cutthroat in the most literal meaning of the term. The two great companies in the field that year were the Rocky Mountain Fur Company, which marketed their furs through

Campbell and Sublette, and the Amercian Fur Company, organized by John Jacob Astor.

There would also be at the rendezvous this year a large, elaborate trapping and trading expedition under Captain Benjamin Louis Eulalie de Bonneville, on leave from the United States Army and bent on making a quick fortune for himself and his rich New York backers. This officer had gone to the mountains the year before with the most elaborate and expensive outfit the mountain men had ever seen, his guide and lieutenant the famous mountain man, Joseph Reddeford Walker. He had even brought wagons all the way from Independence, but with so much struggle and effort that Bonneville declared the project impracticable and abandoned them in the Rocky Mountains. Old hands at the fur trade observed Bonneville with considerable skepticism, tinged with amusement. They were looking forward to discovering at this year's rendezvous how such a complete greenhorn had made out.

There were some highly deplorable aspects to the bitter rivalry between the fur companies. Whenever possible, they lured away the other men's trappers and almost indispensable Delaware hunters by offering them higher wages. They destroyed or stole each other's traps and beaver plews every time they got a chance. There were rumors of murders committed on lonely creeks, and of Indian bands armed and incited to set upon small groups of trappers working for a rival company.

But when the gentlemen who headed the fur brigades met, they greeted each other with the utmost courtesy and even cordiality. They dined, drank, played cards together as if they were bosom friends, instead of ruthless enemies, obeying no law but their own wills. The fur business was one that sorted out the men from the boys.

Into such a situation, with its added hazards from implacable savages and the inescapable dangers of mountain and prairie travel, Captain Stewart, of Grandtully and Murthly Castles, was about to plunge. His journeyings up to now, except for his war experiences, had been altogether in the highly civilized countries of Europe and Asia. His background, it would seem, was not one to fit him for the kind of adventure on which he was about to embark. A few months hence he would be in the Rocky Mountains. Then he might go on to the Pacific Coast, although it didn't seem likely—and in fact, it didn't take place until late fall of the following year. However, just on the chance, he stowed his letters to the Hudson's Bay officials in a waterproof bag and put them in his pack.

During his stay in St. Louis Captain Stewart presumably received letters from Christina telling him of how she was getting along in Edinburgh, and of her son's welfare. Nor was he as unmindful of little George as it might have appeared to some people. Months before, he had written to a friend in Edinburgh asking him to call on Lady Stewart—he always accorded to her her rightful title—and report how he found her and the boy. The friend replied that he had been delayed in going by a "severe pain in his haunch," but when he had done so he found them both well, the child healthy and growing fast.

At last it was time to start on the first lap of Campbell's journey, which would take them to Lexington, twenty-five miles east of Independence on the Missouri River. Campbell's stores were sent to Lexington by keelboat, but the men of the party rode overland on fine horses from Sublette's farm. Sublette and his heavily laden boat, which was to make the long haul up to the Yellowstone, was delayed for a few days.

Arriving at Lexington, Campbell made his final purchases at Aull's store, bought pack mules and horses at Jem Hicklin's farm near by, and rounded up the more than forty men he needed as packers and hunters. Here Captain Stewart learned to pack a mule, an art at which he soon became expert; first came a folded blanket, then a piece of buffalo robe called an apishemore (variously spelled according to the notion of the contemporary writer). Two side bales hung on a pack saddle and were protected from the weather by being rolled in black domestic, a kind of cotton cloth. Small objects needed every night were usually placed on top, and the whole bound securely to the animal's back.

Part of the food taken along consisted of a band of twenty sheep. These would furnish fresh meat until the caravan reached the buffalo country on the Platte. To supplement mutton, there were two mule loads of bacon, 500 pounds of cornmeal, salt, coffee, and sugar; the last two items in short supply, since they were luxuries. Two experienced mountain men were employed by Campbell to keep the caravan in order on the trail: Louis Vasquez, to look after the pack train, and Basil Lajeunesse, to bring up the rear, take care of stragglers, and so on.

Sublette arrived at Lexington about May 1. Several days were consumed in transferring the keelboat cargo to Campbell, camped about five miles away, and in conducting necessary business with the firm of Aull Brothers, merchants at Lexington. He brought with him a packet of mail—the last Campbell's party would receive until they returned in the fall. This packet contained a letter for Captain Stewart, written by faithful brother George, telling him of the death of their mother in March. Though Captain Stewart and his mother had never been especially close, the message brought grief.

Still further pain was inflicted by the second paragraph of the letter, which conveyed the information that Catherine had left her estate of Logiealmond unconditionally to John. This action showed Captain Stewart his mother's complete lack of faith in him as a practical man. The hurt must have been deep.

Campbell's caravan set off May 7, 1833, across a prairie thickly carpeted with grass and wild flowers. The party was made up of about forty-four men, each with three mules: one to ride, the other two serving as pack animals. There were also the leader, Robert Campbell, Captain Stewart, Edmund Christy, a man named Brotherton whom we never hear of again, Dr. Benjamin Harrison, and four men whose names were not recorded. Almost a thousand twisting miles, much of it without even a trail to follow, lay between them and the Valley of the Green.

CHAPTER V

Follow the Rolling Rivers

ع‍ For the first few days the pack mules indulged their mulish natures by kicking, plunging, throwing off their 300-pound packs, making sudden, unpredictable sorties into the prairie at every opportunity. Finding these antics futile, they at last settled down to their work, with only now and then a lapse from propriety.

After the caravan passed the Shawnee Mission a few miles from Westport, Campbell organized the "enlisted men," or employees, into messes of five or six, and assigned specific duties to each man. Night guards were appointed, with a two-and-one-half-hour tour, during which time they did not move from the place assigned to them. This enforced inactivity made it very hard to keep awake. But a moving human being was easy to spot by Indians bent on stealing horses and only a little less easy to kill, almost silently, with a club or an arrow. The guard made ineffective, picket stakes were pulled up and horses stampeded.

The loss of pack and riding animals was one of the most serious disasters that could happen to a caravan. Indians coveted horses and made off with them whenever they could. The number of horses a red man owned determined to a large degree the extent of his wealth and influence.

The night guards, therefore, held the safety of the train in their keeping. Sleep sometimes overcame a tired man unaware. Every twenty minutes an officer called, "All's well!" If the guard failed to answer, he was presumed to be asleep, fined five dollars, and made to walk for three days. Since Charles Larpenteur, hired in St. Louis as a clerk, received only a trifle over sixteen dollars a month, and the "enlisted men" must have been paid even less, the subtraction of five dollars from a man's monthly stipend would come as something of a disaster. This, with the additional burden of being jeered at by his companions as he plodded along while they rode, added up to an embittering experience.

Dr. Harrison appears to have chosen to retain his status as a paying guest, with no responsibility, not even that of picketing his horse and catching it up in the morning. Captain Stewart accepted every duty that came his way, ranging over the prairie with the hired hunters, bringing in more than his share of small game to vary the tiresome diet of mutton and salt pork. There would be no buffalo until they were well up the Platte. He also lent a hand to Vasquez and Lajeunesse as they struggled with the problem of keeping the caravan in uninterrupted and orderly motion. When otherwise unoccupied, he rode with his friend Campbell at the head of the train, absorbing prairie and mountain know-how from his talk. The two men found many areas of agreement, including the absolute necessity of discipline, whether among military forces or in an expedition to the Rocky Mountains.

It wasn't long until Campbell appointed Stewart captain of the night guard. Not long after he had assumed the responsibility of this position, he came upon a guard who was asleep. He peremptorily awakened the man, sent him to his blanket, and took his place until relieved by the next guard.

When morning came Stewart summoned the unfortunate fellow and announced his punishment—five dollars and "three walks," or three days afoot leading his horse. The disgruntled man went to Campbell, complaining about the severity of his punishment and saying that he felt under no obligation to submit to the orders of a greenhorn.

Campbell replied that greenhorn Captain Stewart might be, as far as prairie travel was concerned, but he was a military man, a hero of Waterloo, and now the captain of the night guard. All orders issued by him in line of duty were to be obeyed without question. The man returned to his companions, relaying to them what Campbell had said. Impressed by the fact that they were under the command of a man who had fought at Waterloo, there was no more grumbling. Captain Stewart continued to hold them strictly to the proper discharge of their duties.

Traveling almost due west, they crossed Muddy Creek and turned northward two days' journey to the Kansas River, sometimes called the Kaw. Here they camped three days at the Kaw Indian agency, administered by a relative of General William Clark. Their halt at this point was made to give their horses and mules a chance to graze as long as they wished. Spring not being far advanced, the prairie grass was still sparse and short, putting the animals on short rations. But the days were warm and from now on food for the stock would be increasingly plentiful. Taking up the march again, they crossed the Big Blue and reached the Platte River. A few early spring flowers added occasional flecks of color to the prairie's lush green carpet.

The usual weather of the plains at this time of year brought frequent harassment to the travelers. Black clouds suddenly boiling up from the horizon would cut off the sunlight as though a great curtain had been drawn across the sky. Torrential rains drenched men and animals. Thunder crashed, lightning leaped from sky to earth in flashing bolts; hail battered the caravan with balls of ice, sometimes as large as marbles, so that mules bolted and horses became unmanageable.

At other times the caravan struggled through quagmires of mud and across creeks, bank-full of cold, rushing water. Occasionally the sun came out long enough for them to dry their clothes and gear. The men cursed and grumbled. Campbell took whatever came with stoic calmness, but Captain Stewart seemed to welcome each untoward happening as a personal challenge to his resourcefulness, courage and endurance.

The caravan pushed on, the men wet and cold and most of the time hungry, too. The sheep had been eaten and in stormy weather the grouse huddled under clumps of brush, the rabbits in their burrows. Boiled corn meal and salt pork became tiresome provender.

On May 23 the party reached the forks of the Platte, at this point a wide river, shallow in spite of the spring rains and treacherous with quicksands. They followed the South Fork for a while, then crossed with only minor mishaps and made their way over the intervening plain to the North Platte, heading westward along its placid course. A wide plain stretched in every direction almost as far as the eye could see.

Captain Stewart, riding at the head of the train, was the first to note a landmark familiar to all prairie travelers—Chimney Rock, thrusting itself up not far from the stream. The base from which the "chimney" rose had the appearance of a square stone roof, rising sharply almost to a point. From the apex the slender stone chimney rose thirty or forty feet into the air. The whole formation, standing as it did in a flat plain, arrested and held the eye of everyone who passed that way.

A few miles farther on, the travelers came to an isolated hump of ancient rock rising at a little distance from the trail. It looked like a great fort with bastions and battlements and low, squat towers. Scott's Bluff was a sight that caused even the roughest packer to pause, feeling for a moment the magic of wonder.

The caravan was now approximately 500 miles northwest of Independence, a distance easily covered today by many motorists in one day. With the increasingly warm weather, the grass sprang up almost magically fast, soon reaching the horses' knees. On an occasional flat, sandy space Stewart was amazed to see circles made of gleaming white buffalo skulls, noses pointing outward. These rings varied in size, some being twenty-five to thirty feet in diameter. Campbell, an experienced prairie traveler, said they had been made by Indians as "medicine" to draw buffalos to the spot. Unfortunately, the "medicine" wasn't working at the moment. The hunters ranged for miles on either side of the caravan, hoping to sight even one small herd of the lumbering, shaggy animals whose flesh was incomparably better than beef.

Even before they reached the Platte the men of the party, with one exception, stopped shaving and let their hair grow, thus taking on a wild and rugged appearance. The exception was Captain Stewart. Every morning he repaired to the side of a stream, preferably one of the many small, clear creeks flowing into the muddy

Platte, laid out on a flat rock the several pieces of his carved ivory
toilette set, and propped the mirror up with a stone. He then
proceeded to shave himself as meticulously as though he were about
to attend a dinner party with his friends, Lord and Lady Breadalbane. After some inquiry, he discovered a former barber of sorts
among the packers. He engaged this man to cut his hair from time
to time. So among a company of uncouth-looking mountain men,
he managed to maintain something very like his normal appearance.

A few days farther on, one of the hunters—possibly Captain
Stewart—killed a female buffalo whose calf lumbered off down a
ravine and could not be found. Other hunters rode up; together
they butchered the cow and brought the meat into camp on a
sumpter mule. Everyone was elated at the prospect of feasting on
buffalo meat. The cooks took their kettles from the mule packs,
cursing because they were so small.

When it came to making fires, they found that the only
available substance that would burn was dried sunflower stalks.
For some reason the buffalo had not come down the river early that
year, as they usually did, so there was none of that dependable
prairie fuel, dried buffalo chips. The flimsy stalks of last year's
sunflowers were no fuel with which to cook even the finest, fattest
hump ribs, much less the lean, stringy flesh of a buffalo cow who
was nursing her calf and therefore in poor condition. Usually cows
offered the choicest fare, but not in the spring, when their calves
were not yet old enough to graze.

The men spent much time and effort gathering a great pile of
sunflower stalks. These smoldered exasperatingly under the cooking pots, or went up in one quick burst of flame. After a while the
men tried to eat the meat. They found it hard to cut, even with
their fine Green River knives, and impossible to masticate sufficiently to be swallowed. Morosely, they returned to corn meal and
salt pork.

Next day detached and deeply eroded hills began to break
the monotony of the level plain. Buffalo appeared, at first singly,
then in small herds of twenty-five or so. For the first time Captain
Stewart experienced the excitement, the danger, of "running" these
great beasts. They were the largest animals he had ever hunted;

also the stupidest and, unless wounded, the least aggressive wild animal he had ever shot at. The greatest danger of the buffalo chase was that the hunter's horse might stumble or fall, throwing its rider in the path of the herd's pounding hoofs.

The charge of a wounded buffalo was something to be feared by the bravest man. Clumsy as a buffalo appeared, with his heavy shoulders and awkward gait, he could outrun a horse and his short, sharp horns were weapons he could use with lethal effect on either horse or man.

The members of Campbell's party now feasted on tender hump ribs, choice roasts, liver and tongue. The experienced mountain men ate the liver raw, seasoned liberally with bile, and seared the fat-encrusted *boudins* over glowing buffalo chips, these small intestines being swallowed by the yard. At first the greenhorns were revolted at this crude fare, but soon freed themselves of their high-falutin' ideas and consumed with equal gusto whatever parts of the buffalo their comrades found pleasing to the palate. The hungry days were forgotten.

There is little doubt that Captain Stewart's horse was better than any other mount in the train except Campbell's, and his Manton rifle more accurate than even the finest Hawken. He outrode and outshot everyone else. The men accorded the Scottish nobleman a new, a deeper respect, for he proved to be a mighty hunter. A buffalo was a difficult animal to kill. It had few vulnerable spots that even a high-powered Manton would pierce and it wasn't easy to hit those spots from the back of a galloping horse. The ability to bring in meat was highly prized in the Far West, and understandably so. The men no longer considered Stewart a greenhorn, and a foreign one at that; they gave him their respect and unquestioning obedience.

They reached the junction of the North Platte and Laramie rivers. Here were almost level meadows stretching toward the Black Hills that could be clearly seen in the distance, with Laramie Peak rising against the blue sky. Grass and many-colored wild flowers blanketed this lovely plain. Wild currant bushes grew in profusion, frosted now by innumerable small white blossoms, promising a heavy yield of clustered red berries in the late summer. A place of serene beauty, having nothing in common with the awe-

some crags and peaks, the turbulent, foam-whitened streams of
the Rocky Mountains, still far ahead.

Following the clear, sparkling Laramie River for about a mile,
the party stopped and made preparations to cross. The stream,
though flowing placidly enough at this point, was so deep the
animals would have to swim in order to reach the other side. This
necessitated the removal of all the goods from the backs of horses
and mules in order to prevent damage, and the building of a bull
boat to transport supplies and trade goods across the river.

Stewart watched with lively interest as a detail of men assigned
to the task built the first bull boat he had ever seen. First they
gathered a supply of stout, but pliant, willow branches from trees
growing by the river, bent and fastened them with withes into a
framework the shape of a bowl some eight feet across. Three buffalo hides sewn together with animal tendons were then stretched
over this framework, the seams calked with buffalo grease mixed
with ashes. Experienced hands made short work of this task.
Though the boat looked clumsy, it was handled easily in the comparatively quiet waters of the Laramie. A few hours later the party
was encamped for the night on the north bank of the stream. A
year later, William Sublette would start building a great fort here,
but when Stewart first saw this pleasant spot it lay virgin, untouched by the hand of man.

The word "fort" given these great stockades built by fur
traders is misleading. They were not forts in a military sense, but
trading posts, centers where furs were collected from Indian and
white trappers, payment being made in trade goods. The men in
charge of these establishments were adequately armed, of course,
and care was taken that only a few Indians at a time were admitted
into the inner courtyard where trading was conducted, but the self-
interest of both whites and Indians insured a watchful peace in
their vicinity. The immediate area near the forts was considered by
the Indians to be neutral ground, where the representatives of
even the most warlike tribes met in a truce, that they might trade
with the white man.

Not far from the confluence of the Platte and the Laramie,
Campbell waited for the arrival of Thomas Fitzpatrick, a famous
field man employed by the Rocky Mountain Fur Company, and

his party with their winter's catch of beaver. The timing of the two men in keeping a rendezvous arranged almost a year before was excellent, for in two days Fitzpatrick arrived, accompanied by Henry Fraeb and Andrew Drips, two men well known throughout the fur country. The pelts they brought were soon packed into the bull boat constructed for the crossing of the Laramie, and dispatched down the Platte to St. Louis. Fitzpatrick, Fraeb and Drips went off on another hunt for beaver, promising to show up at the Green River rendezvous about the same time that the slower-traveling cavalcade of Campbell's would arrive there, though as yet neither Campbell nor Fitzpatrick knew the exact location where the rendezvous would be held that year.

Not wanting to wander around with his long train of animals, Campbell sent Vasquez and two companions to hunt up a group of trappers and find out from them where the fur company's brigades would come together. Life became dull as the men waited on the banks of the Platte for this information to be brought to them. But one day the monotony was broken by a burst of excitement spiced with danger.

CHAPTER VI

Destination, the Shining Mountains

ᘔ By midmorning the men were through with their few camp chores. Some lounged on buffalo robes in the scant shade cast by willow trees, or played the game of Old Sledge with cards brought from St. Louis, now roughened and frayed from the rigors of the trail. The cards would last until others could be made by the men themselves from buffalo hides, and marked with their distinctive red and black symbols by means of vermilion from a trade-goods pack and charcoal from the campfire.

One of the men sighted a huge she-grizzly bear wandering through the brush on a hillside not far away. He shouted the news of his discovery. Several of the men grabbed their guns, sprang to their feet and rushed toward the animal, shooting indiscriminately in her direction. She started to lumber off, when one of the bullets must have wounded her. Grizzlies are always ill-tempered, but she probably had a cub somewhere near by, and was in an even more belligerent mood than usual. She now turned on her enemies with awful fury, advancing with her cavernous mouth wide open, uttering terrifying growls, presenting an appalling sight. The men scattered, but continued to fire on the beast. She came on, apparently unhurt.

Captain Stewart's entry into the fray was delayed because he

had to load his gun. That done, he jumped on his horse and galloped to the scene of battle. The bear, which stood six feet high
when rearing on her hind legs, charged him, eyes glaring, froth
whipping from her mouth. Stewart raised his gun and fired, seemingly without taking aim. The grizzly pitched forward, dead. Fifty
bullets were found in the bear's carcass, but only the one fired by
Captain Stewart had reached a vital spot. The men gaped.

The incident of the bear and the foreign sportsman made a
story that for years to come would be told—embellished according
to the fancy of the narrator—beside many a campfire throughout
the Rocky Mountains. In time, the climactic moment of the encounter between Captain Stewart and this particular grizzly was
reproduced, life-size, in wax and exhibited in a St. Louis museum
where it stood for many years. What finally became of it is not
known.

After the brief excitement caused by the grizzly, four more
days dragged by, with no sign of Vasquez and his men. Campbell
became increasingly impatient. Every day his party was late in
arriving at the rendezvous meant decreased profits for him, as the
fur companies already on the ground bought furs from the Indians
and free trappers, selling trade goods to eager buyers at the fantastic prices charged in the Rocky Mountains. Boredom gripped the
men, and fights started for no apparent reason other than to break
the monotony of inaction.

In order to give them something to do, Campbell assigned six
of the most unruly men to go along the river, even into the wooded
Black Hills if necessary, to search for bee trees and bring back a
supply of honey. Such a treasure trove would not only be a pleasant
change of diet for the party, but would provide a considerable
quantity to be used for a definite purpose at the rendezvous. There,
the thick, amber sweetening would be mixed with watered-down
alcohol to make the drink called metheglin, a potion highly es-
teemed by white men and Indians alike.

Campbell knew that if his men were to sell metheglin at the
rendezvous he would have to lay in a supply of honey soon, and
this might be his last opportunity. Bee trees became more and
more infrequent as the settlements were left behind. Bees were
not native to North America, but had been brought to this conti-

nent from Central and Southern Europe by immigrants who settled
on the Atlantic Coast. As the more restless of these families
pushed westward, they took their bee colonies with them. When
this adventurous tide of pioneers reached the Missouri River, it
hesitated there for a long time. But the bees, who unwittingly
serve man but have never been domesticated by them, did not
recognize the boundary to their further advance. Truant wanderers
from the hives belonging to the settlers started colonies of their
own in hollow trees bordering the creeks and rivers flowing into
the Missouri and Mississippi from the west. The bees advanced
a few miles each year until in 1833 their wild breed was well established along the lower and middle reaches of the Kaw, the Republican, the Platte, and their tributaries.

The Indians were inordinately fond of honey, a delight recently come to them, apparently a gift from the Great Spirit. It
was the only sweetening they had and they resented the white
man's appropriation of this delectable treat even more immediately
than they did the slaughter of the buffalo. Only the wisest and
most foresighted men among the tribes could look far enough
ahead to see the end of their way of life as the inevitable consequence of the decimation of the buffalo herds, which came about
gradually.

The six men started joyfully on their errand, taking with them
as many buckets as they conveniently could, supplemented by a
number of stout buffalo-hide bags, and a mule to carry their gear.
On the day following their departure, they returned with all the
honey they and their mule could carry. The men gorged themselves that night on the laboriously gathered harvest of the bees.

At daylight next morning, Vasquez and his two men rode into
camp after an absence of seven days, bringing with them the information that the rendezvous would be held four miles north of
Horse Creek on the Green River. At shouted orders from Campbell, the camp boiled with activity. The cooks hastily served breakfast, horses were caught up, and the caravan strung out along the
trail.

Soon the country was broken by sharp ravines that caused
trouble and delay in getting the horses and mules down the steep
declivities and up the ridges. Campbell urged haste and Captain

Stewart was everywhere, helping to keep the straining pack animals intent on their tasks. Campbell knew how disastrous it would be to arrive late at the rendezvous—the cream of the trading having gone to other fur companies.

Reaching the Sweetwater, Campbell's party followed that swift-flowing stream for a day's march, coming then to another landmark well-known to all western-faring men of the era—Independence Rock. It heaved itself up near the bank of the river like a great turtle. On this giant autograph album were carved many famous names, among them those of James Bridger, Robert Campbell, William Sublette, Nathaniel Wyeth, and most prominent of all, Captain Benjamin Louis Eulalie de Bonneville—what a job it must have been to carve that one—who had marched by at the head of his fancy outfit the year before. His party had been the wonder of the mountains, with its lavish equipment, its twenty Delaware hunters, and, as sub-lieutenant, that great mountain man, guide and leader, Joseph Reddeford Walker.

Five miles beyond Independence Rock, the Sweetwater dashed and tumbled between vertical-walled cliffs 400 feet high, forming a passageway barely wide enough for the crowding turbulent river. This was Devil's Gate. Here the party was forced to detour, returning to the Sweetwater several miles farther upstream.

It wasn't long until the party could see Cut Rock off in the distance to one side of the trail, a clean-cut triangular notch of giant proportions slashed in the crest of a mountain. On July 2 they came to South Pass, a high, almost flat tableland along which runs the invisible spine of the continent. Water falling on the eastern side flows at last into the Gulf of Mexico, but if it falls on the ground imperceptibly sloping toward the west, it goes at last to swell the Pacific Ocean.

Before them loomed the great, snow-crested peaks of the Rockies, mountains far more majestic and overpowering than any other range Captain Stewart had ever seen. Looking at those heights, his thoughts must have strayed to their antithesis, the low, rounded hills that bordered the gently flowing Tay in far-off Perthshire.

Even this early in July, the middle of the day brought real warmth, but at night the men found comfort in their three-point wool blankets. On the morning of the 3rd of July there was ice a quarter of an inch thick in the water buckets.

Campbell and the other men in the train who had passed this way before knew that the fur companies' rendezvous was not far off. On the 5th of July their start was delayed for several hours while the men washed their shirts in a clear mountain stream, shaved, trimmed each other's hair, and otherwise readied themselves to meet old friends, make new acquaintances, and impress the Indian girls. For most of them, a rendezvous was their greatest social event of the year, looked forward to with eagerness, its gambling and drinking and lovemaking remembered on many a lonely bivouac. So they made themselves as presentable as possible, the change in some of them being so great that they were almost unrecognizable to their companions.

Captain Stewart's appearance, when he had finished with his toilette, stunned all of them, even Campbell, into momentary immobility. Having secured his pack of clothing, unopened since it was lashed shut in St. Louis, he donned certain items therefrom, and appeared before his companions wearing a white leather hunting jacket with innumerable pockets and a pair of snug trousers known in Scotland as trews, made of the green, royal blue, red and yellow of the Stewart hunting plaid, all fashioned by a London tailor. On his head rested a Panama hat of the finest texture.

It is a certain indication of the respect and liking in which these rough mountain men held him that no one laughed. They simply stared, while here and there one swore softly, unbelievingly, below his breath. Campbell recovered himself first and gave the order to start. The long train of men and animals moved out on the last lap of their journey.

For several hours they advanced with accelerated pace, even the horses and mules appearing to sense that the long labor of the trail was almost ended. Suddenly a group of horsemen came around a hill and galloped toward them, yelling, waving, firing their guns. They were immediately recognized as men of the Rocky Mountain Fur Company's encampment who, having sighted high in the air the cloud of dust raised by the long train of pack animals, were riding out to give them a trappers' welcome. With them rode Thomas Fitzpatrick, the skilled partisan, who had arrived at the rendezvous the day before, bringing the beaver skins he and his men had taken on their way from the camp on the Platte.

The astonishment of the impromptu greeting committee at the sight of Captain Stewart, garbed as he was in all the accouterments of a Scottish nobleman hunting the stag in the glens of Perthshire, all but overwhelmed the tatterdemalion men in buckskin. But since he rode at the head of the cavalcade, side by side with their old friend, Robert Campbell, they withheld the uninhibited comments they would otherwise have made.

There was a boisterous reunion between old companions of the trail and beaver stream, who had perhaps not seen each other for a year or two. There were letters for some, newspapers two months old for a few, talk of the "settlements" for all. Among the noisiest of this band of greeters was Joe Meek, only twenty-three, brash and cocky, with four years' experience in the mountains. No longer working for wages, he was a free trapper who had come to the rendezvous with plenty of beaver to trade for anything he wanted: a new outfit, a warm capote, all the whisky he could drink—a large order in itself—and to deck out the prettiest young squaw he could find with all the foofaraw her heart desired. Though enjoying the status of a free trapper, going where he wanted and trapping where he pleased, the Rocky Mountain Fur Company furnished him his traps, and he sold his catch to them.

Finally, the shouting, the laughter, the bragging, died down and the augmented party moved on toward the camp of the Rocky Mountain Fur Company, already established by several of its brigades, in the Valley of the Green.

CHAPTER VII

The Greatest Rendezvous of All

꙳ The cavalcade of more than forty men and three times that many horses left the sheltering mountains, to ride out into a great sagebrush plain. Miles away, clumps of willows and an occasional cottonwood marked the course of the river. Dwarfed and blued by distance, far to the west rose the peaks of the main Rocky Mountain chain. The dry air shimmered with heat, the scent of *artemesia* rose, sharp in their nostrils.

Time passed. Finally, they could see the more than a hundred tepees, clustered in uneven ranks, that made up the Shoshone village. Farther along the river smaller encampments appeared. These were the villages of the Blackfoot, Nez Percé, Flathead and other tribes of the mountains and prairies.

As the party rode into the camp of the Rocky Mountain Fur Company's waiting partisans and trappers, there were more welcoming yells, firing of guns. The sights that met Stewart's eyes were like nothing he had ever seen before. Indian braves dashed up on curveting horses, their faces and bodies brilliant with streaks of vermilion, wearing many strings of colored beads, bear-claw necklaces, eagle feathers in their hair, and not much else. Dogs dashed here and there, barking wildly at anything or nothing. Dignified chiefs and head men strode about, draped in fine wool trade blankets that hung about their dark-skinned torsos like Roman togas. Women, garbed in whatever finery they possessed of porcupine-embroidered shirts, beaded leggings and moccasins, flying ribbons, and hawk's bells, hurried up, hoping to see what foofaraw the caravan had brought and to charm some trapper or member of the caravan to buy for them.

By this time it was midafternoon, too late to get the goods unpacked and start trading. The men of the caravan set themselves to readying the trading tent with log shelves and tables, arranging the goods they had brought to the best advantage for tomorrow's business. A detail went to work setting up the only other tents belonging to the party: Campbell's, which he used as an office as well as shelter, and a larger one which was the abode of Dr. Harrison, his gentlemen companions, and the clerk, Charles Larpenteur. As the shadows fell, some of the men who had slept under the open sky all the way from Independence, made themselves small rude brush shelters which they romantically called "bowers." In case of rain a blanket could be thrown over the top, thus protecting the occupants from the worst of the downpour. The most commodious of these shelters could accommodate no more than two men, most of them only one. Captain Stewart had become friendly with a pleasant, well-educated young man named George Holmes, a packer, who had apparently come along for the adventure. From all accounts, Holmes was a handsome, good-humored fellow with an unusually attractive smile. His companions nicknamed him "Beauty," which displeased him greatly.

Now, Captain Stewart and George Holmes combined their efforts and built a better and more nearly waterproof bower than most of the others bothered to do. This shelter they planned to occupy together.

After his goods were unpacked and properly disposed for the night, Campbell asked if Bonneville's party had arrived at the army man's stockade five miles down the Green, built the year before. He was relieved to hear that Fort Nonsense, as the mountain men called Bonneville's stout enclosure, was still unoccupied. Nor had Fontenelle's train bringing American Fur Company goods reached the Green. Campbell may have hoped that Bonneville would not arrive at all. The army man had the reputation among fur traders of being dogged with misfortune, mostly of his own making. He could have had no such hope regarding Fontenelle, a highly intelligent man with years of experience in the Far West behind him.

For the present, at least, Campbell was on the ground ahead of his rivals, but this advantage was not likely to continue very long.

As darkness descended over the valley, the trappers went back to their bivouacs, the Indians to their tepees. Campbell and Stewart ate their supper together in the leader's quarters close by the trading tent, taking a little comfort now and then from Captain Stewart's silver whisky flask, which was engraved with the word *Provyd*, and the crest of the ancient House of Stewart.

After a while the two friends said good night. Captain Stewart checked the night guards to see that all was well, every man awake and watchful. Then he made his way to the sylvan shelter where George Holmes already lay asleep.

It had been a long day for the man from Perthshire. He had seen more strange peoples and savage customs than had ever come his way before. And, however faintly, he must have felt even that first night his deep kinship with the wild mountains, the proud, arrogant red men, the vast, untamed country around him. For this valley in the Wind River Mountains became his home base, its fascination drawing him back year after year during all the time that fate willed he should remain in America.

Reaching his shelter made of willow withes, he wrapped himself in his blanket and lay down beside the gently snoring Holmes. He stayed awake a long time, listening to the alien sounds about him: the howl of a distant wolf, the slow, muffled beat of an Indian drum across the river, the rustle of a bird stirring in a near-by tree.

At daylight next morning Campbell, accompanied by two men, set off to "raise a cache" at Pierre's Hole, leaving Fitzpatrick to manage the trading. Larpenteur felt slightly indisposed, so did not go with Campbell. Redman, the man who was to have helped Fitzpatrick with the trading, soon became so drunk he was useless. Larpenteur was called in to sell the liquor and help out generally. His comment on the situation was, "Such drinking, yelling and shouting went on as I had never heard before . . . soon there was not a sober man to be found in camp but myself." Mr. Fitzpatrick, Larpenteur made clear, was not included among the inebriated men to whom he referred, nor were the other "gentlemen" of the party. The whisky, much diluted with water, sold for five dollars a pint, metheglin for as much more as men befuddled by drink could be induced to pay.

For three days business boomed. Then, on July 8, Fontenelle got in with his train, camped a few miles up the Green; but trading kept up with almost no lessening. Customers crowded eagerly at both camps. A whole year's needs and desires of trappers and Indians had to be supplied here in three or four weeks and buyers were plentiful. Campbell and his men came back with the furs they had recovered from the cache; ten packs with ten plews to a pack. The beaver skins had been carefully handled by experienced trappers, and were undamaged by their storage underground. It took skill and experience to prepare a good safe cache. First, a place was selected where the soil was fairly dry. Then a circle of grassy sod was removed intact and carefully laid aside. Next, the men dug a hole three or four feet deep, barely large enough to accommodate a man. This hole resembled the neck of a bottle. Immediately below it a chamber was excavated large enough to hold the furs or supplies the men wanted to store there. The chamber was then lined with whatever stout greenery was available, in order to avoid cave-ins and to protect the goods from any possible dampness or seepage of water. The entrance was then filled in with earth, the sod carefully replaced. Left-over dirt was dumped into the nearest stream, or distributed over the surrounding terrain in such a manner that no passerby, white or Indian, would notice it and so suspect the presence of a cache somewhere near. All that being done, horses were driven over the area to hide the last trace of disturbance, or a campfire was built on the spot where the opening had been made.

Sometime during the first days of the rendezvous Captain Stewart met that great hunter, Antoine Clement, half Cree Indian, half French-Canadian, admitted by all to be the best shot in the mountains. This year he had come to the rendezvous with one of the partisans of the Rocky Mountain Fur Company, so he was more or less attached to that group.

Antoine was an unusual man—not just another half-breed—
and accounts of his exploits brighten most of the journals and
memoirs of fur-trade days. He was a handsome man by white
standards, of medium height, with no perceptible trace in his
appearance that even hinted of his Cree heritage.

Antoine's hazel eyes were clear and frank. Fine auburn hair fell
to his shoulders. His skin remained fair in spite of its almost constant exposure to sun and weather. His features were more nearly
Greek than Indian or French. He had no education except in the
crafts and skills of the mountain man and Indian, but in all
of these he was adept. For the most part, Antoine cast his lot with
the white man and so acquired many of the white man's ways and
modes of thought, though he never completely broke the ties that
held him to the aboriginal life.

He owned a fine Hawken rifle and used it with admirable
skill. At the same time, he rarely went on a hunting expedition
without a good bow and a quiver full of arrows slung on his back.
He used these weapons interchangeably, as the occasion seemed
to warrant, and with uniformly good results. His usual clothing
was finely made, thong-fringed antelope-skin shirt and leggings,
worn alike by Indians and white men as they went about their
business in the mountains and on the prairies (in the case of full-
blooded Indians the fringes were made of human hair from scalps
taken in war).

It would be difficult to find two more completely contrasted
human beings than the Scottish nobleman and the half-breed who
knew little beyond the way of life as it was lived in the Rocky
Mountains. But from almost the moment they met, they appeared
to recognize their equality in matters that most deeply concerned
both men. They became friends.

The grass gave out in the vicinity of the Rocky Mountain Fur
Company's encampment and Campbell moved several miles down
the Green, where he continued to do a rushing business. The
rendezvous of the fur companies was in some ways like a dozen
fairs rolled into one, without a single policeman on the grounds.
There was drinking, fighting, gambling, horse racing, feasting. The
Indians staged nightly dances, accompanied by the beat of drums
and singing that sounded to white men more like the howling of
wolves than festive chants.

The old squaws did the work of the Indian villages, preparing the food, butchering whatever game the hunters brought in, caring for the horses of their lords, gathering wood and packing it in on their backs to keep alight the most constantly burning cooking fires. They also prepared the skins of deer and antelope for clothing, and did beautiful embroidery, using dyed porcupine quills and many-colored beads. Their own saddles, high at both back and front, were artfully ornamented. Putting up and taking down the tepees was also their work.

The young girls, often unbelievably pretty, learned from the older women the skills they would be expected to use as wives and mothers. At the rendezvous they spent most of their time charming trappers into buying them strings of beads, cheap jewelry, gaudy silk handkerchiefs, small mirrors; all the gewgaws, the foofaraw, their savage hearts coveted. The Indian girl who won the favor of a white man thereby raised her social and economic status among her own people. The cheapest trinkets given to her by the poorest trapper were wealth beyond imagining. Among the white men the competition was fierce as to which one should give his Indian "wife" the most and costliest presents. These favored squaws received the finest blankets, yards of crimson cloth, quantities of silver bells with which to deck themselves and their horses, the best satin ribbon St. Louis had to offer. She—and her horse— gave tangible evidence of the generosity of her temporary lord, so she reflected credit on him. However, the favors of dusky beauties did not always have to be paid for. The head men of the tribes sometimes offered their wives or daughters to trappers as a gesture of friendship and hospitality.

The Shoshone girls were prettier than the Utes or the Crows— cleaner, too—and so more desirable. But after a womanless winter in the mountains, few of the men were particularly discriminating.

The Indian men did little except hunt, race their horses, dance around a campfire counting coups—a brag session with scalps—paint their bodies and faces with vermilion, play the game of "hand," eat, and drink whisky when they could get it. This left them plenty of time to plot deviltry of all sorts.

A few days after Campbell had moved to his new location, a proud and dignified old Shoshone chief invited him to a ceremonial smoke and dog feast at his tepee. They had been friends for years, trusted and respected each other, having done business together and exchanged hospitalities before. Campbell, experienced mountain man that he was, felt no repulsion toward eating young, tender dog meat, especially when cooked with the skill for which Shoshone women were noted. In fact, he as well as many another leader often took dogs along on their trips as a dependable and convenient supply of fresh meat. This custom was not often mentioned, except obliquely, in their journals, and not at all around the china-and-crystal-laden dining tables of St. Louis and New Orleans. It was, however, an accepted custom in the beaver country, where expediency, and in some cases extreme necessity, overrode squeamishness that sprang from civilized notions.

Campbell, addressing the chieftain in the Shoshone language, suggested that Captain Stewart be included in the invitation. This the old man did with great urbanity. With Campbell as interpreter, Stewart accepted with phrases no less stately than those used by the chief.

CHAPTER VIII

Meet the Mountain Men

꒳ When the appointed time came for the dinner with the Shoshone chief, Stewart and Campbell mounted their fine blooded horses and rode through the camp of the Rocky Mountain Fur Company in the direction of the Shoshone village. Campbell, clad in the usual fringed buckskins of the mountain man, attracted little attention, but Captain Stewart's fashionable garb caused great astonishment as well as some unconcealed amusement. Here was a man the likes of which these white men and Indians had never seen. Well, he had never seen the likes of them, either.

Some of the trappers wore buckskin shirts made by the squaws. A few of these garments were new, but mostly they were blackened by the smoke of many a campfire and made slick with grease from countless feasts of fat buffalo cow. Here and there was a capote of proper cut and material, fashioned back in the settlements by experienced hands. But there were also many a rough jacket, obviously cut from an old blanket with a butcher knife and stitched up by the wearer himself. Head coverings presented an infinite variety. Hats, even of the sturdiest kinds, quickly disintegrated under the hard usage that was their lot during a winter in the mountains, battered by rain, hail, snow and wind. When a man's hat was gone, he fashioned another according

57

to his own ideas, from whatever materials were at hand. The results were usually grotesque, but occasionally a wild, barbaric beauty would be achieved. One head covering that arrested Stewart's amazed attention was a turbanlike arrangement of two pale, lustrous stone-marten pelts with the wings and breast of a bluebird ornamenting one side. Others bore such whimsies as a cluster of drooping eagle feathers, a bunch of ermine tails, a few loops of snakeskin. Bizarre as these head coverings appeared, they were wholly practical, protecting the head of the wearer from the inclemencies of the weather and from overhanging tree limbs that might otherwise crack the skulls of inattentive travelers.

A free trapper rode past Stewart and his companion, followed at a respectful distance by his Indian wife on a pony. Evidently the trapper had had a successful season and brought many beaver plews to the rendezvous. One look at his wife and her mount, however, and the question arose as to whether he had much left to show for his months of arduous labor in the beaver country. The Indian woman rode proudly, as well she might, decked out in every finery to be found on the trader's tables that happened to appeal to her barbaric taste.

A silk kerchief of brilliant colors fluttered its corners from her head. Bright ribbons dangled, beads clinked, cheap rings sparkled on brown fingers, small mirrors and silver hawk's bells jingled with every step taken by her gaudily caparisoned pony. Life for her had never been so good, and probably never would be again. The Indian brave had no notion of pampering his wife in this fashion—or any other—much preferring to decorate himself with whatever white man's trinkets he could buy or steal.

When Stewart and Campbell reached the outskirts of the Shoshone village they saw aboriginal life lived in the open. Young men raced their horses, gambling on the outcome. Others sat, painting themselves for a visit to one of the American camps, or reclined before their tepees while the women cooked, dressed hides, made moccasins, or did their colorful and intricate porcupine-quill embroidery, the sheer beauty of which has seldom been surpassed by the work of any savage people. Perhaps the strangest sight of all to Stewart was the many children, both boys and girls, practicing with

their small bows and arrows, not as a game but with great seriousness.

At last the two white men arrived at the chief's tepee. Dis-
mounting, they unhesitatingly handed bridle reins to waiting
youths who led the beautiful animals away. The Shoshones were
the cleverest, most notorious horse thieves in the whole West and
their mounts were the finest obtainable. No scrawny bang-tails
for them. Under other circumstances, these young men would have
joyously tomahawked half a dozen white men if by so doing they
could have made off with such horses as these. However, to steal
horses belonging to guests who trusted them was unthinkable—
though they might steal the same animals at a later date and
under different circumstances with no compunction whatever.
Indian ethics, or at least those held by the Shoshones, had some
strange twists, but you could be sure that these ethics never would
be violated, regardless of temptation. It is more than can be said
of the white man's ethics.

Before the chief's tepee stood the insignia of his rank as chief
and status as a warrior. From a tripod formed of straight willow
wands dangled his medicine bag, one of his most prized possessions.
It was made from the whole skin of a small white wolf cub. What
strange, nondescript, and perhaps mildly revolting items it held
was any man's guess, but every object was sacred, adding its medicine to the already powerful medicine of the chief himself. From
half a dozen wands stuck in the ground dangled as many freshly
taken scalps, each stretched on a small hoop to dry, each with its
long strand of black hair gently swaying in the breeze. Captain
Stewart would have looked with interest at the chief's shield, made
of buffalo hide and painted with strange—but, to an Indian, mean-
ingful—designs that hung on the tepee beside the drawn-back flap
that served as a door.

On entering the dimly lighted interior of the lodge, the two
white men were given a dignified welcome. Half a dozen other
important men of the tribe, besides the chief, were present, seated
on folded buffalo robes. Campbell presented his gifts to the chief:
a fine red woolen shirt, several strings of the especially desired blue
beads, and a long Green River knife made in Sheffield, England.

To the other guests he distributed mirrors, envelopes containing vermilion, and tobacco. Grunts of satisfaction expressed the pleasure felt at receiving these extravagantly generous gifts.

The chief then called in two women, who came bearing his presents to the white men. Campbell received a beaded and fringed shirt made of antelope hide and a buffalo-skin bag packed with a special pemmican: jerky pounded to a powder and mixed with dried berries and the marrow from buffalo bones—the most highly prized delicacy of the Indian cuisine and one that kept indefinitely. Stewart was given a painted buffalo robe and two pairs of soft beaded and embroidered moccasins.

These gestures of friendship concluded, the chief indicated where the white men were to take their places in the circle. An aged squaw brought a container of live coals to the chief. One of these coals served to light the tobacco in the chief's peace pipe, the bowl of which was made of a certain red sandstone named Catlinite from a quarry on the upper Missouri. From this sacred quarry came the material for all peace pipes from the Atlantic Seaboard to the Rocky Mountains and beyond. The stem of the chief's pipe was formed from a carefully polished river reed and decorated with eagle feathers and blue beads.

The old chief solemnly placed the mouthpiece of the long pipe stem between his lips, took one slow puff, pointed the stem west, north, east, south, toward the sky, then downward to the earth in the prescribed sacred order. He passed the pipe to Campbell, who followed the chief's example in every particular. No move of this important ceremony escaped Captain Stewart's eyes and when his turn came, every detail was executed with precision. His careful observance of this rite would not have gone unnoticed by the Indians; to them the smoking of the peace pipe was a sacred ceremony in which the smallest deviation might evoke displeasure in the spirits of earth and sky.

After the pipe had passed around the circle, women brought in the feast: dog-meat stew in a great pot from which each guest selected portions, putting them on pieces of bark that served as plates. There were boiled camas roots which to the white men seemed a stringy kind of potato, not very palatable.

After the feast was over and long-winded speeches expressing undying friendship had been made by both sides, Stewart and Campbell returned to their new location on the Green. Campbell went to his tent where, he said, he had work to do on his reports to the company. Captain Stewart chatted with the trappers and men who served at the trading post. As night fell, he checked the horse guards to make sure all were on duty and sober. Even here at the rendezvous a stray band of Crows or the ever-treacherous Blackfeet might try to make off with a dozen or so horses, if given the slightest chance.

Next morning, which was July 13, a wandering trapper brought the news to the Rocky Mountain Fur Company's encampment that Bonneville, with 110 men and about 300 horses, had arrived the day before at his stockade, only four miles away. Stewart quite possibly had heard of Bonneville during his stay in New York, for it was in that city the year before the Scotsman's arrival that Bonneville had raised funds for his adventure in the mountains, mainly from friends of John Jacob Astor.

In any event, Stewart would certainly have heard more than one discussion of Bonneville's plans in St. Louis, where Senator Benton and others there must have known of them. It was common knowledge among the inner circles of the federal government that a gentleman's agreement had been reached with Bonneville, that in return for a leave from the army for two years, he was to bring back surveys, maps and any other information that he could come by about the country that lay in the Rocky Mountains and beyond—how far beyond never being stated, but as later events showed, quite clearly understood by those in the inner councils. Ostensibly, however, Bonneville went into the West for the sole purpose of cleaning up a fortune in furs for himself and his wealthy New York sponsors.

The stir occasioned by Bonneville's arrival, along with Captain Stewart's natural interest in meeting an officer of the United States Army, would have impelled him to visit that gentleman as soon as possible. They were both educated men, adventurers at heart, connoisseurs of fine food and drink, who, when they could, surrounded themselves with luxury, though never sidestepping hardship. While widely different in background and experience, they had so much in common that they must have spent many hours together in Bonneville's plush headquarters within the rough log stockade of what the unthinking and uninformed called Fort Nonsense.

In fact, the location of the stoutly built fort had been chosen, probably in Washington, with foresight and wisdom. It stood in the very center of the fur country and would, if required to do so, provide a base for any expedition, military or otherwise, planned to invade the Oregon Territory. If a military force came out of the Columbia region—where the British were established—to threaten the American fur trade, or to challenge the claim of the United States on Oregon, Fort Bonneville was there to block further progress. Strengthened and armed, the log enclosure would serve as a defense against any unwelcome visitors approaching the South Pass. It sat fairly astride the Humboldt River route to California, a potentially rich and important area on which powerful figures in Washington had been casting speculative eyes for years. That the project, given into the hands of Captain Bonneville came to nothing at the time was not the fault of the far-sighted men in Washington, but of this inept army officer from Fort Gibson whose mind was more on immediate personal wealth and aggrandizement than on the future of his country.

During the visits which Captain Stewart made to Bonneville's camp, he had the opportunity to become acquainted with Joseph Reddeford Walker, one of the greatest of the mountain men, who had outfitted and organized Bonneville's party for the army man at Independence in the winter and spring of 1831–1832. Walker was sub-chief of the outfit and one of Bonneville's most valued guides and advisors. Another famous man with Bonneville at this time was Michael Silvestre Cerré, of St. Louis, a member of the great Cerré fur dynasty.

Captain Stewart may have witnessed the arrival at Fort Nonsense of the ragged and starving remnant of the Gant and Blackwell party. This expedition had set out from St. Louis in the spring of 1831 with a force of seventy men, well-equipped and with more than enough horses for riding and packing. The surviving members, who had met with incredible misfortune, were now reduced to "one dirty blanket and a rifle with a few rounds of ammunition" for each man. These unfortunate adventurers were well received by Bonneville and employed by him in one capacity or another. Among them was a New England man of some education named Zenas Leonard, who was to perform a signal service for future historians and lovers of the Far West.

The saturnalia of the rendezvous grew wilder and noisier and more violent as trappers continued to stream in, singly and in parties of four or five, with their beaver packs and occasional skins of marten, mink and otter. A rumor spread that a mad wolf had run amuck in one of the upper camps of the fur trappers, biting several men. Campbell, when he heard of it, shrugged the story off. There was always some wild tale going around in the mountains, he told Captain Stewart. The reputation of the trappers for fabricating stories was well known. No one thought it necessary to take precautions against a possible repetition of the incident. Days went by. The story of the mad wolf was forgotten. The men went about their business and pleasure as usual.

CHAPTER IX

Off to the Big Horn

꙳ June was half over. Though the rendezvous would not break up for another week or ten days, the trappers began to plan where they would make their fall and winter hunts. There appeared to be as much shouting, gambling, fighting, and horse racing as before at the several encampments, as much buying of foofaraw for the Indian girls as ever, but the high tide of excitement ebbed a little. Campbell, Fitzpatrick, Fontenelle, and Bonneville sat in their tents, mapping out their strategy for the coming year, plotting and scheming to outwit each other.

Campbell called Captain Stewart into councils held in the Rocky Mountain Fur Company's tent. Both Campbell and Fitzpatrick had come to trust the Scot, not only for his skill with the Manton rifle and for the military fashion with which he handled the men under his command, but for his quick grasp of the complexities of the fur trade. Here, they realized, was no ordinary playboy sportsman, but a mature, intelligent man who could shoulder large responsibilities with credit to himself and to those associated with him.

As the rendezvous neared its end, Stewart's thoughts turned to what he would wear, once he was on the trail again. The rough garments he had bought at Aull's store in Lexington had become worn beyond further usefulness by the rigors of the trip out. He knew that his white leather jacket with its many pockets and the trousers of Stewart hunting plaid were completely unsuitable to wilderness travel. Taking Campbell's advice, he commissioned a squaw with a reputation in such matters to make him a shirt, trousers, and leggings of buckskin. These handsome and practical garments, plus half a dozen pairs of moccasins, would be ready for him when it came time for him to leave the Green River valley.

One evening as the rendezvous neared its end, Captain Stewart suggested to George Holmes that the younger man sleep somewhere else that night than in their bower, as he was expecting a pretty Blackfoot girl. Holmes may have grumbled a little, though good-naturedly, as was characteristic of him, but he agreed, taking his blanket to an open, grassy space where he lay down and went to sleep.

Shortly after midnight, turmoil broke out. Dogs barked, men shouted, there was the sound of running feet. Captain Stewart hurried toward the center of this confusion, belting on his capote as he ran. By the light of an almost full moon, he saw Holmes sitting on the ground, one ear and the side of his face bleeding. A few feet away a gray wolf glared, standing its ground defiantly, seemingly without fear.

"Mad wolf! Mad wolf!" men shouted. Larpenteur lifted his gun to shoot the animal. Stewart, exercising his authority as night captain, ordered him not to fire because of the danger of wounding someone in the milling group crowding close.

Intimidated finally by the noise, the wolf slunk away in the darkness. Dr. Harrison was sent for, but he could do little except bathe Holmes's wounds and stop the flow of blood. After a while the camp quieted down, all except young Holmes and Dr. Harrison. The physician stayed with the injured man for the remainder of the night.

The only man in the whole encampment of the Rocky Mountain Fur Company who slept through the disturbance was Joe Meek, so drunk even the Angel Gabriel's horn hardly would have roused him from his slumbers. Joe was young and feeling his oats. Next morning Captain Stewart happened to encounter the irrepressible if now sober Joe.

"You were so drunk last night the mad wolf might have bitten you, too," Stewart said, frowning.

"Shucks," Joe is supposed to have replied, "if that wolf had of bit me, it would of cured him, sure—if it hadn't killed him!"

Stewart regretted bitterly that he had been the cause of Holmes's sleeping in the open that night. The young man seemed all right, however. His wounds began to heal quickly in the clean mountain air. But he lost his light-hearted gaiety, becoming morose and melancholy, predicting that he would shortly die of hydrophobia. He showed no symptoms of the disease and continued to discharge his camp duties as before, though, so anxiety regarding him subsided. The men were not aware that hydrophobia gives no sign of its presence until the virus, creeping along the nerves, reaches the brain.

Bonneville no doubt told both Campbell and Captain Stewart that he was sending Joe Walker with a party of men to California, via the Great Salt Lake. Several of the men who were going knew their destination. The California aspect of the undertaking was later denied by Bonneville, through Washington Irving, in Irving's book, *The Adventures of Captain Bonneville*, but contemporary evidence shows that Bonneville made no secret at the time that the goal of this expedition was the Pacific Coast.

Zenas Leonard, of the bankrupt Gant and Blackwell outfit, went along as a clerk. He left the only first-hand account of this momentous journey that has so far come to light. He stated in this record that he joined the party because he "was anxious to go to the coast of the Pacific." Joe Meek, who was no fool even though he had been too busy living to acquire such trifling skills as reading and writing, also indicated that his reason for joining was that he wanted to go to California.

Stephen Hall Meek, Joe's older brother, went along on this same expedition, and mentions the fact in a short autobiography written fifty years later. Bonneville outfitted the expedition, consisting of thirty-four men and three times as many horses and mules, for one year, which was extravagant, even for him, if the party was to go no farther than the Great Salt Lake, as he later declared.

As further evidence that this was no mere trapping expedition,

Joseph Reddeford Walker was appointed to lead it. Walker, then thirty-five years old, was one of the greatest—and least publicized —mountain men, explorers, and guides the West ever saw. In his twenties he had helped organize Jackson County, Missouri, where he served two terms as sheriff, and to found Independence, suggesting the names for both county and town. His choice indicated clearly his political leanings. A Jackson man as well as a Benton man, he was in favor of "manifest destiny," with all that phrase meant in the way of Western expansion for the United States.

It now seems clear that Walker, under the guise of leading a trapping expedition, was dispatched to California for the purpose of gathering information and to report the political situation in Monterey, its capital. His task was to determine how much opposition, beyond a token resistance, would be encountered if the United States annexed California in the near future. That he carried out his mission well is indicated by ensuing events.

Walker took his party to Great Salt Lake, trapping as he went, though with scant success. They killed their last buffalo near the western shore of the lake, jerked the meat, and set off into the Great American Desert. At the far side of that appalling stretch of wasteland, Walker discovered a lake and a river that emptied into it, both of which were named for him. Following this river, he came to the Sierra Nevadas, precipitous, snow-topped at this time of year, beautiful and threatening.

Walker and his party made a homeric crossing, the first white men to see the Yosemite Valley. During the passage they lost twenty-four horses, seventeen of them killed to provide food for the all but exhausted explorers. It was lean, tough and stringy food. The men would, Leonard states with obvious horror, "take only such parts of the flesh as extreme hunger will render it possible for a human being to eat but—it was the only thing that saved us from death."

Once they were over the mountains and down in the lovely valley of the San Joaquin, their troubles were over. They lived sumptuously on antelope, deer and the large sweet acorns so liked by the friendly Indians who lived in that grassy, well-watered and well-wooded paradise.

At last they came to Monterey, where they were hospitably

received. Walker, handsome, six feet tall, was as much at home in the political and social circles of the capital as Bonneville or even Captain Stewart would have been. He spent the winter there, and returned to meet Bonneville at a designated rendezvous in 1834. He brought back little fur, but appears to have given the army man the information that influenced the government to proceed—but slowly and cautiously—with its plans to end Mexico's rule of California. Not until two years later did Bonneville make the attempt to lay the blame on Walker for his own failure to amass a fortune in the fur trade for himself and his New York backers.

The departure of the Walker party from Bonneville's camp on the morning of July 24, 1833, was a matter of considerable interest to trappers and partisans alike. Captain Stewart rode over to witness this picturesque leavetaking for romantic California. One wonders why he didn't go along. The expedition offered the kind of adventure that would have afforded him keen delight: uncharted trails, unknown dangers, and at last the fabled land of California.

Perhaps he was restrained from accompanying Walker and his band of daring men because he had committed himself to help Campbell and Fitzpatrick get their furs safely to the Big Horn at a point far to the north, where the river first became navigable after its tumultuous plunge through the mountains. Campbell planned to take the company's furs down the Big Horn and the Yellowstone to that river's confluence with the Missouri. There Sublette would be waiting with the keelboat which, it will be remembered, he had taken far upstream the previous spring. Then the two partners, with their furs and buffalo robes, would float down the river to St. Louis.

Later the same day that Joe Walker and his long train of men and horses left for California, Captain Stewart departed from the now almost deserted site of the rendezvous. The party with which Stewart found himself associated was a curiously assorted one. There were Campbell, of course, and Fitzpatrick with his party of twenty trappers, along with clerk, Charles Larpenteur, Antoine (who was apparently employed by Captain Stewart), Dr. Harrison, and the melancholy George Holmes, plus the usual complement of pack horses to transport the furs.

At the last moment, Nat Wyeth joined Campbell's brigade. His own party, consisting only of himself, Milton Sublette, and four assistants, two white men and two Indians, was inadequate to travel safely through Indian-infested country. He, too, was headed for the Big Horn, to take his season's catch down the river.

On the following day, July 25, Bonneville, with Silvestre Cerré and the rest of his party, left Fort Nonsense, taking with them their disappointingly small amount of furs. Cerré would go with them to St. Louis by the same water route that Campbell planned to use, but neither had confided in the other regarding the matter. No fur trader ever told his competitor anything, except perhaps—and with caution—the time of day.

Bonneville's leave from the army would expire in November. According to a statement made later—much later—by him, and repeated by Irving in *The Adventures of Captain Bonneville,* Cerré carried in his pocket a letter from the captain to the War Department in Washington, D.C., asking for an extension of his leave. The letter was never received by those to whom it was addressed.

There was no reason to believe that Bonneville did not write such a letter. Headstrong and willful he may have been, but he was not so lacking in common sense as to take liberties with the War Department. It is equally clear that he had no intention of returning within a reasonable length of time to his duties at Fort Gibson. He undoubtedly had powerful friends in the top echelons of the government, so the leave surely would have been granted, had the request for it been received. However, somewhere along the way, Bonneville's letter disappeared. The failure of the letter to reach its destination set in motion a curious sequence of events, to be touched on later.

Now two sizeable caravans were traveling toward the Big Horn River, neither with any knowledge of the other's whereabouts. Matters began to take on more than a tinge of comic opera. After a day or two, Bonneville came upon unmistakable signs that Campbell was ahead of him. Some obscure train of reasoning made him decide that Campbell was marching in this direction in an effort to deceive Bonneville—that Campbell really intended to make his winter hunt in the Crow country, where Bonneville planned to go as soon as his furs were shipped down the Big Horn. So Bonneville kept a discreet day's march behind Campbell.

Campbell, who had no idea that Bonneville was in the vicinity, and couldn't have cared less, continued on his way. At last Bonneville realized that Campbell was going openly about his business, making no attempt to throw the army man off the track. He immediately detached a party of men and sent them to the trapping grounds he had selected. A day or two later he sent another body of men to follow the first.

While all this was transpiring, George Holmes developed the violent, horrifying symptoms of hydrophobia. Many contradictory accounts of the details of this tragedy have survived; but all narrators agree that during a violent paroxysm, the frenzied young man broke away from his companions, rushed into the woods, and was never seen again. Years later, Captain Stewart declared in his novel *Edward Warren*, "There has never quitted my breast a reproachful remorse for the part I played that sad night." (He meant the night Holmes was bitten by the wolf.)

Immediately after he dispatched the second contingent to the Crow country, Bonneville abandoned his policy of secrecy and caught up with the Campbell party. Thereafter the two brigades journeyed together toward their common destination, the Big Horn River. Complete amity, even cordiality prevailed—on the surface, anyway. They proceeded, "In great good fellowship," as Washington Irving had Bonneville say. At the moment, neither partisan could harm the other, so why not enjoy each other's company? It was an attitude that prevailed throughout the fur country.

Arriving at the banks of the Big Horn where it escaped from the rocky defiles of the mountains, the three parties set about building the necessary bull boats. Campbell had thirty packs of beaver, ten hides to the pack, amounting to about 1200 pounds in weight. There was also an indeterminate number of buffalo robes. Here Captain Stewart had his second experience with bull boats. Campbell built three, seeing to it that their seams were well caulked with buffalo grease and ashes from the campfire.

Bonneville and Cerré built three boats also, for though Bonneville had comparatively few furs he had to furnish transportation for thirty-six of his men who desired to return to the settlements. Nat Wyeth contented himself with one boat, but it was unusually large and more strongly constructed than the others. It would not only carry his furs, but his four assistants, Milton Sublette, and himself; it was eighteen feet long, five and a half wide, and pointed at both ends instead of being the usual circular shape. It took three buffalo skins to cover the framework and Wyeth made sure the hides came from venerable bulls, so they were extra thick and strong.

Wyeth, nervously urging his men to hurry, characteristically was ready first, even though he admitted his boat leaked a little. They shoved off and the swift, deeply flowing current of the river took them out of sight. He was shortly followed by Cerré, boats laden with furs and the band of erstwhile trappers, now homeward bound. Vasquez was sent overland, accompanied by Larpenteur and three assistants, to drive the horses Fitzpatrick did not need, along with two cows and a bull. Finally, Campbell embarked, shouting unnecessary admonitions to that astute mountain man, Fitzpatrick, until the last possible moment.

After that, Fitzpatrick and his twenty trappers, Captain Stewart, Antoine, and Dr. Harrison waited for Bonneville to start for wherever he intended to go. Bonneville, having lost confidence in himself as a sleuth, left almost at once. Then Fitzpatrick and his party started for the Crow country, where they had intended to go all along, as soon as they had attended to the shipment of their furs. These Indians had always been friendly to Fitzpatrick and he did not know that their hearts had changed toward him because of a little trouble he had gotten into with a wandering band of the tribe the year before.

On September 5 his scouts reported a near-by village of Crows, numbering about a hundred tepees, whose chief was a wise old red man whom Fitzpatrick knew well. Thinking this a piece of good fortune, he encamped about three miles from the village. Next morning he made preparations to ride over alone, make a courtesy call on his friend, the chief, and at the same time see if he couldn't drum up a little business in beaver plews and buffalo robes. Before leaving, he made arrangements to leave Captain Stewart in command of the party, numbering about twenty-five men, with the usual complement of horses. This action was a mark of great trust, and an indication of the esteem in which Fitzpatrick held Stewart.

Unknown to the white men, Crow scouts had been watching their every move, with malice and motivated by the worst of intentions. Shortly after Fitzpatrick left, a very large party of young Crows rode into the encampment. Having been assured that these Indians were friendly and could be trusted, Stewart received them cordially. The braves, however, were arrogant and surly, and had their medicine man along, a very bad sign, as Fitzpatrick would have realized, but which meant nothing to Stewart. The Indians began to appropriate small articles to which they took a fancy, then items of greater value.

Stewart's temper rose, and he told them in words they plainly understood what he thought of them, but hesitated to make any threatening movement because of the great disparity of numbers between the white men and the Indians, it being about four to one. Antoine, who spoke the Crow language, took Stewart to one side and explained to him that the only way they could save their lives was by maintaining complete calm, no matter what happened. The medicine man had told the young warriors that if one of them committed the first act of violence, they would be defeated. Their plan, then, was to force Captain Stewart to shoot, or even strike, one of the marauding band, upon which they could, with safety to themselves, tomahawk every man, take his scalp, and steal what they wanted.

So Stewart, with Antoine at his side, faced the murderous horde quietly and silently. Tomahawks were brandished in their faces, insults shouted at them, but the men retained their composure—at least in appearance—made no hostile move, exhibited no anger. The Indians' purpose was defeated by their own superstitious belief in their medicine man, and the self-restraint and cool courage of Stewart, Antoine, and the other men in the party. But when the savages left, they took horses, guns, trade goods, everything the party possessed—even Stewart's fine watch.

When Fitzpatrick returned from a pleasant visit with the old Crow chief, who knew nothing of the extracurricular activity of his young men, and heard the appalling bad news, he had only praise for Stewart, whose self-control had saved the lives of every man in camp. But anger against the renegade band of Crows rose in him with all the fury of a prairie thunderstorm. He rode back, defiantly alone, to the Indian village, and demanded full restitution from the chief. Fitzpatrick had the reputation of being able to handle Indians better than any other man in the fur trade, and he must have earned it, for he got some of his property back: a handful of horses, a few traps, some rifles, and a pack or two of trade goods.

He could do no more, so with Stewart and the remainder of his party, he got out of the country, losing more horses to the Crows on the way. There were well-substantiated rumors that the attack on Fitzpatrick's party and the extra horse stealing that followed were incited by Jim Beckwourth, a mulatto who was sometimes alleged to have Crow blood in his veins. This swaggering, boastful fellow did hold a position of influence in the Crow tribe, called himself a chief, and married a Crow woman. He was on the American Fur Company's payroll and was generally regarded as the most inveterate liar in the West, a considerable distinction among men who practiced the telling of tall tales as an art.

Beckwourth later dictated an "autobiography" which included a long account of how Captain Stewart came to him, hotly accused Jim of complicity in the Crow affair, and demanded that Jim see to it that his best horse was returned. The passage is replete with elegant dialogue, written by Beckwourth of course, in which Jim nobly denies Captain Stewart's accusations and completely humbles the proud Scottish nobleman. It was pure fantasy, spun from Beckwourth's conceit and imagination, but it is probably true that Captain Stewart's attitude toward him was one of anger strongly impregnated with contempt.

Where Captain Stewart spent the winter of 1833–34 is not known. There is no evidence to show that he was in either St. Louis or New Orleans, nor is his name mentioned as a member of any party that remained in the Rocky Mountains. There are some vague hints that he traveled as far south as Taos and Santa Fe. If so, he may have seen Indian and Mexican workers building the three-foot-thick adobe walls of Bent's Fort on the north bank of the Arkansas. This fort, built by the Bent Brothers and Ceran St. Vrain, became the largest and most important trading post to be erected in the West during the era of the fur business.

That spring, though its location cannot now be pinpointed, there occurred an incident involving Captain Stewart, his prized "fast-running" horse, Otholo, his Indian servant, a young man of the Iowa tribe called Marshall, and Markhead, a man famous in the West for his unflinching courage, although it is doubted that he possessed even a modest degree of intelligence. The Indian, following a number of small depredations, stole Stewart's horse and his best rifle—both irreplaceable here in the mountains. Stewart's temper, as we have already seen, had a low boiling point. Rage consumed him. He said, in Markhead's hearing, that he would give $500 for the thief's scalp. Easy money, Markhead thought, taking the words literally.

Setting out in search of the Indian, Markhead found him riding Captain Stewart's horse, shot the savage dead, scalped him, and recovered both horse and rifle, all in what seemed to him the simple line of duty. Pleased with himself, he rode exultantly into camp leading Otholo, gun held aloft, the Indian's bloody scalp dangling from the barrel. Stewart, not at all averse to shooting an Indian in a skirmish, was shocked by this coldblooded murder, the result of his own words spoken in thoughtless anger. He flung the scalp into a clump of bushes, to Markhead's complete confusion. However, he paid Markhead the reward he had so rashly offered.

The first dependable report we have of Stewart's whereabouts in 1834 is of him, in the company of Jim Bridger, riding in a northerly direction to that year's rendezvous. It was to be held on Ham's Fork, a clear, pleasant stream flowing into the Green River from the west. Sheltering mountains protected the valley of Ham's Fork, grass grew thick and tall, cottonwoods cast their thick shade against the rays of the burning summer sun. It was a good place to hold a rendezvous.

The man from Perthshire had received no news from home since he had left Lexington about a year before. Surely Campbell, or Sublette, or whoever might lead the Rocky Mountain Fur Company's train to the mountains that year, would bring letters from Scotland.

CHAPTER X

Fort Laramie Christened
With Champagne

ঠ৺ It is probable that as far back as the spring of 1833, William Sublette and his partner, Robert Campbell, planned to build a fort at a strategic point in the West. Early in 1834 Sublette returned to St. Louis from a business trip to New York and Philadelphia. He began immediately to put this plan into effect, though apparently he told no one about it. Men in the fur trade learned early to play their cards close to their chests.

On April 13, 1834, he secured a license to trade for one and one-half years at several specific locations on the prairies and in the mountains. One of the places mentioned was on the Laramie. This site seemed of no particular importance to General William Clark, Superintendent of Indian Affairs for this region, who issued all such licenses; but Sublette and Campbell had selected it with all the sagacity for which they were famous.

This license in hand, Sublette set off at once for Independence, where he would ready the train for the long journey to the rendezvous. He hurried, for his rival, Nathaniel Wyeth, was also taking a train that year and Sublette wanted to beat him to the rendezvous.

Tension between the leaders of the two expeditions was still further increased by the fact that Milton Sublette traveled with Wyeth instead of with his brother William. The relationship between Milton and William was an interesting one. Throughout Milton's active life in the fur trade, he refused to ally himself with William or to be guided by him—as, indeed, he had no need to do, having proved his ability to take care of himself over and over. Somehow, William could not accept the situation and kept on trying to get Milton to work with him. Yet the two brothers, in spite of their differences, remained steadfastly loyal and affectionate toward each other.

With Bill Sublette went a young greenhorn, William Marshall Anderson, who made a name for himself by keeping a light-hearted journal of the expedition. Arriving at Independence, they found Nat Wyeth there, grimly determined to get started first.

The preceding winter and early spring had been more rainy than usual, and now it had turned warm. The grass was up and growing fast. Soon there would be sufficient feed on the prairie for the stock. Wyeth, active as a whirlwind on the Kansas prairie, was buying trade goods and supplies for his men, as well as superintending the shoeing of his pack and riding animals, urging his men to ever greater exertions. Nat's hopes of traveling faster than the partners were pinned on the extra-fine horses he had bought at St. Louis, at ruinous prices.

His party of trappers, packers, hunters, and swampers numbered fifty men, with 140 horses and mules, plus twenty cattle for an emergency food supply. Milton Sublette had twenty men and three times as many horses, the usual ratio on these expeditions. There was also a strange assortment of people going along, with a diversified array of talents and occupations. Among this group were two Methodist missionaries, Reverend Jason Lee and his nephew, Reverend Daniel Lee, who were making the journey to save the souls of the Flatheads and the Nez Perces. With them were three lay assistants: Cyrus Shepherd, P. L. Edwards, and Courtney Walker, young men whose sole purpose seems to have been to see the West, expenses paid.

This group had with them the invariable encumbrance that

seemed to go with all missionaries—cows. In this case, there were two.

Other men of note who accompanied Wyeth were Thomas Nuttall, distinguished mineralogist and botanist, John K. Townsend, ornithologist, and four assistants. There was also Captain Joseph Thing, a distinguished navigator of Boston, who went along to measure the distance from Independence across the Rocky Mountains, all the way to Fort Vancouver, by observations made of the stars. He was employed by the Boston company that financed Wyeth's expedition, operating under the name of the Columbia Fishing and Trading Company. In midsummer Captain Stewart would join Wyeth's party and journey with them to Dr. John McLoughlin's empire on the Columbia.

How Wyeth thought his fine horses would keep him ahead of Sublette is not possible to comprehend, since his party could move no faster than the small herd of cattle that belonged to him and the plodding milch cows of the missionaries. It appears that Sublette took one look at his competitor's outfit and stopped worrying about the possibility of Wyeth's beating him to the rendezvous. After that, he concerned himself only with getting the goods packed and seeing to it that the horses and mules were properly shod in the blacksmith shops facing the square at Independence.

Wyeth did succeed in getting away first. On the 27th of April he had gathered the bulk of his party four miles out on the prairie west of Independence—all except the missionaries. The two Lees were so zealously engaged in spreading the gospel among the sinners of the brawling frontier town on the Missouri that they couldn't tear themselves away, though Wyeth had, in angry desperation, told them he would not wait on their appearance for so much as one hour.

They didn't believe he would have so little regard for the work of the Lord as to make his threat good, but on the morning of the 28th, Wyeth's caravan moved out into the seemingly endless prairie without them. The two preachers and their assistants spent a hurried and anxious three days catching up with him, prodding their cows to unprecedented exertions as they went.

Friction began to develop almost at once. The two missionaries made the mistake of expecting the men of the train to accord them the same deference which they had received, as minis-
ters, in their former environment. They also freely expressed their
disapproval of the language the men used in addressing recalcitrant
mules. The fact that the party traveled on Sunday was an abomina-
tion and a stench in their nostrils, and they said so, clearly and
often. They held themselves aloof and apart from all and sundry,
even Wyeth, who now and then committed the unpardonable sin
of distributing a ration of whisky to his men at the end of a particularly hard day's work.

Hardly surprisingly, the two missionaries began to suffer from
an unprecedented number of petty mishaps. The load of one of
their animals slipped and no packer was available to get it back
in position and secure it properly. A picket rope disappeared just
when it was needed. The man whose duty it was to tell them when
a meal was ready forgot all about it. There seemed no end to the
ingenuity of Wyeth's men in thinking up small but irritating ways
to harass and annoy Jason and Daniel Lee.

The sanctimonious and overbearing conduct of these two missionaries made more difficult the western journey of better men of
the same calling who followed them. Wyeth, not renowned for
his patience, remained courteous, with what prodigies of self-
control we can only imagine.

On the tenth day of travel, Milton Sublette's "bad leg" began
to give him such serious trouble that he was forced to turn back
and return to the settlements. The difficulty resulted from a bone
injury suffered several years before when he was wounded by an
Indian arrow. Later that year the leg had to be amputated.

On Wyeth's thirteenth day out of Independence, Sublette's
train passed him, a bitter moment for Nat. It took Sublette almost
a month to reach the fork where Laramie Creek joins the Platte.
The train crossed the Laramie and encamped on the north bank
of that stream about a mile above its confluence with the Platte.

There Sublette started to carry out his long-considered plan
of building a fort which, though not in size but in importance and
fame, would equal Bent's Fort, then being constructed far to the
south on the Arkansas between Timpas and Purgatory creeks.

Strenuous activity filled the next few days. Men were sent to the Black Hills for stout tree trunks of fir with which to form a fifteen-foot-high stockade, approximately 167 feet long and 120 feet wide, with two bastions at opposite corners, a blockhouse over the entrance gate, and whatever interior walls were necessary.

When the end of the first log was lowered into the trench provided for it, young Anderson, who had a feeling for drama and a sense that history was in the making, insisted there should be some sort of ceremony. After some good-natured argument between him and Sublette, the name of Fort William was decided upon. Anderson's enthusiasm so far outran his taste for fine liquor that he smashed against this first upright log a bottle of champagne he had cherished in his pack all the way from St. Louis. So, technically, and by the potency of bubbling champagne, the great trading post became Fort William, though the trappers and mountain men never called it anything but Fort Laramie. Within a day or two after the actual building began, Sublette hurried on to the rendezvous, leaving thirteen men to complete the fort and fourteen muleloads of food, ammunition and trade goods.

No site in all the surrounding area other than this one on the Laramie could have been as favorable for trading purposes. There was navigable water from this point all the way to St. Louis. Its location was almost in the center of the country frequented by the Oglala and Brulé Sioux, near to the ranges of the Arapahoes and Cheyennes. Practically everyone going to or coming from the richest beaver country on the continent followed the Platte. The fort would be finished, ready for the fall trade. Sublette and Campbell never showed greater wisdom than when they selected this pleasant meadow sloping to the Laramie on which to build a trading post.

Wyeth arrived at the Laramie on Sunday, the 1st of June. He recorded that the partners' fort was well along, and that Sublette had gone ahead. He noted the strange sight of men planting corn between the fort and Laramie Creek. Agriculture had come to the Platte. With no more than one day's rest, he hurried on—if it could be called hurrying when one's steps were matched to those of cows with swaying udders.

At Ham's Fork the clans began to gather. Captain Stewart and

Jim Bridger, whether together or separately is not known, rode in
during the second week of June. Indian villages came streaming in,
tribe by tribe, to set up their tepees with the usual initial uproar
and confusion, out of which the squaws somehow brought order.
Trappers, singly and in small groups, appeared, leading pack animals loaded with beaver. Everyone was waiting for the curtain to
go up, the play to start.

On the 18th of June Sublette and his train, with its trade goods
and its liquor, reached Ham's Fork. The rendezvous exploded like
a sky rocket into a burst of sustained sparkle, fire and color. Captain
Stewart was welcomed into Sublette's camp and the two men
drank each other's health in the best vintages St. Louis had to offer,
the bouquet of the wines made even more delightful by the wild
scenes amid which they were consumed.

There were letters for Captain Stewart. Some may have been
from his faithful Christina, telling him of the boy, George. An
envelope from Stewart's attorney in Perth brought a remittance
from John, but only a part of what was due. Then there was a long
letter from brother George with disquieting, even infuriating news.
George, pleasantly excited by what was going on, reported that
Lord Breadalbane was making extensive additions and improvements to Taymouth Castle. When they were completed, Taymouth would be one of the show places of Scotland. Brother John,
not to be outdone by Lord Breadalbane, whom he seemed not to
like very well, had undertaken to build something that would
throw Lord Breadalbane's puny efforts quite in the shade. He was
having a magnificent new castle constructed—appropriately named
New Murthly—not far from the ancient seat of the Stewarts—
actually almost in its front yard. Three stories high, it would be,
with fancy towers, turrets, embrasures—all the newest architectural fancies. Several years would pass before New Murthly could
be completed, and John said it would cost over a million pounds,
but its magnificence would humble Lord Breadalbane once and
for all.

In spite of the unhappy, stormy years he had spent at Murthly,
the captain loved the place deeply. The thought of John's monstrosity of a castle defacing the lovely estate, of the money his
brother was squandering on it for no reason but petty spite against

Breadalbane, Captain Stewart's friend, and that he couldn't get even what was due him from property rightfully, even legally, his —all this no doubt added up to a bitter draught for Captain Stewart to swallow. The taste was not soon forgotten. But, younger son that he was, he could do nothing about any of it.

After three days, Wyeth came in, with his entourage, stepping up the excitement by opening his trading post. Cerré appeared, bringing Bonneville's furs, taken during his winter hunt. The army man did not come to the rendezvous that year, as he had other business to attend to.

The combination of business, debauchery and frolic was now in full swing for miles along Ham's Fork. Some accounts say that 600 whites and 1500 Indians were there, shouting, cursing, drinking and fighting, with only now and then a sober head among them.

Amid all this turmoil there suddenly appeared a young man named Ashworth, an Englishman, blond, with tattered clothing and elegant, supercilious manners. He claimed to be the son of Sir Richard Ashworth, a peer of the realm. He had neither money nor its equivalent, beaver pelts; he was unarmed and on foot. Unfortunately no one took the trouble to record the story he told to account for his presence at the rendezvous in such a destitute helpless condition.

By common consent, responsibility for him was turned over to Captain Stewart, and because Ashworth declared himself to be a countryman of his, he accepted it. In his usual openhanded fashion he gave Ashworth a horse, a gun and a Hudson's Bay blanket, and made the young fellow welcome at his mess. Ashworth tried to improve his condition by a little dishonest gambling. His victims grumbled and threatened but did nothing except to shut him out of their games of Old Sledge. His attitude became insufferable toward everyone, with the exception of Captain Stewart, who had generously assumed responsibility for him and his immediate needs.

Even Stewart began to feel some qualms as to the wisdom of what he had done, at the same time aware that no other course had been possible to him. All he could do now was hope that Ashworth would not misbehave too badly before an opportunity arose to get rid of him.

CHAPTER XI

The Indians and the White Man's God

ह∾ Almost as soon as Jason Lee, king-pin of the missionaries, arrived an eager delegation of Flatheads and Nez Percés hurried to call on him. They had come to the rendezvous hoping to find someone there who was qualified to tell them about the white man's God.

In order to understand the urgency of their mission and their great joy at finding that missionaries had come with Wyeth's caravan, it is necessary to go back a few years; take note of the first chapters in one of the strangest serial stories ever to be enacted in the Far West. It is a story that began in simple faith and ended in brutal mass murder.

The Nez Percés and the Flatheads were among the most peaceful and well-intentioned people on the North American Continent. Their home ground was vaguely in what is now Montana and Idaho, but they traveled and hunted over a much larger area. In the late 1820's they became imbued with the idea that the white man's God had a more powerful medicine than was possessed by any of their own deities. Jedediah Smith's passage through their country on his way to Fort Vancouver on the Columbia may have implanted the idea, or at any rate, strengthened it, for Smith was a sincerely religious man. A Bible accompanied him on all his

82

travels and he spoke often of the power and glory of the Divine Being he worshiped.

In 1832 the two tribes appointed a delegation to go to St. Louis and ask that a religious teacher be sent to them. The original group consisted of six, but two of the older men died before a start could be made. This left four: two chiefs, one called Man-of-the-Morning, the other Black Eagle, and two trusted young men, Rabbit-Skin-Leggings and No-Horns-on-His Head. They made their way to Green River, expecting to join a fur brigade there and return with it to St. Louis. But no rendezvous was held that year. The Indians went on for a while alone, but somewhere along the way they met a party under Lucien Fontenelle and accompanied it to St. Louis.

In that busy city the four proud savages were like lost souls in an alien world. No one, not even William Clark, could talk to them, understand what they said. They could only communicate by signs. Clark provided a place for them to stay and strange food for them to eat. In time, he found an interpreter, and then the days were not quite so terrifying for the men of the wilds. But city life imposed terrific strains. Black Eagle, the Nez Perce war chief, died in October and Man-of-the-Morning soon followed him.

That left No-Horns-on-His-Head and Rabbit-Skin-Leggings to wait out the dreary winter in St. Louis. In the early spring of 1833, William Clark arranged passage for them on the steamboat *Yellowstone*, which would take them to a point about 800 miles from their home. To an Indian, that was practically next door. Before they left, Clark promised he would do his best to send missionaries to them with one of the fur-trade caravans that same year; however, he was not able to find a sufficiently dedicated—or financed—group to undertake the project in 1834.

On their way up the river on the *Yellowstone* they had as a fellow passenger that adventurous artist, George Catlin, and he became much interested in the young men and their story. At Fort Pierre, in what is now South Dakota, the steamboat laid over for a few days. A large village of Sioux was encamped there. The head men gave a great feast for No-Horns-on-His-Head and Rabbit-Skin-Leggings, presented them with elaborately decorated Sioux deerskin garments, bead and bone necklaces of fine workmanship.

Catlin painted portraits of both young men arrayed in all their finery.

Near where the Yellowstone River flows into the Missouri, No-Horns-on-His-Head sickened and died. Some distance farther on, Rabbit-Skin-Leggings set off overland alone. On the way he came on a band of his own tribe, the Nez Percés, and told them his story and of Clark's promise to send missionaries to the rendez-vous that summer. Later the party engaged in a skirmish with the warlike Blackfeet and Rabbit-Skin-Leggings was killed, but those of the party who survived took the news of William Clark's prom-ise to the tribe.

The tribesmen mourned for their dead emissaries but rejoiced in the success of the expedition. A large body of Nez Perce Indians went to the 1833 rendezvous, where Captain Stewart must have seen them there and heard their story. They were grievously disap-pointed, no one having come to tell them of the white man's God. Still hopeful, they had come again now in 1834. In the persons of Jason Lee and Daniel Lee, they believed that their prayers at last had been answered.

Jason Lee, face to face with the Indians whose souls he had come so far to save, became indifferent to the whole project. On the long journey from St. Louis he must have heard Wyeth talk of Fort Vancouver, its rich farm lands, the fertile well-watered Willamette Valley on the south side of the Columbia just waiting for settlers. After one look at these Nez Percé Indians his eyes turned to a bigger and better vision far down the Columbia, where there was land for farming and who knew what great things to come? When the Nez Percés learned his decision, they went patiently home, with the avowed intention of coming back next year, when they might have better luck.

While Nat Wyeth was trying to straighten out his tangled business relationships with Fitzpatrick and Bridger and Captain Stewart renewed friendships with Antoine and other men he had met the year before, another reunion was taking place a few days' journey to the west. Here, somewhere in the vicinity of the Bear River the Walker party, returning from California, was searching for Bonneville. On the 12th of July they found him. The two parties camped together and Walker made his report.

Not many furs, he said, but he had crossed the mountains to

California by a new route, spent the winter at the capital of the
Mexican province, discovered an easy pass farther south. What
other information he imparted is not known, but Bonneville appeared entirely satisfied with what Walker had done. The two
men waited amicably together for Cerré to bring supplies purchased at the rendezvous.

Cerré shortly appeared with goods sufficient, Zenas Leonard
said, "to outfit our present company for a whole year." Bonneville
dispatched Walker with fifty-five men and the usual number of
riding and pack animals to cross the Rocky Mountains and trap
the beaver streams eastward as far as the Missouri River. He would
then return, hunting and trading on the way, to join Captain
Bonneville, in June of the following year, near the mouth of the
Popo Agie where it meets the Wind River and they become the
Big Horn. It was a strange arrangement to make with a man
who Bonneville later declared had disobeyed his orders and
wasted his substance in debauchery and riotous living during his
winter in Monterey.

The frenzy of trading, drinking, lovemaking, gambling and
bragging that made up a rendezvous did not last long that year.
The first sign of the break-up came from the Shoshone village,
largest of the Indian camps. Moving was the squaws' business, and
they did their work well. First, the conical skin tepees, with their
framework of long, tapering lodge poles, came down in what seemed
hopeless confusion, but was really well-planned and organized activity. Skins and poles were packed on horses. Travois, made of
two poles fastened to the shoulders of other horses, with a raw-
hide platform out of reach of their kicking heels, were piled with
blankets, robes, kettles, clothing, household gear of all kinds,
lashed securely for the rough ride ahead. Dogs, trained to drag
small travois, were laden with articles. Yelling women and barking dogs made a prodigious uproar.

Small children rode the horse travois—stoic, for the most part
silent. Braves raced and circled grandly about, doing nothing and
with no responsibilities. Ready to go, after not more than a half
hour of preparation, a hundred or so braves, twice that number of
women and children, horses and dogs, streamed away—an Indian
village on the move.

Wyeth, too, was soon ready to pull out, having disposed of

only a small part of the trade goods he had brought so far. He
gathered his party together and headed toward Oregon, planning
to make one important stop on the way. With him went Captain
Stewart and the nuisance, Ashworth, who apparently had nowhere
else to go, and could not be abandoned here in the heart of the
Rockies. The missionaries were there also, in eager search of spirit-
ual fields to glean, or new lands to colonize—it is hard to tell
which. There is no more word of the cows; maybe the Indians got
them, perhaps with an assist from Wyeth's packers. There went
also the scientists, Nuttall and Townsend, and the navigator,
Captain Thing. There is no mention of Antoine Clement, who
probably spent the winter hunting and trapping in the mountains.
Neither the hardships of the trip, a twice-told tale to him, nor
the white man's way of life at Fort Vancouver, of which he had
heard many stories, would have appealed to his taste.

A few days west of Ham's Fork, Wyeth's party came upon the
camp of Thomas McKay, a quarter-breed—some said a step-son
of the great Dr. McLoughlin. His brigade was made up of French-
Canadians and half-breeds. They had a few squaws along and lived
in skin tepees—a picturesque lot that Captain Stewart found most
interesting. McKay was, as far as training and education went, a
white man, but he found it easy to adapt himself to Indian ways
when it seemed expedient to do so. For the rest of the way Wyeth's
party and that of McKay traveled in close conjunction with each
other, now separating for a few days, then coming together again.

Before Wyeth's party reached the Snake River, they met Bonneville and a party of ten men, starting for the Walla Walla country where Bonneville had spent the previous winter. At that time
the army man had made the acquaintance of Pierre Pambrun, in
charge of Fort Walla Walla, who had treated him with the utmost
courtesy—until Bonneville asked to buy some supplies he needed.
Pambrun's curt refusal, which changed the social atmosphere
from warm to chilly, was in conformance with the practice of the
Hudson's Bay Company. Hospitality was to be dispensed freely,
but no help whatever was to be given anyone who might encroach
on its territory, considered to be any area where it cared to send
fur brigades, whether north or south of the Columbia.

As a consequence of Pambrun's refusal, Bonneville and his

men had spent the winter short of traps and other supplies, so that he had returned with little to show for the season's effort—barely enough furs for Cerré to secure in trade sufficient goods to outfit him for another year. Now Bonneville was camped here on a tributary of the Snake, hunting buffalo and drying the meat.

Captain Stewart and Wyeth rode over to call on Bonneville. Possibly Townsend and McKay went along. Two accounts have come down to us of how they were received. Washington Irving gives a happy picture of old friends meeting, of open-handed hospitality offered them. Bonneville, his chronicler says, offered his guests a great feast of buffalo tongues, hump ribs and boiled marrow bones, accompanied by hearty potations from a "mellifluous keg."

Others present saw what happened in a slightly different light. They say that Bonneville gave them a feast, all right—he had plenty of buffalo meat—but brought out the metheglin, which often filled the "mellifluous keg," with reluctance. Seeing this, Stewart and Wyeth developed an extraordinary thirst and with much gusto drank the proffered liquor to the last drop. It was Rocky Mountain style humor. Fortunately, their horses got them safely back to camp; they could hardly have made it under their own power.

Wyeth's party resumed its march and about July 12 reached a site near the mouth of the Portneuf River, a tributary of the Snake. The location was a familiar one to Wyeth, who had decided to build here his trading post, where he could dispose of his trade goods and have a permanent headquarters from which to carry on his business. With his usual energy, he set about collecting timber for a stockade. Cottonwoods were plentiful and much driftwood was readily available on the banks of both nearby streams.

Food was of immediate concern. A group of men was sent off to search for buffalo, among them Captain Stewart, whose prowess in bringing down the great beasts was becoming a legend in the mountains. On their return a few days later, well-supplied with roasts and tongues, they fired a volley of rifle shots to announce their approach and narrowly missed being wiped out by their friends as a band of marauding Blackfeet.

Under Wyeth's urging, the fort took shape rapidly. Proper tools were lacking, but the building was strong. McKay and his brigade came up and camped near by. On Sunday, July 27, McKay did what none of the other men had the grace to do, asking Reverend Jason Lee to preach a sermon. He agreed at once, having been longing to bring the gospel to this godless crew.

A strange group gathered in a little cottonwood grove at three-thirty that afternoon, prepared to listen to what is thought to be the first sermon ever preached in the Rocky Mountains. Captain Stewart, a Catholic though not a practicing one; Wyeth, who some say was an out-and-out infidel but tolerant of the religious beliefs of others; the scientists, who may have been anything or nothing as far as religious convictions went; the Indians from McKay's brigade; the rough men of the train; and even Ashworth—all listened gravely while the man of God preached a wandering sermon replete with quotations from the Bible.

The post began to approach completion. The stockade was eighty feet square, with two bastions at opposing corners, the classic plan on which most trading posts of the West were constructed. Meat became scarce again, but Wyeth would not send men away for a sufficient distance to find buffalo. Grizzly bears were plentiful along the Snake, but the men grumbled at having to eat their tough meat. On the 4th of August the work was finished and the next day the American flag was unfurled at the top of a tall pole set up in the center of the stockade. This post was no second thought of Wyeth's. He had planned to build it even before he left St. Louis, the last place on his route where he could buy an American flag the size of this one. So much for the foresight of Nat Wyeth.

Fort Hall, named for the senior partner of Wyeth's sponsoring firm in Boston, was then dedicated by a liberal allowance of liquor to the men, who got gloriously drunk. The two Lees deplored in their journals the sinful and wicked waste of this event.

On the morning of the sixth Wyeth left the fort with the working segment of his party still unsteady on their feet from the libations of the day and night before. The new post was well-stocked with trade goods. A Mr. Evans, with eleven men and fourteen horses, was left to take care of it.

After a few days' travel the going became rough for Wyeth and his party. Great chasms split the plain. Sharp ridges obstructed the men's path. There were beds of tumbled lava to cross. Everyone took the hardships without complaint, with the exception of Ashworth, who groused continually, always showed up when a meal was ready, but was somewhere else when there was hard work to be done. Captain Stewart, who labored with the others getting the pack horses over the difficult terrain, became more and more impatient with the chap's unpleasant ways and treated him with less and less courtesy. Beyond showing disapproval, however, nothing could be done. In the wilderness no man was deprived of food, access to a campfire, or the protection offered by being one of a well-armed and experienced group.

At last they reached Fort Walla Walla, situated on the east bank of the Columbia, which flowed almost due south at this point. The fort, though an important outpost of the Hudson's Bay Company, was a small edifice built of driftwood. Pambrun, an old friend of Wyeth's, received them with courtly expressions of welcome. His wife was an Indian woman of great goodness as well as common sense, and he had several half-breed children.

Here Nat Wyeth, Captain Stewart, the missionaries and two scientists disposed of their horses and transferred their goods to boats of the dugout variety. Starting down the great Columbia, they portaged around the Cascades, then re-embarked and were borne swiftly toward Fort Vancouver, on the north bank of the Columbia and six miles west of the mouth of the Willamette. News of their coming went ahead of them to Dr. John McLoughlin, Head Factor of the Hudson's Bay Company, king of the vast territory that stretched north and east of the Columbia River.

CHAPTER XII

Kingdom on the Columbia

ᘐᕥ The long train of boats carrying Wyeth's party floated down the wide river headed by a large pirogue carrying Stewart, Wyeth, the scientists and the missionaries. As the boat swept toward the Fort Vancouver landing, there came to the ears of these men the strident skirling of a bagpipe, mingled with the clear notes of a great bell. It was midafternoon, September 16, 1834.

On the shore stood a group of gentlemen wearing dark suits, black stocks, white collars, and tall beaver hats. Behind them, only a few hundred yards from the river, Captain Stewart could see the great stockade of split cedar logs that enclosed the two-story white-painted house of the factor and perhaps twenty-five small log buildings. From a tall pole waved the Union Jack. A detail of the occasion which Captain Stewart was not likely to have missed, even in the confusion of stepping ashore, was the piper, wearing a magnificent Highlander's costume, the kilt being made of the Royal Stuart Plaid.

Dr. McLoughlin came forward to welcome his visitors with all the ceremony for which he was noted. He was fifty years of age and had been chief of Fort Vancouver for almost a decade—ever since he had built the first fort there in 1825. This renowned gentlemen stood six feet, two inches in height and weighed close to 200 pounds. His white hair, parted slightly on one side, hung almost to his shoulders, framing a healthily florid face. Garbed in a fine black broadcloth suit, he was an imposing and authoritative figure. The Indians called him White Headed Eagle.

The welcoming ceremonies concluded, Dr. McLoughlin and his entourage, consisting of his chief aides, escorted Stewart, Wyeth, Nuttall, Townsend, and the two Lees through the gates of the stockade. Here they passed armed guards wearing Scottish costumes only a little less splendid than the one worn by the bagpipe player. The packers and other employees of Wyeth's train, to whose company Ashworth had been relegated by common consent, were directed to lodgings in the village that huddled close outside the walls of the fort.

The missionaries were assigned to what Jason Lee described as "comfortable and spacious quarters" in one of the log buildings within the stockade. Stewart, Wyeth and the two scientists were given rooms in the factor's residence, which, unlike the other structures at the fort, was built of planed boards turned out by the company's own sawmill.

As he stepped inside the walls of Dr. McLoughlin's home, Stewart might almost have imagined himself in a Scottish castle. Thick rugs covered the floors. Oil paintings and engravings of hunting scenes in the Highlands hung on the walls. Shelf after shelf held the factor's books. This was Dr. McLoughlin's famous library, from which volumes went out with every brigade that left for the beaver country and to each trading post in his vast territory.

That evening the gentlemen of the fort gathered in the great dining room, wearing formal attire as was their custom. Logs blazed in the two fireplaces, one at each end of the hall, tempering the cool September air. When Stewart and Nuttall entered, they saw a long table covered with a fine linen cloth. Tall candles shed their light on delicate china, gleaming silver, sparkling crystal goblets. Wyeth and Townsend were already there, as were Dr. McLoughlin and the other gentlemen of the fort. A few minutes later the two Lees appeared, and with them Ashworth, whom Dr. McLoughlin had not invited.

What Captain Stewart's thoughts were on seeing this fellow appear it is not difficult to imagine. Dr. John McLoughlin seated his unexpected guest with distant courtesy and an appearance of unruffled calm. Taking his place at the head of the table, he invoked a divine blessing, then proposed the customary toast, "To the Honorable Hudson's Bay Company." With the exception of their host, all the men gathered around the table and drank the toast in good red wine; even Jason Lee, who so often deplored the consumption of strong drink on any occasion whatsoever, joined in. Dr. McLoughlin's glass contained water. He partook of spiritous liquor but once a year, at the starting out of the first fur brigade of the season, when he drank a cup of brandy with the men, wishing them good fortune in their season's work.

Dinner progressed, with half-breed and Kanaka servants, clad in livery designed by Dr. McLoughlin, bringing in course after course of well-cooked food. A typical dinner at Fort Vancouver included roast beef, caribou steaks, ham raised and cured on the home farm, a variety of vegetables, and a dessert, perhaps baked apple duff delicately flavored with spices. Throughout the leisurely meal the piper marched about the hall playing pibrochs—softly, it is to be hoped.

Captain Stewart may have felt the illusion that he was dining with the Breadalbanes at Taymouth Castle, or with his old friend, Lord Glenlyon of Blair-Athol. Such a feeling could have been only temporary, as awareness would have returned of the miles of wilderness surrounding this little island of civilization, of the crowding primeval forest, the near-by Columbia sweeping grandly to the sea.

Dinner over, the company adjourned to a large room known as the Bachelor's Quarters. Here they sat until a late hour, discussing books, philosophy and politics. It was a far cry from the roistering, drinking, yelling and shooting of the rendezvous where Captain Stewart had been only a few months before.

Although Stewart's host had been born in Quebec, Scotland was the land of his forebears and it lived in his heart as his true home. Hence the music of the bagpipes, the Highland dress worn by some of his retainers, the engravings of Scottish scenes that hung on his walls.

By a pleasant coincidence, Napoleon was McLoughlin's hero. The good doctor considered the little Corsican a brilliant master of military strategy and was familiar with every battle in which Napoleon had engaged. His interest on discovering that Captain Stewart had fought in the Peninsular War and had received a decoration for bravery at Waterloo can be imagined. His alert blue eyes must have sparkled under their thick sandy brows as he and the visitor from Perthshire discussed the personality and military genius of Napoleon. The development of the friendliest feelings between the two men was natural and inevitable.

Their talk went on and on. Finally the hour grew late. Dr. McLoughlin's guests rose, the missionaries prepared to take their leave. Ashworth, encouraged by his host's politeness, pushed his luck too far and was given his come-uppance. The manner in which this happened is described in a report sent several weeks later by Dr. McLoughlin to the Governors' Committee of the Hudson's Bay Company. After giving an account of Captain Stewart's arrival, and his letters to the several Hudson's Bay Company officials, McLoughlin wrote as follows:

> . . . when I found this out and that he [Ashworth] had introduced himself into the Room I had given the missionaries and taken his lodging with them (which I did not know until the evening when I sent for the missionaries to supper) and had followed them into our house, I allowed him to take his supper at our table on account of the missionaries with whom he had obtruded himself, but as he was withdrawing and seeing that he was inclined to make himself at home, I told him that this house was not an Hotel and desired the servant to open the doors of the Fort and let this gentleman go out. As we could not allow him to starve alongside the Fort I have given him the same rations as to our own men, salmon and biscuit or potatoes and salmon, as it occurred. I do not know what he intends to do, but I am told he is desirous of going to Woahoo [Oahu?] and to get rid of him I will give him passage to that place and which I mention that, in case he is what he states, and complains of not being better treated, your honors will know what I have done. . . .

Exit Ashworth. His further movements are unknown to history. The man's only claim to distinction is that he successfully imposed on the generosity of Captain Stewart and by his bad manners roused indignation in Dr. McLoughlin's breast.

Captain Stewart, standing by the window of his room later that night, would have heard the familiar rhythm of Indian drums coming from the cluster of tepees outside the stockade, and the chant of red-skinned gamblers crouched around a small campfire. Turning down the coverlid of his bed, he quickly fell asleep, lulled by the unaccustomed comfort of a mattress made in a London factory. His last thought before unconsciousness claimed him may well have been that the English way of conducting the fur business bore little resemblance to the fashion in which Americans went about the same pursuit. The first was a monopoly governed by a small group of men in England; the other operated under the free enterprise system, and so was fiercely competitive, every man for himself.

Wyeth curbed his restless energies for a few days, permitting his men a brief rest. The delay in getting to the Pacific was all the more difficult for him to endure, since bad news had awaited him here at Fort Vancouver. His supply ship, the *May Dacre*, out of Boston, had been badly damaged at sea by lightning. She was forced to head into Valparaiso, where it took three months to complete repairs and refitting. That meant she had missed the salmon season, of which her Boston owners had expected her crew to take advantage, storing away a cargo of salted fish to make her return journey profitable. Now she awaited orders at the mouth of the Columbia.

Wyeth, never long cast down, formed a plan to send the ship to the Sandwich Islands with a cargo of lumber. As soon as possible, he hurried on. White Headed Eagle prevailed on Dr. Townsend to remain at the fort as its surgeon. Nuttall was happy to stay on any terms, as long as he was allowed to pursue his study of the wild life thereabouts.

For a few days the strange world within the walls of the stockade held Captain Stewart's interest. Sturdy cedar pickets fifteen to twenty feet high enclosed an area 660 feet long by 300 feet wide—considerably larger than either Fort Bent or Fort Laramie. A twenty-foot-square blockhouse stood on the northeast corner, housing a cannon firing three-pound balls. The Hudson's Bay

Company ruled the Indians with a firm hand, tolerating no non-sense and at the same time dispensing impartial justice to white man and red man alike. The factors of the Hudson's Bay Company had little trouble with the natives in their territory, a situation in sharp contrast to the dark and bloody deeds—on both sides—that marked the American advance across the continent.

Grouped around the factor's residence stood more than a score of small, neatly built log houses. Some of these structures housed the married officials of the company and their families. Others served as a blacksmith shop, pharmacy, storehouse, and so on.

A few Indian women, some accompanied by their children, walked about inside the stockade, or went to visit their relatives in near-by tepees. These women looked quite different from the buckskin-clad, gaudily ornamented young females Captain Stewart had seen at the two rendezvous he had attended. Still less did they look like the old women who did the camp drudgery. These women were neat and clean. They walked proudly, their demeanor modest and dignified. Thick braids of black hair hung down over red and purple shawls that only partially concealed dresses made of silk or velvet, cut in the latest fashions of Montreal or London. Now and then there appeared on the finger of a brown hand a beautiful jeweled ring that had not been designed for trading purposes. In only one particular did these daughters of the forest and river maintain their own style of dressing. They would not give up their comfortable embroidered and beaded deerskin leggings and moccasins.

These women, who aroused Captain Stewart's astonishment as well as his admiration, were the wives of the Hudson's Bay Company officials permanently stationed at Fort Vancouver. The men who assisted Dr. McLoughlin in the management of his fur empire were not permitted to take up with any likely-looking Indian woman met casually on the trail. They married only the daughters of chiefs or head men after proper negotiations, the nuptial rites being solemnized with full tribal ceremonies. An account of one such wedding states that when the Hudson's Bay Company man went by boat to claim his bride at her father's village, he stepped ashore and walked to the family tepee on a pathway of beaver skins—the Indian version of the red-carpet treatment. Dr. McLoughlin, who always set an example for his men, married the daughter of a chief and had several children by her.

These Indian wives often had a servant or two, and were taught the amenities of civilized living to whatever extent the men were capable of imparting them. At the time Captain Stewart was at Fort Vancouver the husbands had not been able to cope with the task of teaching their wives proper table manners, and consequently the men dined without feminine society. Later, Narcissa Whitman, that blithest, most beautiful and most tragic of all women missionaries to the Indians, taught these same women the art of using the knife, fork and spoon, and of draping a napkin across the lap.

They already knew how to sit on a chair. After Narcissa's brief stay at the fort, the brown-cheeked beauties "took supper" with their husbands in the great dining room. Maybe Narcissa did not save their souls as she professedly yearned to do, but she taught them good manners.

The Hudson's Bay Company's policy regarding the marriage of their officials to Indian women was based on plain common sense and strictly practical considerations. White women were unable to endure the isolation and the hardships which the life imposed. The arrangement affiliated the powerful chiefs and head men with the Company's interests and secured their loyalty and engendered good relations between the two races. The male children of these marriages were often sent away to school, given advanced education, and in some cases, travel in Europe.

The few weeks of Indian summer that followed Stewart's arrival at Fort Vancouver gave him the opportunity to ride over the vast properties and inspect the surprising variety of enterprises belonging to the Hudson's Bay Company here on the Columbia. There was also considerable private industry going on here in the hands of individuals.

Within a radius of a few miles, over 2000 acres of rich farm land were under intensive cultivation. Expert husbandmen raised corn, wheat and other grains, all harvested at this time of year. They also grew strawberries, melons, apples and other fruits. Grist and saw mills, their wheels busily turning, stood on small, rushing

streams that tumbled into the Columbia. There were herds of fat
cattle, thousands of sheep, hogs, poultry, and the horse paddock
that must have reminded Captain Stewart of Sublette's horse farm
on the outskirts of St. Louis. Nor was there too much difference
between the McLoughlin farming enterprise and what went on in
the estates of Grandtully and Murthly.

Flanking the cleared land were the limitless forests. Great
mountain peaks, their tops white with snow now that winter approached, gave a sublimity to the landscape: Mount Hood across
the Columbia to the south, Mount Adams northward, and far
beyond Mount Rainier lifting its majestic bulk into the sky. All
these could be seen from McLoughlin's empire.

Captain Sir John Simpson, one of the founders, wrote: "I have
rarely seen a gentleman's seat in England possessing so many natural advantages and where ornament and use are so agreeably
combined."

Jason Lee took only a passing interest in the home farm at
Fort Vancouver. He was eager to be about the Lord's business,
which in this case was strictly real-estate business. Astutely directed
by Dr. McLoughlin, who wanted no American settlements, missionary or otherwise, on what he considered his territory, Jason Lee,
with his nephew Daniel, who appears to have been a first-class yes-
man, explored the beautiful Willamette Valley through which
flowed the river of the same name. Here was unbelievably fertile
land, an abundance of water, and a mild climate. The Indians were
friendly and there weren't too many of them. Jason was sure that
the Hand of the Lord—and his own good sense—had led him to
the right place.

Dr. McLoughlin sent the two Lees on their way to the location where they had decided to settle, with a princely gift of
horses, calves, cows, oxen, and a boat. He even presented the missionaries with a substantial contribution of money. The Hudson's
Bay factor was more than generous with every worthy person who
didn't get in his way, commercially speaking. At least one layman
of Jason Lee's party hired out to Dr. McLoughlin and remained
at the fort.

What Captain Stewart did the remainder of that winter is a
matter of conjecture. Judging by the detailed information about

the surrounding country that he later gave Dr. Whitman at the 1835 rendezvous, and in 1836 to both Dr. Whitman and his companion, Mr. Spalding, he must have visited the Lees' settlements on the Willamette and explored the rich valleys to the north of Fort Walla Walla. It would have been in character for him to have traveled 115 miles down the Columbia to the Pacific to give Nat Wyeth a hand loading the *May Dacre* and get the ship off to the Sandwich Islands. That done, he would have examined Dr. McLoughlin's efficient salt works, situated not far from where Lewis and Clark's men had made salt by boiling ocean water in iron "kittles" more than thirty years before. He probably visited the ruins of dreary Fort Clatsop, where those two intrepid men spent a cold, wet and hungry winter, having brought the flag of the United States for the first time to that far Pacific shore.

With good luck, Captain Stewart would have seen a whale spouting in the watery distance, or even one stranded on the beach. If the latter, we may be sure he sampled whale steak and good greasy blubber. He was not a man to draw back from any experience that was new and strange.

In the early part of February, 1835, evidence shows that he was at Fort Vancouver, making plans to meet his friends at their yearly rendezvous in the Rockies.

CHAPTER XIII

Captain Stewart—
Address: Rocky Mountains

ই Winter still gripped the Oregon country. One cold day of slashing wind and stinging rain Captain Stewart said good-by to Dr. McLoughlin and set off up the Columbia. He traveled with a small body of men headed by Francis Ermatinger, one of the brigade leaders of the Hudson's Bay Company. They had three large pirogues loaded with supplies for the small scattered trading posts up the river.

On the 11th of February Ermatinger and Stewart met Wyeth at the end of the Cascades. Nat was making his way downstream alone through the spring storms in a leaky dugout that he barely managed to keep afloat. Matters at Fort Hall had not been going well. The Kanakas Wyeth had sent up from the coast had deserted, taking with them what supplies and traps they could carry. Indians had stolen his best horses. He had gone to his establishment on the Snake in the dead of winter, attempted to get some order and discipline established there. Now he was hurrying back to his fort on Sauvies Island at the mouth of the Willamette.

Ermatinger and Stewart, exasperated at Wyeth's foolhardiness, even while admiring his courage, watched the valiant Nathaniel as he disappeared in the rain around a bend in the river. Then they turned to the back-breaking, muscle-straining task of portaging their boats and goods around the miles of white water known as the Cascades.

On the 10th of June they reached Fort Hall on the Snake, near the small Portneuf River. Why it took them four months to get this far toward the rendezvous can be explained only by the supposition that their party trapped on the way. Here at Fort Hall they outfitted themselves with horses and, after two days' rest, rode up the Snake, reaching New Fork, the site of that year's rendezvous, about June 20. This was too early to expect trappers and Indians to be there, and much too soon for the caravans to arrive, which they rarely did before the first or second week in July.

However, within a few days bands of Utes, Snakes, Blackfeet, Sioux, and a small, still hopeful delegation of Nez Percés began to set up their tepees along the course of the New Fork. Parties of trappers rode in, bringing their beaver packs and an enormous thirst. Three weeks went by; still no caravan, and consequently no money and no liquor. But there were beaver plews and buffalo robes in plenty. These skins were the banknotes of the mountains. So gambling and racing and lovemaking made life interesting. Then there was hunting, part sport and part necessity, since an encampment of this size required a lot of meat. Buffalo were near by, and in the mountains there abounded deer, antelope, grizzly bear and wild sheep.

More weeks passed. Still no caravan. Frolic changed to boredom, then to anxiety. Perhaps no trading party was coming this year. There had been rumors—the price of beaver was down.

Finally it was the first of August. There was talk of breaking up—though what the trappers would do without new traps to replace those broken and lost, without warm clothing, blankets and a supply of ammunition, no one knew. Captain Stewart began to feel deeply concerned about how he was going to get back to St. Louis. No white man could make that trip alone and come through alive. Everyone stayed on, hoping that the next day would bring the solution of their problems.

The only caravan to go into the mountains that year belonged to the American Fur Company, though evidence fails to show that either its leaders, or those who anxiously awaited its arrival at New Fork, knew that this was to be the case. The Rocky Mountain Fur Company had sold out its interests to the American Fur Company. Bonneville, broke, left the mountains in July. Wyeth had more troubles than he could manage at Fort Hall and on Sauvies Island and was to leave the West forever the following year.

Lucien Fontenelle, of the American Fur Company, was late getting his caravan to Independence, for reasons unknown, but they must have been valid ones, since Fontenelle was both wise and experienced. He did not get his party on the road until April 15. Then, instead of heading across the prairie to the Platte, he followed the Missouri to Bellevue, near the mouth of the Platte.

Traveling with the party were Dr. Marcus Whitman, a Presbyterian missionary who was also a medical man, and his companion, Reverend Samuel Parker. They had been dispatched by the American Board of Commissioners for Foreign Missions to find out what had become of Jason and Daniel Lee, sent West the year before, and from whom no word had come. They were also enjoined to answer the cry for enlightenment that had reached them some time before from the Nez Percé Indians. Fate was bringing these two religious emissaries to New Fork, where they would meet Captain Stewart, even then traveling toward them on the other side of the Rockies. Stewart was as unaware as they that through them he would give a nudge to American history.

The "enlisted men," or employees of Fontenelle's train, had heard about Jason and Daniel Lee, the two missionaries who had gone West with Wyeth the year before and their "holier-than-thou" attitudes. The stories, we may be sure, had lost nothing in the telling. Now here were more, the men thought, of the same breed. Reverend Parker they dismissed as inconsequential—not worth noticing—and singled out Dr. Whitman as the object of rough, even malicious, practical jokes. Once they went so far as to throw a few ancient eggs at Dr. Whitman. He held his peace, did not complain to Fontenelle, attempted no retaliation.

When the caravan reached Bellevue, there was another unexplained delay of a few days. Then cholera, that terrible scourge of the river towns, struck Fontenelle's party. Nearly all the men, including Fontenelle himself, were laid low by this swift and fre-

quently fatal disease. Dr. Whitman, never robust and suffering
from a chronic ailment that caused great pain in his side, worked
day and night, dosing and nursing the sick. He insisted that the
camp be moved to higher ground away from the river, cared for
the men with unflagging, almost superhuman devotion. Only two
men died. In twelve days the disease had run its course.

For the first time since they had left Independence, the
packers and hunters were grateful that Dr. Whitman was with
them. Though a preacher and a greenhorn, he had saved their
lives. From Bellevue on, they showed him the ultimate of which
they were capable in the way of respect and helpful consideration.
With all possible speed the caravan pressed on up the Platte to
Fort Laramie, now completed and doing a large business in beaver
and buffalo robes, some brought in by Indians, others by free trappers. At Fort Laramie Fontenelle turned the party over to Fitzpatrick, who drove men and horses to the limit of their endurance
in a desperate effort to reach New Fork before the assembled
trappers and Indians left.

On August 12, over a month late, Fitzpatrick brought his
train to its destination. The joy and relief was so great on each
side that pandemonium reigned for a couple of days. Then everyone settled down to business and trading went ahead briskly.
September, a good time to start the fall hunt, was approaching
and there was no time to lose.

Fitzpatrick, of course, brought to Captain Stewart mail that
had been accumulating at St. Louis since the year before. George
wrote happily in his artless fashion that the building of New
Murthly was progressing. When completed, its roof, domes, turrets—everything—would be given some kind of treatment (George
was characteristically vague about this) which would cause it to
sparkle in the sunlight as if it were covered with gargantuan jewels
of many colors, something new and sure to be beautiful. John said,
he rambled on, that when New Murthly was finished it would be
much finer and more impressive than the addition of Taymouth
Castle that Lord Breadalbane was currently engaged in building.
Of course New Murthly would cost a great deal of money, but if
it gave John pleasure, why not?

Captain Stewart could think of a number of reasons why not.

The revenues of the estates of Grandtully and Murthly—Logieal-mond, too—would be poured into the building of this monstrosity with the fancy towers and bejeweled roof. And he would wait interminably for the small sums due him.

It was probably at this time that he received a letter—perhaps two letters—from New Orleans, suggesting that he make certain business arrangements in that city that would be materially advantageous, not only to himself, but to the economy of his country. One of these letters was almost certainly from the British Consul's office in New Orleans. These communications set up a train of events that we shall come to later.

Antoine Clement appeared at the rendezvous. He and Captain Stewart renewed their friendship and went on hunting expeditions together. It took much meat to keep the American Fur Company's party supplied and these two hunters could be depended on to bring it in.

The Nez Percé delegation believed, with deep joy, that the long-delayed answer to their prayers had come at last in the persons of Dr. Whitman and Reverend Parker. However, neither of these two white medicine men knew exactly what to do about it. When Dr. Whitman discovered that Captain Stewart had recently traveled through the country of the Nez Percés, that he knew where Jason Lee had gone, he was overjoyed. Here was a source of first-hand knowledge which he badly needed.

The two missionaries were shocked to learn that Lee had abandoned the Nez Percés and the mission on which he had been sent; even more shocked when Captain Stewart told them, in plain language, why. Whitman and Stewart, in spite of their wide differences of background and modes of thought, had a common integrity of purpose and sense of devotion to duty. They talked for hours, with Reverend Parker a passive but interested listener.

Stewart was well-equipped to tell them about the rich, well-watered valleys of the Nez Percé and Cayuse Indian country in the vicinity of Fort Walla Walla. He told them it would be wise to start their settlement not too far distant from Fort Walla Walla, where, in case of emergency, they could get supplies. He assured them that since their proposed mission would hold no threat to the profits of the Hudson's Bay Company, they could be

almost certain of being given aid and co-operation by Mr. Pambrun, factor of Fort Walla Walla, and even by the great Mc-
Loughlin of Fort Vancouver, overlord of the Hudson's Bay Company's empire north of the Columbia. He may have spoken of
suitable locations for their mission, and if so, among them he
would have mentioned Waiilatpu, twenty-five miles up the Walla
Walla River from Fort Walla Walla, where the related tribes,
Cayuse and Nez Percé, roamed at will.

Now a question of immediacy arose. If both Dr. Whitman
and Reverend Parker went ahead to reconnoiter, decide where
they would settle, then return east the following year to recruit
more missionaries and secure financial backing, it would be 1838
before the mission could be established. Neither man liked the
idea—the Nez Percés had waited long enough.

The upshot of it was that Parker was delegated to go on, visit
Jason Lee on the Willamette, then examine the territory ad-
jacent to Fort Walla Walla. Parker accepted this responsibility
with trepidation, but seems to have carried out his mission well.
While he was doing this spade work, Dr. Whitman would return
east to recruit more people and get the necessary financial assistance.

Captain Stewart saw that these two missionaries had no
thought of promoting settlements for their own aggrandizement
and financial gain, but were genuinely interested in spreading the
gospel to the benighted, and in curing their ills as well as teaching
them to live more healthfully and comfortably. So he helped them
all he could and was to do Dr. Whitman and the people who
heeded his appeal an even greater service the following summer.

The rendezvous drew toward its close. Reverend Parker got a
small outfit together—not over five men in all, including a young
Nez Percé named Bull's Head and a youthful *voyageur* called
Compo. They set off bravely on their long and dangerous journey
with Jim Bridger, that skilled mountain man, to aid them as far as
Jackson's Hole, among the Tetons in the northwest corner of what
is now Wyoming. After that they would be on their own.

While Parker made his preparations to depart toward the
northwest, Dr. Whitman was making his arrangements to go almost across the continent in the opposite direction. He found a

Nez Percé boy who knew a few words of English, and secured permission from the youth's father to take him along as Exhibit A to back up his plea for cash donations to the cause of enlightenment for Indians as wild and untutored as he. The boy's heathenish name was Tackitonitis, which Dr. Whitman promptly changed to Richard. Then another Nez Percé father brought his young son to the missionary, pleaded that the boy be taken along and taught religion on the way. This boy was named Aitz; Dr. Whitman called him John.

On August 27, after a stay of fifteen days on New Fork, Fitzpatrick headed his caravan, consisting of sixty men, 200 mules and horses, plus six wagons, now loaded with packs of beaver and buffalo robes, back toward the Sweetwater on the first lap of his journey to St. Louis. With him went Captain Stewart, Antoine, Dr. Whitman and his two Nez Percé wards. Stewart had been in the Far West for three summers and two winters. During this time his only contact with what could be called civilized living had been at Fort Vancouver. Much as he loved adventure and the sight of new places and strange peoples, he would be glad to experience again the soft and elegant life that had been his for most of his forty years.

With their long pack train winding behind them, bearing the winter catch of furs, Stewart and Fitzpatrick came at last to Fort Laramie, now the well-established center of the fur trade of the Northwest. This was the Scotsman's first view of the fort's high log walls with their two bastions set diagonally across from each other and the American flag bearing twenty-four stars flying from a lofty pole in the center of the courtyard. To the west stretched the Black Hills, dark with a dense stand of fir trees. In the vicinity of the fort the ground sloped gently to the clear waters of the Laramie. Here on this grassy meadow wild-currant bushes held thick clusters of crimson berries ripening to luscious tartness in the September sun.

Close by the stockade Captain Stewart saw a dozen or two tepees of the Sioux and farther off a small encampment of the Snakes and Blackfeet. Here self-interest took precedence over ancient enmities. They all wanted to trade their furs and get in return the fabulous treasures of the white man, free from the imminent possibility of losing their scalps. The only way to secure the in-estimable blessings of guns, ammunition, blue beads, red cloth, and now and then a swig of firewater was to keep the peace among themselves. The same considerations, of course, kept their mur-derous propensities in check at the rendezvous.

Fitzpatrick, Stewart, and Antoine, followed by the other men of the party, rode through the zaguan gate under the cannon and into the courtyard, where Fontenelle welcomed them. Small rooms built of logs lined the stockade walls, except for a small space at the rear, where a low-railed balcony gave access to a nar-row, easily guarded door leading to the horse corral. The small rooms clinging to the stockade housed a smithy and a storehouse, and provided sleeping quarters. At one side of the main entrance a stairway led to the large blockhouse above the gate, where the small cannon was kept to quell any trouble that might possibly arise outside the walls. A half-dozen Indians were in the courtyard trading. As a precaution against treachery, only a few at a time were allowed inside the fort.

After a few days' rest for men and animals, the long caravan went on down the Platte, passing the familiar landmarks of Scott's Bluff, then Chimney Rock. St. Louis was still a lot of miles away.

CHAPTER XIV

King Cotton's Capital City

৯ৡ At last the great cavalcade reached Bellevue on the Missouri, near the mouth of the Platte. There Antoine turned back toward the mountains, whether alone or with a party of trappers we do not know. Fitzpatrick paused for a few days to rest his pack animals.

On October 16, Captain Stewart wrote a letter to William Sublette at St. Louis, date line Council Bluffs. This letter would go down the river by steamboat and reach its destination long before the train arrived in St. Louis, for Fitzpatrick was taking his furs overland, the way Fontenelle had come the previous spring.

In due time Captain Stewart reached St. Louis and established himself in his old headquarters at the City Hotel. There letters awaited him, among them a delicately phrased communication from the "Leddies o' Logie," hoping their nephew was well and inquiring when he would come back to Scotland and resume the life of a gentleman. There was also another letter from faithful George, recounting the progress John was making in building New Murthly and enclosing a small portion of an overdue installment of his annuity, sent by John's attorney in Edinburgh. Captain Stewart found these two communications almost equally irritating. Taken together, they were enough to tip the scales of decision in favor of his embarking on his next adventure.

In view of his luxurious, even extravagant, tastes he needed money and he needed it badly. As much as he enjoyed adventure, a certain amount of elegant living was possible, even in the most remote wilderness—providing one were able to expend sufficient money to achieve it. He considered once more the business letters he had received at the rendezvous and decided to journey soon to New Orleans so he could talk to the gentlemen there who had written to him. In the meantime he would enjoy the many balls and parties to which he was invited, renew his acquaintance with the businessmen and the beautiful ladies of the city.

Here in St. Louis news was available concerning Captain Bonneville. That redoubtable adventurer had shown up at Independence in August, about the time Captain Stewart left the rendezvous. At Independence Bonneville had been apprised that, because he had overstayed his leave by two years, his name had been stricken from the army lists. He immediately made the claim that he had sent a request for an extension of leave in 1833, by special messenger—the letter that was never received.

Most men in his position would have felt they were in deep trouble and hurried to Washington to see what they could do to save their careers. Not Bonneville: he traveled unconcernedly to New York, where he was a guest at the home of John Jacob Astor. Almost at once President Jackson reinstated Bonneville and gave him back his rank of Captain, in spite of the fact that seventeen officers of Bonneville's former command at Fort Gibson signed a protest.

The conclusion seems obvious. Captain Bonneville apparently had performed some great service for the government, the nature of which it was not politically expedient to reveal. What Captain Stewart thought of all this we do not know. He had seen Walker and his party depart from Bonneville's camp in 1833 and it is reasonable to suppose that he knew at least as much as Joe Meek did about what was afoot and probably a good deal more.

A few weeks later Stewart was in New Orleans. What he did that winter is surmise, based on such elements as a known fact or two, authenticated evidence furnished by a family in Texas, and Captain Stewart's subsequent actions. He associated himself with a young businessman named E. B. Nichols, who had made quite a reputation as a cotton broker in New Orleans. Mr. Nichols came from a wealthy family of Cooperstown, New York, and no doubt started his career with considerable financial resources. At first the connection between these two men was on an entirely business basis, but it soon changed to friendship that, years later, was to have strange consequences for both of them.

Captain Stewart began to buy, through Nichols as broker, large quantities of cotton for the looms of England and Scotland. He was engaged in no small enterprise, for Great Britain was at that time by far the greatest cotton-goods manufacturing nation of the world. The commissions Stewart received for securing the cotton fiber so badly needed by his country would have been substantial. The sudden change in the captain's financial situation that took place during the winter of 1835–36 has puzzled those who have followed his career. Only recently have the facts come to light regarding his purchasing large amounts of cotton through Nichols.

Captain Stewart also formed a mysterious partnership that winter with Mr. Crawford, the British Consul in New Orleans. What business they engaged in is not known, but it was of enough importance to require them to have a representative in London for two or three years, a Mr. Vernunfft.

As the winter months drew to a close, Stewart had his business activities so well organized that he was able to visit Cuba, a place he long had wished to see. Returning to the United States late in February, he wrote the following letter to William Sublette from Charleston, South Carolina:

> I have just arrived here from the Island of Cuba on my way to St. Louis by way of Washington, Philadelphia, and Cincinnati. I hope this finds you well and planning a western trip. I am not sure how I shall go, but still intend proceeding to the West in April. I shall learn at Washington if there is to be a party sent by the U.S. to make a survey of the country and shall let you know as soon as I hear. I write this to let you know that there are two guns in cases that I have directed to be sent from New Orleans to your care. I must also remind you of your promise of a black horse. I beg you to get me one

other as fast a horse as you can secure and two hardy, quiet mules. Mr. Sillem, a German gentleman who accompanies me, begs you will be good enough to procure him 3 good horses and 4 mules—saddle, pack saddles, etc. I am answerable for all this. I must draw upon you for $200 which I hope you will honor. I make no apologies for asking you to take all this trouble, presuming on the friendly aid you have hitherto offered me. I start for Washington in a day or two.

WDS

Since Captain Stewart asked Sublette to buy these horses, pack mules and other equipment for himself and Mr. Sillem, he evidently did not plan to go with a government survey party leaving from Washington, even if there should be one. His interest seems to have been entirely concerned with whether or not a survey party was going into the West that year, and the subject was evidently one of importance to Sublette.

In later accounts, Mr. Sillem's name appears with a variety of spellings: Celan and Sellam, among others. W. H. Gray, whom Captain Stewart and Mr. Sillem were to meet later that year, even changes his nationality, referring to him sourly as a "young English blood."

The implications of Stewart's request that Sublette buy for him "as fast a horse as you can get," are clear. He intended to indulge in a little serious horse racing at the rendezvous with the Indians, as well as with any white man who possessed animals suitable to compete in such contests. This year he was determined not to be beaten, as he probably had been the year before.

Two days later, on shipboard en route to Washington, D.C., Stewart wrote to Robert Campbell expressing regret that Campbell had resumed his "shaking habits" and stating that the writer would "strongly recommend some other religion. Take a dose of morphine when you first feel the chill and one of quinine every two hours and I think with the bitters you will get the better of this accursed ill." He went on to ask Campbell to buy him a "good running horse," as his had foundered. He also wanted a pair of holsters to replace ones he had lost.

The Rocky Mountain Fur Company had sold its interests to

the American Fur Company and in the spring of 1836, the leadership of that organization's yearly caravan to the mountains was placed in the capable hands of Thomas Fitzpatrick. Black Harris, a man well known in the fur trade, was engaged as a kind of sub-lieutenant. Milton Sublette, a partner in the enterprise and famous for his courage and drive, determined to go, too, in spite of serious disabilities. He had only partially recovered from the amputation of his leg the year before. This ordeal had been followed several months later by a second operation to excise—it was hoped—the last trace of diseased bone. William Sublette had provided his brother with an artificial limb made of India rubber, but walking was still difficult for Milton, and horseback riding impossible. A charette was assigned to him, the vehicle to be drawn by two mules hitched tandem.

When Captain Stewart and his friend, Mr. Sillem, arrived in St. Louis they began the task of buying their extensive supplies. The Scot now had sufficient means at his disposal to travel in a style somewhat more suited to his station and his tastes than heretofore had been possible. He purchased an assortment of luxury foods and liquors such as the mountains had never seen.

Included in the lot, which before he finished was sufficient to to fill two wagons, were canned goods which had only lately become available, such as sardines, ham, plum puddings and preserved fruits. Then there were dried fruits, sugar, much coffee, fine tobacco, cheeses and a large supply of brandies, whisky and vintage wines; also, a stout canvas tent large enough to accommodate him and his companion, Mr. Sillem. In all his previous journeyings in the mountains he had had no more shelter than could be afforded by a blanket or two. With him also went three servants, two dogs and two "fast-running horses." This trip, the sportsman from Scotland was going in all the style his resources would permit, promising himself no doubt that he would do still better another time.

Weeks before the caravan was ready to start, Dr. Marcus Whitman, with his missionary party, arrived in St. Louis and reported to the American Fur Company. The Secretary of the Board of Missionaries had made arrangements for this group to travel up the river on a company boat, then go with the caravan as far as the

Rocky Mountains. From there they would make their way to Oregon, where they intended to establish a mission at some place still to be selected.

Dr. Whitman was accompanied by his wife, Narcissa, to whom he had been married only a few months, Reverend H. H. Spalding and Spalding's wife, Eliza. Reverend and Mrs. Benjamin Satterlee, assigned to the Pawnee Mission on the Platte, journeyed with them. Mrs. Satterlee suffered from tuberculosis, a matter of deep concern to the Missionary Board. Dr. Whitman had prevailed upon the officials to let her go, since the West so often brought about a cure of this disease. Also in the party were Richard (Tackitonitis) and John (Aitz), the two Nez Percé boys who had accompanied Dr. Whitman on his return to Boston the year before.

Dr. Whitman and Captain Stewart were old friends, happy to see each other again, and pleased at the prospect of being travel companions on the long journey to the rendezvous. For some reason not quite clear, the officials of the American Fur Company requested the missionary party to proceed at once upriver on one of the company boats, the *Chariton*, to Liberty and outfit themselves there. Later, on an appointed date, another company boat, the *Diana*, would pick them up and take them to Bellevue. From there the caravan would start up the Platte.

CHAPTER XV

Men, Mountains and Missionaries

ह्ब्ब The missionary party arrived at Liberty and within a few days were joined by W. H. Gray, hired by the Boston Missionary Board as lay assistant and mechanic. Characteristically, Gray called himself a "secular agent." His job was to get the oddly assorted group, plus what was possible of their equipment, horses and cattle, to Oregon, which he did, accompanied by whole-hearted applause furnished by Mr. Gray himself.

According to Gray, he and Dr. Whitman spent $3000 at Liberty, outfitting for the journey and for establishing a mission in the Oregon Territory. The vehicles consisted of one large farm wagon and a light Dearborn carriage, this last mainly for the comfort of the ladies when they grew tired of riding horseback—on side-saddles. Gray deplored many of the articles purchased as unnecessary, even useless, predicting that most of them would be thrown away before the party reached its destination. Gray was a practical man and his prediction was fulfilled long before they came to the banks of the Columbia.

There was urgency in their preparations, for they must be ready when the *Diana* came to pick them up. While the men selected and bought the multitudinous items Narcissa Whitman and Eliza Spalding made a tent. Narcissa described it in a letter to her sister.

Since we have been here we have made our tent. It is made
of bed ticking and is conical in form, large enough for all of
us—*viz*, Mr. Spalding and his wife, Dr. Whitman and his
wife, Mr. Gray, Richard Tackitonitis and John Aitz; quite a
little family—raised with a center pole and fastened down with
pegs, covering a large circle. Here we shall live, eat, sleep, for
the summer to come, at least—perhaps longer.

Narcissa, with her beauty, her red-gold curls, her vivacity and
charm, seemed not at all the missionary type, but in fact she was
dedicated to the work she had undertaken, and to her husband. In
contrast to Narcissa, Eliza Spalding was a dark, pious woman,
with no sense of humor whatever, and a critical eye firmly fixed
on the shortcomings of others, as measured by her rigid code of
moral standards. Frail, ill most of the time, she found no lightness
or joy anywhere in this vale of tears. That the two women got along
as well as they did is a credit to them both; they must have worked
hard at it.

At last the party was ready, waiting only for the steamboat to
arrive. Unexpectedly, Mrs. Satterlee became critically ill and died
within a span of two days. The missionaries were conducting her
funeral services when they saw, far down the river, the boat that
was to take them to Bellevue, two days early. Hurrying to the river
bank, they shouted to the captain but, paying no attention, he
steamed on past. As they discovered much later, he was not the
same man who had expected to bring the boat upstream, and no
one had told him about the Whitman party.

Almost stunned by this turn of events, they concluded the
last rites for Mrs. Satterlee, did what they could to bring religious
comfort to the bereaved husband. He decided not to go on with
them. Then they took counsel together as to their next step. A
real crisis confronted them. Was their whole undertaking to fail
here at Liberty before it was even well started? They decided,
courageously, to go overland and make every possible effort to
catch up with Fitzpatrick at Bellevue.

They started off with the farm wagon, the Dearborn, twelve
pack animals and sixteen cows, four of them giving milk. Most of
the time Narcissa and Eliza rode horseback, twisted uncomforta-

bly on sidesaddles, as became modest females. When this mode
of locomotion became too much for even their Spartan endurance,
they betook themselves to the Dearborn for a while. Spalding
drove the heavy wagon, Gray piloted the carriage. John and Richard drove the cows and kept the pack horses in line.

The small cavalcade followed the east bank of the Missouri
for a short distance, crossing the river near Fort Leavenworth. A
few miles farther along they came upon a lean, gaunt boy of sixteen or so. His clothing was not only inadequate, but ragged, he
had no gun, and he was on foot. He had come from somewhere
in Iowa, he said, and wanted to join a fur caravan going to the
Rocky Mountains. It was a moment in history, though none of
them suspected it, not even the boy, whose name was Miles Goodyear. Dr. Whitman, understandably doubtful of the wisdom of
adding to his already almost overwhelming responsibilities, furnished Miles a horse, gun, ammunition and stout clothing. Gray,
observing all this through the clouded lens of his own personality,
disapproved heartily. The boy was, Gray felt dourly sure, a deserter
from Fort Leavenworth, and a less than useless addition to their
party. In this Gray was mistaken. The boy made a good, dependable "hand" as long as he stayed with them, which was many an
arduous mile beyond the Rocky Mountains.

Not long after Miles joined the party, Narcissa, writing again
to her sister, related a few details of their manner of traveling:

> Mary, you ask concerning my beds and bedding. I will tell
> you. We . . . spread our India rubber cloth on the ground,
> then our blankets, and encamp for the night. We have plenty
> of Mackinaw blankets, which answer for our bed and bedding,
> and when we journey we place them over our saddles and ride
> on them.

Eliza's endurance gave out, and she had to ride most of the
time in the Dearborn. They hurried on—if it could be called
hurrying when there were sixteen cows to be urged along, and a
four-horse farm wagon lumbering at the rear.

While the missionaries struggled forward, at Bellevue the
appointed time came for the fur caravan to start up the Platte.

Fitzpatrick departed on schedule, unaware of what had happened to them, and probably relieved by their absence. Missionaries were always a nuisance anyway. Complaining about everything, indignant because they had to travel on Sundays—and now women! Mrs. Whitman and Mrs. Spalding were the first females to intrude themselves on a train going to the Rocky Mountains. It was more than a man should have to put up with.

The outfit as it started up the Platte was an impressive sight. More than 400 horses and mules, seventy employees, and a considerable train of wheeled vehicles, including nineteen carts, strung out across the prairie. At its head rode that skilled mountain man, Thomas Fitzpatrick. By his side, mounted on a fine black horse, went Captain Stewart, with Mr. Sillem, also on a blooded horse, near by. Close behind them rode Milton Sublette in his cart with its tandem hitch of mules. Farther back in the train rolled Captain Stewart's two wagons, one requiring two, the other four, animals to pull it over the rough terrain. With the wagons were Captain Stewart's three servants to wait on him and Mr. Sillem, and two more "fast-running" horses with which to pursue the buffalo and antelope, or race anyone foolish enough to bet on his own steed. Black Harris ranged along the sides of the caravan and at the rear, taking care of small emergencies, keeping the horses and wagons moving.

For four uneventful days they followed the shallow Platte. Finally, one by one, the wheels of the carts and wagons began to complain, then to screech, then to scream as if in agony. Fitzpatrick wheeled his horse and rode furiously back, demanding why. He was told the awful truth. In the excitement and press of many duties, no axle grease had been provided at Bellevue, an oversight of the first magnitude. Fitzpatrick exploded in sulphurous profanity. Until a lubricant was provided, they could take the wagons no farther. They made camp.

The country was treeless. Yet they had to have ashes. Fitzpatrick sent men out to find wood where, so far as the eye could see, there was no wood. Two oxen were slaughtered, men rendering out the fat of these animals in maddeningly slow motion over inadequate wisps of flame coaxed from a scanty supply of dried sunflower stalks. Four precious days went by before the men returned with a small supply of wood, which was quickly reduced to ashes. Darkness overtook the men as they blended the two ingredients to make what would have to pass for axle grease until the party reached Fort Laramie. The men of the train, some bedeviled by impatience, others by exhaustion, found it hard to sleep that night.

While all this was happening to Fitzpatrick and his train, the missionary party was having a very bad time indeed. The whole success of their venture, into which had gone so much labor and money and faith, depended, it seemed, on the whim of an indifferent, even hostile providence. They prayed that a miracle would be performed, bringing them to Bellevue in time. They finally arrived at that point—but no miracle. Fitzpatrick had left several days before. They could not know that what would pass for a miracle, except to a mind like Gray's, was even then in the making far ahead on the trail to Fort Laramie. They knew that if they did not catch up with Fitzpatrick within a few days, they would have to turn back, all their hopes blasted for this year, perhaps forever. Yet, in the face of what looked like utter impossibility, they put their small party in motion and started to follow the Platte.

On the 25th of May, 1836, the last vestiges of hope began to fade. Yet they would not give up. Darkness came. The cattle could not be urged beyond a snail's pace. It was decided that the wagons and horses should go on, leaving the two faithful Nez Percé boys to keep the exhausted cattle moving. Dr. Whitman and Narcissa could not bring themselves to leave the Indian boys alone and rode slowly with them through the night.

Spalding, Eliza, Gray, and Miles Goodyear, accompanied by the wagons and the pack animals, forged ahead. Dr. Whitman, Narcissa, Richard, John, and the cattle plodded along far in the rear. Nine o'clock came and the animals could be pushed no farther. With only their blankets for shelter and covering, the weary little party made ready to get what rest they could. Dr. Whitman, making use of the tin cup belted to his waist, brought Narcissa her supper: warm, frothy milk from one of the cows. She accepted it, cheerfully grateful for the Lord's bounty and her husband's thoughtfulness.

Bestirring themselves before daybreak next morning, they went on. At five o'clock they came up to the rest of their party and Fitzpatrick's caravan, encamped together near the confluence of the Platte and Loup Rivers. The contingent under Spalding and Gray had come up to the fur company at midnight. The long anxiety, the incredible exertions of the Whitman party were over. From now on until they reached their destination, there would be for them only the normal hardships of the trail.

The delay of the fur caravan, made imperative by the absence of axle grease, had saved the missionaries from failure and made possible the opening of a whole new chapter in the expansion of the United States. Now, wheels would roll for the first time beyond the Rocky Mountains, and for the first time white women would go beyond the missions planted sparsely here and there a few miles west of the Missouri River. A truly vital step would be taken in the nation's march to the Pacific.

Dr. Whitman and Captain Stewart greeted each other cordially. The eyes of everyone, from Fitzpatrick, the rugged man of the Far West, to the lowliest packer, were gladdened by the sight of Dr. Whitman's bride. There were, of course, two men who at least pretended that they were somewhat less than admiring of Narcissa: William Gray and Henry Spalding. Gray protested altogether too much in his book, leaving the reader with the inescapable conclusion that he was very much conscious of her at all times. Spalding, a man of great and almost continuously vocal piety, saw little but sin in the behavior of his fellow human beings, including the fair Narcissa, of the flashing smile and the twinkling blue eyes.

There is a well-authenticated story that Reverend Spalding had fallen in love with Narcissa, proposed, and been rejected, before she met Dr. Whitman. It does much to explain Spalding's attitude toward both Whitman and his lovely Narcissa, especially since Mrs. Spalding was a plain, serious woman, in poor health, whose aim in life was to do the Lord's will—as she saw it—which, on the whole was a pretty dreary business, not only for her but for everyone else.

Fitzpatrick, gaunt and tireless, took his long caravan of wagons, carts, horses, and cattle, now increased by the missionary party, up the Platte as fast as he could. He had succeeded in making a good, early start, but the missing axle grease had created a serious delay. A whole season's profits depended on his getting to the rendezvous before his competitors acquired most of the beaver plews and buffalo robes brought in by the free trappers and the Indians, who, unlike company employees, sold where they pleased.

After a few days' travel up the Platte, Narcissa invited Captain Stewart, Milton Sublette, Fitzpatrick, Gray, and her missionary companions to "tea." Spreading an India-rubber "cloth" on the ground, she served tea in tin "basens" with all the grace she had learned in the home of her father, Judge Prentiss, of Steuben County, New York.

Narcissa brought gaiety to her brave little party, disregarding the sand that blew into everything, and the absence of chairs that forced her guests to sit cross-legged on the ground. Captain Stewart, who admired courage as well as beauty, was completely charmed. William Gray's comment on the blithe Narcissa—made in the book he wrote later—was that she was a flirtatious woman. In the next sentence he grudgingly admitted that she was also a lady.

When Fort Laramie was only a day or two ahead of them, Fitzpatrick sent a messenger to announce the approach of the train and also to impart the astonishing news that he was bringing with him the first white women ever to journey up the Platte beyond the Pawnee Mission, only a few miles from Bellevue. There were men at the fort who had not seen a white woman for five or even six years. The Indian wives of the men there had never seen one. There ensued much bathing in the clear waters of the Laramie, followed by wholesale shaving and hair trimming. The Indian women readied their handsomely beaded and embroidered skin clothing and the equally elaborate garments of their half-breed children. Even the Sioux and Utes, encamped in their lodges close to the stockade, felt the stir of excitement and curiosity.

The men in charge of Fort Laramie rode miles down the Platte to welcome the train. Their Indian wives, colorfully and beautifully clad, accompanied the men in order that they might fittingly welcome the missionary ladies. There was great commotion as the long caravan forded the Laramie, spread itself out, and encamped on the open space sloping toward the river. Here they would necessarily pause for a few days while goods from the wagons and carts were transferred to the backs of pack animals. Fitzpatrick did not plan that any wheeled vehicle except Milton's cart should go beyond Fort Laramie. The trail was too rough.

He reckoned without Dr. Whitman, who intended to take his heavy wagon and the Dearborn all the way to Oregon. Compromising, Whitman finally agreed to leave the heavy wagon behind, while Fitzpatrick consented to his taking the Dearborn for ailing Eliza Spalding. Narcissa needed no special consideration. Her vitality and energy seemed boundless.

The second day at Fort Laramie, while the re-packing was going on, Captain Stewart returned Narcissa's hospitality of the trail by inviting her and the other members of the missionary party to a tea served inside the fort. Here there were chairs to sit on (very comfortable, with buffalo-hide bottoms, as noted in her journal by a grateful Narcissa), a table, plates, cups and saucers. Captain Stewart offered fine potted meats for his guests' pleasure, along with yellow slices of imported cheese, green mango pickles from India, and honey-colored marmalade, the product of Seville oranges and English skill. All this delighted Narcissa, even as it appalled Eliza Spalding by its worldly extravagance.

While the whole company hesitated here at Fort Laramie, Captain Stewart made the acquaintance of Major Joshua Pilcher, an old hand in the fur trade. He had been associated at different times with General Ashley, Jedediah Smith and other greats in the business during the twenties and thirties. He had also made several not too successful ventures of his own.

Major Pilcher proposed to accompany Fitzpatrick to the rendezvous, where he had business to transact. His mount was a particularly fine white mule, an animal of which he was exceedingly proud. He was likewise vain of his costume, which consisted of a skillfully tanned and fashioned buckskin coat trimmed with red wool cloth and tastefully embroidered with red and blue porcupine quills, a red cloth shirt, buckskin pants, and moccasins ornamented with blue beads.

William Gray was a man who disliked practically everyone on sight. Major Pilcher's peacock attire did not endear him to the "secular agent" of the missionary party. A few days out on the trail from Fort Laramie, Major Pilcher, white mule, and all, fell into a deep mudhole, which brought great and pleasurable satisfaction to the vinegar-minded Gray.

The first day out of Laramie the train made its tortuous way through bottom lands strewn with fallen cottonwood trees. At night Dr. Whitman came into camp exhausted but jubilant, declaring he had had a fine day—the Dearborn had overturned but once, Milton's cart only twice. Fitzpatrick recognized Dr. Whitman's stamina, both of body and spirit. He assigned two men of his own force to help the missionary.

When the party reached Independence Rock, Fitzpatrick dispatched a messenger to the rendezvous, giving the approximate time he expected to arrive there. Probably he encamped near the spot. At any rate, the names of Eliza Spalding and Narcissa Whitman were carved on the great stone, very likely by Major Pilcher and Captain Stewart, the two "gallants"—Gray's word for them—of the party.

On July 3 they reached that bare, flat, undramatic stretch of country known as the Continental Divide. In the distance five horsemen galloped wildly toward them, yelling and brandishing rifles. The men of the party grabbed their guns, prepared to defend themselves from what looked like a band of tomahawk-happy savages. Their fears were soon dissipated; the galloping horsemen were a welcoming party of trappers riding out to meet Fitzpatrick and his train. Another two days brought them all to the rendezvous, held that year between the forks of Horse Creek and Green River.

There were about fifteen hundred whites and Indians already encamped there. The tepees of the Snakes and Bannocks were scattered for three miles along Horse Creek, while still farther upstream clustered the Flathead and Nez Percé villages. Also present were about a hundred Americans—hunters, trappers, and traders—and some fifty Frenchmen. The arrival of Fitzpatrick's train compounded the confusion, noise, and turmoil.

Fitzpatrick had his men throw up a rough log enclosure, waist high, to protect his goods from pilfering hands, and began the business of trading for furs and robes. There was no lack of customers, either for goods or watered whisky. The rendezvous continued with the usual gambling, shooting, lovemaking, and fighting as a good time was had by all.

The Indians were astounded by the arrival of the white women, the first they had ever seen. They decided to honor them with a grand procession, a custom of theirs when they wished to show great respect for someone. All four tribes represented in large numbers at the rendezvous participated in this spectacular event.

The procession started at the west end of the valley, where the Snakes and Bannocks were camped. The Nez Percé and Flathead warriors joined the cavalcade as it swept past their villages. The participants were dressed for war; that is, they wore small scraps of cloth, supplemented by many stripes and circles of vivid vermilion, blue and yellow paint decorating their bodies, and carried spears, lances, war clubs and guns.

As the 200 or more yelling warriors galloped across the plain, they presented an alarming sight. Some of the white men snatched up guns, expecting to fight for their lives, but the more experienced ones realized what was afoot and reassured their comrades.

Captain Stewart and Major Pilcher hurried to the tent of the missionary ladies, assuring them that there was no danger and that the show they were about to see was staged as an honor to them. The great cavalcade circled the tent of the missionary ladies several times at full speed, whooping and yelling as only a band of red savages could. The two women came out to view the wild and fearsome spectacle. Eliza returned to her tent almost at once, whether because of physical weakness or the outrage to her modesty at the sight of so many practically naked Indians, no one can say. Narcissa remained, apparently enjoying herself, and became the center of attraction for the warriors. Several of the savages dismounted from their curveting steeds to examine the Dearborn wagon standing beside the tent of the missionaries. This strange object roused almost as much wonderment as did Narcissa and her red-gold curls.

Within a day or so, Eliza felt strong enough to start compiling a Nez Percé vocabulary. Narcissa began one also, but didn't get far with it. Gray commented acrimoniously that "She was often interrupted by the attentions thought necessary to be paid to gentlemen callers."

Sour grapes. Gray probably never had a chance to show her any attentions, with Major Pilcher and Captain Stewart on hand.

One deep and almost stunning disappointment awaited Dr. Whitman at the rendezvous. Tom McKay, quarter-breed stepson of Dr. McLoughlin, and John McLeod, both men high in the employ of Hudson's Bay Company, arrived at the rendezvous from Fort Vancouver; but Reverend Samuel Parker was not with them. He was to have brought back with him the detailed knowledge of the country that would have made it possible for Dr. Whitman to decide wisely on a location for his proposed mission.

Reverend Parker, a man fifty-seven years of age, had been unable to face the prospect of the trip back to the Rockies, across that rugged terrain, then—still on horseback—over the prairies to the Missouri River. Instead, he had taken passage on the Hudson's Bay Company boat to the Sandwich Islands. He had waited six months for a boat leaving Oahu, and reached home at last on May 11, 1837, and so passes from our story.

However, Dr. Whitman was not without help in this emergency. Captain Stewart had, as Dr. Whitman was aware, considerable first-hand knowledge of the country under consideration and of conditions there. There can be little doubt that he suggested Waiilatpu as a favorable site for Dr. Whitman's proposed mission. The location was about twenty-five miles north of old Fort Walla Walla on the Columbia, directly up the Walla Walla River. It was in the Cayuse country, but the Nez Percés ranged freely far beyond it to the west. There was good land at that point. The mission would be able to raise most of its food and to keep a plentiful supply of horses and cattle.

Later events made clear that Dr. Whitman decided here at the rendezvous that they would follow Stewart's suggestions. Thus Stewart became an instrument of the destiny that used the Whitman party to blaze a trail for other missionaries, and for an ever-increasing number of settlers who, within a handful of years, took the United States to Oregon. The Whitman mission itself came to an end in horror and tragedy, the price fate sometimes demands of those who take momentous steps in history.

Arrangements were completed with the reluctant McLeod that the missionary party should go with him and McKay to Fort Vancouver. Against the advice of both Indians and white men, Dr.

Whitman insisted on taking the Dearborn wagon. He placed the responsibility for it in the hands of young Miles Goodyear who, though he had reached the Rocky Mountains, his original goal, now was eager to go farther.

After more than three weeks of arduous travel over rougher country than had previously been encountered, on August 5 they reached Fort Hall on the Snake. At this point Miles issued an ultimatum. Either the Dearborn stayed here at the fort, or he did. No longer would he drag, pull, push and coerce the pesky vehicle across sands, up hills, down declivities and across streams that rose above the floor boards. He was through.

Knowing Dr. Whitman's determination, it comes as no surprise that the Dearborn went on. Miles joined a party of Bannock Indians and started on his notable career as a mountain man and friend of the Indians. In course of time he married a Bannock woman, perhaps several of them. In his way, he was no less a man than Dr. Whitman, for he, too, made his dream come true.

Some way beyond Fort Hall, the Dearborn smashed an axle. There was no wood to make another. Dr. Whitman sawed the light wagon in two, made a cart of the portion that still had an axle, and went indomitably forward until they reached Fort Boise, at that time little more than a crude stockade.

Here McKay and McLeod united in assuring Dr. Whitman that, because of precipices and portages yet to come, he must now abandon the makeshift cart. Reluctantly he agreed to their suggestion, which, in effect, was a command. The Hudson's Bay men promised the missionary that later they would furnish him and Gray with a large and suitably equipped party to bring the vehicle through. The promise was never kept. Next year the wheels proved of great assistance to the Hudson's Bay Company in hauling the lumber for the new Fort Boise, constructed at the mouth of the Boise River where it runs into the Snake.

From the first days of Whitman's and Spalding's association there had been a clash of personalities between them. The characters of the two men were so widely divergent that this would have come about even if there had not been the added irritant of Spalding's unmistakable jealousy of Narcissa, which grew into a canker of bitterness. Serious friction developed between the two men. It became clear that they could not work together, even in the business of saving heathen souls.

They arrived at Fort Vancouver on September 12. From there Whitman would go to Waiilatpu, situated in the country of the Cayuses, Indians whose friendship for the whites was uncertain and subject to unpredictable fluctuations. Whitman had been informed that this was the case, but he felt confident he could cope with any situation that might arise. Spalding departed for Lapwai, near where the city of Lewiston, Idaho, now stands.

Winter was approaching and time was of the essence. Both men left their wives at Fort Vancouver under the fatherly care of Dr. McLoughlin, until such time as shelters of a sort could be built at the posts selected for their future labors.

While the noise and milling turmoil of Indians and whites still surged along the riverbanks in the valley of the Green, Captain Stewart, Antoine and the mysterious Mr. Sillem, along with their dogs, horses and servants, disappeared from view. Passages in Stewart's novels lead to the belief that they went on a hunting expedition into the remote fastnesses of the Wind River Mountains beyond New Fork. This wild region must have had an irresistible attraction for the adventurous Scot. In its canyons and gorges could be found most of the large game animals of the Far West: cougar, grizzly bear, antelope, elk, and the uncannily sure-footed Rocky Mountain sheep with their great curved horns. Somewhere in these wilds they met Jim Bridger and a small party of trappers. Together they rode to Fort Laramie.

There, and not by accident, they found Fitzpatrick and Milton Sublette with their caravan, taking the season's furs to St. Louis. But Milton was desperately ill—far too ill to continue the journey, even in his cart. Fitzpatrick paced up and down his small quarters at the fort, consumed with anxiety for Milton, who lay suffering with pain and fever caused by inflammation in the stump of his leg, and at the same time worried by the delay. Finally Fitzpatrick decided to go ahead, leaving Milton in the care of the fort's Indian women.

So one morning the Fitzpatrick train forded the bright-flowing Laramie and set off down the shallow, muddy Platte on the long trek home. Captain Stewart, Mr. Sillem, and Antoine went with it. We never hear of Sillem again. Of Antoine, we shall hear much.

Among the numerous letters waiting in St. Louis for Captain Stewart was one from Archibald in London, expressing a wry pleasure, which somehow held overtones of blame, that William had decided to return from "the wilds" to St. Louis for the winter. Aunt Mary wrote from Logiealmond: she realized poor William hadn't enough money for returning to Scotland and offered to send him £100 to pay his way back home. As for William's brother, Thomas, (now studying to be a cardinal), he was visiting the aunts in Logiealmond, had been made a Knight of Malta, and would return to Rome soon.

George wrote, relating small news of the family and of happenings in Dunkeld. Work was progressing on New Murthly and George was childishly pleased. Several years would elapse before the elaborate building would be completed. But some day it would be one of the show places of Scotland. There was nothing like it in the whole country. A tide of fury must have risen in Captain Stewart as he read George's naïve remarks about the turreted and towered New Murthly, raising its monstrous bulk at the foot of Birnam Hill and overlooking the lovely Tay.

Later events indicate that at this time Captain Stewart received another letter from home—possibly from Christina, though no copy of it has as yet been found. This letter brought the startling information that John had contracted a fatal malady, one that would not be long running its course. Captain Stewart would, then, within a foreseeable future, succeed to the title and estates of his illustrious forebears. It is reasonable to suppose that news of such serious import as this would have been withheld as long as possible from George and the elderly aunts, though Archibald seems to have known the truth. Captain Stewart apparently did not divulge it to anyone, or if he did, they kept the secret well. While still in St. Louis, he received a letter from Archibald that said starkly, "John is in Paris. His condition is very bad."

The ambiguity and lack of detail of these phrases indicate that Archibald knew William to be in possession of the facts regarding John's health. At any rate, it is quite clear that from the fall of 1836 Captain Stewart must have begun laying far-reaching plans for the coming time when he would be master of his family estates.

He stayed a few weeks in St. Louis, seeing old friends and making new ones, attending glittering balls at which the ever-present rich gumbo soup was served between dances. Then he and Antoine went down the Mississippi to the busy, colorful city of New Orleans, with its French charm and its American business push and bustle. Antoine enjoyed the life of the city; he had a useful faculty of adapting himself to any environment. The French blood of his father, which so clearly predominated in his appearance, was no less an influence in his thinking and actions. He thrived in cities as well as in the mountains.

Arriving in the city of the delta, Stewart wrote a letter to John, requesting in terms that were mild for him that long overdue payments of his annuity be made at once. Failing that, he would like to receive the sum of the estate left to him by his father, £3000 in all. He appears to have been very busy that fall, attending to his cotton-buying activities and carrying forward the unknown, but remunerative, business in which he and Consul Crawford were engaged.

In January he received a letter direct from John—usually his older brother communicated with him through an attorney in Edinburgh—refusing curtly to make any payment whatsoever, either of interest or principal. The reason he gave for this action was not one calculated to soothe a man of Captain Stewart's temperament. John required all the money available to him, he stated, for the building of New Murthly.

Stewart, so far as is known, made no reply to this. There was no need for him to do so. His own efforts were bringing him all the money he would require for his plans encompassing 1837, although the amount would be considerable. For the rest he could wait. There had never been any love between the two brothers and William Stewart was too innately honest to pretend to an affection he did not feel.

In the meantime, fate was moving to bring together—apparently by chance—the Scotsman and an artist of unusual training and talents. Their combined efforts were destined to preserve much of the Far West that would within a few short decades disappear forever from the face of America.

CHAPTER XVI

An Artist Goes West

੨ঌ Alfred Jacob Miller was born in Baltimore, January 10, 1810. He was fortunate in that his formative and creative years came at a time when art and artists were well thought of in the United States. Miller lived in the light cast by such painters as Charles Wilson Peale, famous for his portraits of Washington, and his two almost equally famous sons, Rembrandt and Raphael. There was also the renowned Benjamin West, an American, though he lived most of his life in London; and there were many others.

Miller's parents were comfortably well-to-do and they recognized early in his life that their son possessed outstanding artistic ability. Consequently, for him there was no living in a garret, half-starving, freezing in winter, sweltering in summer. Nor did he experience a distressingly long struggle for recognition.

His artistic tendencies showed up first in normal schoolboy fashion. He tortured his schoolmasters by drawing caricatures of them, which they angrily confiscated and burned before his eyes. At the age of seventeen, his sketches showed that he had been given the advantage of some training in using the brush. Three years later he studied for a while with the artist, Thomas Sully, who at that time made his home in Baltimore.

In 1833, the year William Drummond Stewart first went to the Far West, Alfred Miller's family thought well enough of his

128

talent to send him to France and Italy for further art instruction. He remained for a while in Paris, then went to Rome, Bologna, and Venice, assiduously studying the works of the great artists whose paintings were to be found there. Presumably, he made a visit to Switzerland; in his notebook of this period there are several sketches of the mountains and lakes of that country. Young Miller was especially fascinated by Turner's treatment of light, and that painter's influence can be seen in his later works.

Miller returned to Baltimore in 1834, where he rented lodgings and a studio at No. 153 Colonade Row on Baltimore Street, over the music store of Mr. George Willig. We do not know how the young artist made out here financially—not very well, probably. About this time his father died and young Miller found it necessary to make his own living.

In the fall of 1836 he moved to New Orleans, arriving there with only thirty dollars in his pocket. He rented a modest second-story studio at 132 Chartres Street, above a drygoods store owned by one L. Chittenden. Shortly afterward, Miller painted Mr. Chittenden's portrait. Possibly the fee was applied to the rent. At any rate, Mr. Chittenden was so enchanted by the likeness that he recommended other patrons. Some of these people bought pictures Miller had painted in Europe, others sat for their portraits. Soon he was busy and on the road to becoming prosperous. He was now twenty-six years old.

One April morning in 1837, William Drummond Stewart, walking briskly along Chartres Street, stopped in front of one of Mr. Chittenden's windows. A number of Miller's paintings were on display. The Scotsman may not have been there by accident. The wife of his business associate, Mr. Crawford, the British Consul, had made a protracted visit to Baltimore the previous year, where it is likely she met Miller, or at least heard of him.

Turning away from the paintings, Captain Stewart walked upstairs, found himself facing a door bearing the legend, *Studio, Alfred Jacob Miller, Enter.* He walked inside, nodded casually to the artist busy at his easel, and proceeded to inspect the paintings on the walls with a manner of aloof indifference, speaking only in monosyllables. He was observing everything with the closest attention, and not the least, Miller himself.

The artist was sufficiently impressed by the appearance of his caller to note in his journal that the stranger held himself erect with a military air, wore a gray suit with a black stripe outlining the seam of his trousers, and that the handle of a bowie knife could be glimpsed in the opening of his vest. (A bowie knife, Miller commented, was fashionable "jewelry" for gentlemen of the lower Mississippi.) Finally Stewart expressed somewhat guarded praise of a picture of the city of Baltimore and Miller's handling of the evening light that enveloped the buildings. He then took his leave without having introduced himself.

A few days later Stewart called again at the studio on Chartres Street. This time his manner was affable and even friendly. He handed Miller a card on which was inscribed: *Captain W. D. Stewart, British Army.* He then explained to the astonished young artist why he was there. He wanted Miller to accompany him on a trip to the Rocky Mountains for the purpose of making on-the-spot sketches of scenery, people—especially Indians—and interesting incidents. It is possible that he went even further with Miller at this time, revealing to him that he would also be expected—at some later, then indeterminate, date—to go to Scotland and there make large oil paintings from his sketches to adorn the walls of Murthly Castle. Miller would have thought twice about giving up his prospects as an artist in New Orleans, by now looking very good indeed, to set off on a jaunt promising hardships, even dangers, merely to make a bunch of sketches.

The proposition outlined by Captain Stewart could not have failed to excite Miller, but he gave no sign of this, made a half-hearted objection or two, said he would like to think it over. Captain Stewart agreed, told the artist to consult his friends, talk to Mr. Crawford. Miller lost no time in doing just that. The British Consul told him that Captain Stewart was next in line for the title and estates of Murthly and Grandtully Castles and that his present financial status was such that the gentleman was quite able to take care of any financial arrangements he might wish to make. Miller went back to his studio, took an appraising glance at the mountain and lake scenes he had painted in Switzerland, thought they looked pretty good, and accepted Captain Stewart's offer.

The full import of this agreement neither man could have foreseen. In time, of course, Murthly got its great oil paintings of the Far West as it was in the year 1837. But immeasurably more important than that, Miller was to preserve for America and for the world, in his many sketches and in finished pictures he made from them, scenes, peoples, and a way of life that soon vanished from the face of the earth.

While still in New Orleans, Captain Stewart received a letter from his friend, Lord Breadalbane, asking that Stewart send him several buffaloes, "or any other animal of the west that is good to eat." The difficulties of transporting buffaloes from the Rocky Mountains to Taymouth Castle in Scotland appear staggering, but Stewart set about finding a way to overcome them. One can almost see the line written in a firm hand in his notebook: "Buffaloes to Breadalbane, earliest opportunity."

During the remainder of Stewart's stay in New Orleans, he and Miller saw a good deal of each other. Miller met Antoine Clement—they were to be companions for a long time and in widely differing scenes. The artist watched Captain Stewart play cards with the half-breed at the Scotsman's lodgings—perhaps sometimes joining in their games. Three new Manton guns came from London. Captain Stewart gave one—the heaviest—to Antoine. It shot a ball almost an inch in diameter, weighing twelve to the pound. This would stop the largest grizzly in its tracks, or stun a buffalo if it hit the animal's skull. It was to be a marvel in the mountains, become the basis for many a tale of wonder related about lonely campfires and at the few rendezvous that were still to come. Stewart, Miller, and Antoine were invited to make their headquarters at Sublette's country home and stock farm until it was time for them to join that year's caravan to the mountains. A week or two later all four men arrived in St. Louis.

William Sublette provided his guests with the finest city fare, but he also gave them, as a great treat, pemmican and jerky. Every year as long as he lived he had a bale of these delicacies sent to him from the Indian country, enough to last for six or eight months. Captain Stewart purchased from Sublette two magnificent horses, one black, one white. The mounts he bought for Miller and Antoine were hardly less fine.

Pratte, Chouteau and Company, successors of the Western Department of the American Fur Company, were planning to send a caravan to the mountains that year. It would be led by Captain Stewart's old friend, Thomas Fitzpatrick, who knew the Indians, the fur trade, and the trails better, perhaps, than any other man then alive. Stewart, who planned to go with that outfit, began to form his own private company. When assembled it was composed of three engagés, two packers and general roustabouts, François Lajeunesse, a man who shows up here and there throughout the annals of the Far West, a cook, Antoine, Miller, and Stewart— ten in all. Stewart had two sturdy wagons, four mules to each, stocked with every luxury he could afford and was able to transport. He was well aware of the route they would travel, so the wagons were not overloaded. Under the stout coarse linen sheets that covered their bows the wagons carried all the varieties of fine foods he had taken the year before, only more of them: sardines, hams, marmalades, dried fruits—the list was a long one. There were also brandies and fine wines—even separate tents for him and Miller. Antoine, of course, scorned to sleep under canvas.

Here in St. Louis Captain Stewart had a practical as well as beautiful piece of equipment made for his own use and pleasure. This was a combination tomahawk and pipe, the cutting blade fashioned of the best quality of steel, the pipe bowl of red sandstone from the sacred quarry on the upper Missouri. Every act of his in New Orleans, St. Louis, and on the journey in 1837, seems to fall into a pattern showing his belief that this was his last trip West, and he intended to bring back with him everything he could that, through all his years to come, would serve to recall memories of the scenes and activities he had loved.

Stewart and Miller visited William Clark several times during that early spring of 1837. Clark received them seated in a large armchair covered with a grizzly-bear robe. He was sixty-seven, but vigorous and alert in spite of the many hardships he had endured in his youth. Thick white hair framed his face and fell almost to his shoulders in the fashion of the time. He showed his two guests the many trophies he had collected and placed in the museum connected with his office, related many a story of the Rocky Mountains. They told him of their plans for the approaching summer.

He listened, recalling his own adventures amid the wild scenes they would soon look upon, and expressed deep regret that he could not go with them.

Besides the Manton guns, a heavy box arrived from London. Stewart had it stowed, unopened, in one of the wagons, revealing to no one what it contained. From St. Louis the caravan moved up the river by steamboat to Westport, not far from Independence. Here they encountered a party of twenty Delawares, mounted and armed, ready to travel. The head man of this band asked Fitzpatrick's permission to travel with the caravan as far as the rendezvous, where he and his companions hoped to find employment as hunters or scouts. Fitzpatrick readily agreed to this arrangement; Delawares were entirely trustworthy, having long ago allied themselves with the white man, and they would help to provide meat along the way.

In this year of 1837, the United States saw its first great depression. There were riots, bread lines, a rash of suicides. Business firms toppled, banks closed, foreign investors sold their securities for whatever they would bring on a plummeting market.

By a paradox, the cities along the lower Missouri and Mississippi Rivers were riding high on the crest of a boom. The consumption of cotton, especially by England, grew ever greater in volume and was paid for in cash. Trade with Sante Fe had doubled within a few years, and all goods sent to that city in New Mexico brought high prices, payment being made in the form of silver coins. China still unstintedly purchased furs, though the market for beaver in England and on the Continent had sharply declined now that the gentlemen in those parts were wearing silk hats instead of beavers. So for the fur companies it was pretty much business as usual, and Captain Stewart had plenty of money at his disposal.

A misfortune more terrible than financial depression struck the upper reaches of the Missouri and Big Horn Rivers that year. This was the most violent and widespread outbreak of smallpox ever known on the continent of North America. The epidemic, which started with the Mandans on the Missouri, spread with almost the swiftness of a prairie fire. Ferocious and deadly, it leaped northward, then west along the Yellowstone. Whole villages perished, leaving none to bury the dead. Tribes were decimated, their identity as separate peoples wiped out. Indians slew the members of their stricken families, then killed themselves rather than suffer the horrors of the scourge.

Untouched either by the paralyzing depression or by the small-pox horror raging far to the north that together made this year darkly memorable in history, the people with whom we are con-cerned walked a charmed path between them.

On the 5th of April, a short time before the caravan started, Milton Sublette died at Fort Laramie and was buried not far from the fort his brother William had helped to build. Neither Captain Stewart nor his companions knew about it until they reached the confluence of the Platte and Laramie rivers. Not until June 16 did the St. Louis *Missouri Republican* publish the death notice.

At last the long caravan headed out into the seemingly limit-less prairie. At its head rode Fitzpatrick, Captain Stewart, and Miller. Then came Stewart's two wagons, followed by the twenty charettes drawn by two horses hitched in tandem fashion. There were forty-five mounted men, and extra horses to help get the wagons and charettes across rivers and up steep banks. The Dela-ware Indians brought up the rear, when they were not off hunting. Lajeunesse ranged the length of the caravan, seeing that every-thing was kept moving and in order. An impressive sight.

Two days out from Westport, Fitzpatrick appointed Stewart lieutenant of the entire train, second only to himself. The veteran of Waterloo immediately put into effect a strict system of military discipline and enforced it with Wellingtonian inflexibility. The men grumbled, of course, but Fitzpatrick recognized the value of such organization, considering the unruly elements in his caravan, and upheld Stewart in his plans and decisions.

Much to Miller's indignation, he was given no special con-sideration, being expected to care for his horse, picket it at night, catch and saddle it in the morning. One privilege, if such it can be called, was accorded him—that of hiring a man, whom he paid out of his own pocket, to take his place on night-guard duty so that he might be rested for his task of sketching along the way. Miller felt, reasonably enough, it would seem, that he should have been allowed to sleep at night, with no penalties attached; but Stewart refused to relax the rules on his account.

Soon the party reached the Kansas River. Here Miller made a detailed and beautiful sketch of the men struggling to get the carts and wagons across the comparatively shallow stream, while others of the train busied themselves setting up the tents for Miller and Captain Stewart and starting cooking fires on the opposite bank.

As soon as the Kansas River was behind them, Stewart formulated a plan for setting up camp which was followed without deviation from there on until they reached the rendezvous. About an hour before it was time to stop for the night, he dispatched scouts ahead to find a good place to encamp, the requisites being a fairly level site close to water and with sufficient grass for the animals.

On reaching the spot selected by the scouts, the charettes and wagons, spaced about thirty feet apart, were formed into a large circle. The horses were turned loose and allowed to feed. Tired and hungry at the end of the day's march, they attended strictly to the business of cropping grass and did not wander far during the hour or two before sunset. The cooks soon had campfires blazing and kettles boiling for the evening meal. As twilight approached, the horses were driven inside the circle of vehicles and either picketed or hobbled. After supper and a session of yarning and smoking around a campfire, the teamsters and engagés found shelter under the wagons or slept in the open as they wished. During the night they were serenaded by small prairie wolves.

The caravan was now passing through the lands occupied by the Kansas Indians, once a rich and warlike tribe, now reduced to poverty. The herds of buffalo on which they had depended for food, clothing, and tepee skins, had long since been driven away by the white man. They were therefore forced to live on small game and annuities given them by the Great White Father in Washington. Their spirits were undaunted, however, and pride in their past still burned in their swarthy breasts.

One day when the train paused for its usual two-hour nooning, a small band of Kansas appeared, led by White Plume, grandson of the powerful Chief Pawhuska of the Osages. Miller was so struck by the noble features and erect bearing of White Plume that he asked the Indian if he might paint his portrait. White Plume agreed at once, making only one request: that Miller not leave out of the picture the silver peace medal given him some ten years before by President John Quincy Adams, now hanging about his neck on a buckskin thong. Miller of course had no notion of overlooking the thick, heavy two-and-one-half-inch disk. Many similar peace medals, some of them larger than White Plume's, were distributed by the presidents to Indians whom they wished to placate, or honor, or reward for some service. This one was probably the first Miller had seen. No doubt he examined it carefully. On its obverse side he would have seen a profile representation of John Quincy Adams in high relief. On the reverse side, under the word PEACE in large letters, appeared a tomahawk and peace pipe, crossed above two clasped hands and the word FRIENDSHIP.

When Miller painted White Plume's portrait, he served posterity better than he knew. This chief was the great-great-grandfather of Charles Curtis, Vice-President of the United States during the Hoover administration.

Leaving the lands of the Kansas behind, the caravan soon came to the country of the Pawnees, who were a completely different kettle of fish. Bands of them appeared from time to time, each demanding a tribute of presents in return for permission to cross their country. Fitzpatrick and Stewart bluffed them out of it by stern refusals and a show of courage, but doubled the guard at night. The Pawnees followed them for days, watching from distant vantage points, hoping for a chance to steal a few pack horses and their loads. Captain Stewart rode some distance ahead of the train, most of the time accompanied by Antoine. The marksmanship of this pair and the execution they could do with their heavy Manton rifles was not unknown to the savages; and the Pawnees, like all Indians, were exceedingly cautious when the odds were against them. Finally, they gave up their project of thievery as hopeless and moved off in search of more rewarding adventures.

For a while, as the caravan moved on, the men were restive under the firm hand Stewart kept over them. Small rebellions broke out from time to time, which were promptly suppressed. The last incident of this kind that occurred on the journey was a fight

between two men, a violation of the rule that there were to be
no physical combats while en route to the mountains.

Word that the battle was in progress came to Stewart. "Let
them alone," he ordered. Finally one was badly beaten up and
thoroughly defeated. Stewart sent for him and said, "You have
been whipped, I see." The man, hanging his head, agreed that
this was so. "I'm heartily glad to hear it," the Scot replied. "Now
you have nothing to boast of. Go." He then sent for the victor, who
approached with the self-assured look of a man who expects praise
for his exploits.

"You have whipped Louis?" Stewart asked. "Certainly," was
the arrogant reply. Stewart then informed the man that if he
heard of his boasting about it, he would take his horse away and
make him walk for a week. There was no more fighting. Miller's
conclusion was that ". . . our leader understood well the management of unruly spirits." The task was no small one, as Stewart
had a widely assorted group of men under his command: free and
company trappers, engagés, half-breed and full-blooded Indians
—even an artist. His success was a tribute both to Fitzpatrick's
judgment in appointing him and to his own ability as commander
of the train.

The caravan reached the Platte and turned westward, following the river. One day a hunter, ranging far to one side of the
train hopefully looking for buffalo, of which none had yet been
seen, came galloping back to Fitzpatrick and Stewart, yelling,
"Indians! Indians!" Another hunter quickly followed the first, to
report that a band of savages numbering several hundred was approaching. He excitedly urged them to look lively if they wanted
to save their scalps.

The engagés, mostly greenhorns, were terrified. Miller confessed he was frightened out of his wits. But not the old hands.
Fitzpatrick and Stewart rode out to meet the Indians. Even they
must have felt some qualms as the great horde rushed pell-mell
directly toward them, then circled the two white men, yelling and
waving their guns, with which they were well supplied.

However, as the two had suspected would be the case, the
demonstration was a friendly one. The Indians were Oglala Sioux.
They and the white men sat down together on the prairie, smoked

the peace pipe in ceremonial fashion, pointing it west, north, east, south, up toward the sky, downward to the earth in the prescribed fashion. Then Fitzpatrick and Stewart, knowing what was expected of them, rode back to the caravan with the chiefs and there distributed to them, "on the prairie"—i.e., for free—gaily colored shirts, Green River knives, blankets, and whatever else they thought might bring pleasure to their guests' savage hearts. The Sioux were smarter than the Pawnees, more diplomatic, and with no trouble at all secured a far greater amount of the white man's treasures than their less intelligent prairie cousins.

This was Miller's first sight of Sioux warriors: tall, superbly proportioned, with regular features. "Nothing in Greek art can surpass them," he wrote in his journal. His unstinted admiration also went to their beautifully ornamented deerskin and antelope-hide clothing, their bows, arrows, quivers and painted shields, their magnificent war bonnets made of eagle feathers, with richly beaded head bands. Actually, the finest accouterments of the Sioux, acknowledged Beau Brummels of the prairie and mountain, were secured by trading with the Crows. The women of that tribe were not only the most skilled workers, but the finest artists as well.

Arriving at the forks of the Platte, they followed the south branch of the river for a short time, then crossed to the other side. For most of the way they would follow the North Platte. Miller paused at Scott's Bluff long enough to make one of his most beautiful scenic paintings. The great rock rising abruptly from the plain looked to him like "fortifications with towers, battlements, embrasures, scarps, and counter-scarps." Perhaps some of this was the imagination of an artist, but Scott's Bluff, dramatically breaking the monotony of the prairie, must have been an astounding sight to the traveler of that day.

Still they had not sighted buffalo, or any other large game, so the men were restricted to a monotonous diet of bacon and coarse camp bread. But Captain Stewart and Antoine, assisted by a group of the Delaware Indians, began to bring in prairie grouse, more commonly called sage hen. These birds resembled the gray-and-white Barred Rocks of our own barnyards, but were more plump. They fed mainly on sagebrush leaves, supplemented by what few small seeds they could find. Miller complained that the flesh of these birds had an unpleasantly pungent flavor. Their mess cook must have been a greenhorn who did not know enough to remove the crop as the bird was delivered to him. This done, young sage hen is as delicately flavored as chicken.

At last buffaloes appeared, first in small groups of two or three, then herds of twenty-five or more. Now the men of the caravan feasted morning, noon, and night on succulent tongues, hump ribs, liver, and that favorite of the real mountain man, broiled *boudins*, crisped before the fire and dripping fat.

One morning Stewart and Antoine rode out from camp immediately after breakfast with a special purpose in mind. Before noon they rejoined the caravan, driving before them three half-grown buffalo calves. These ungainly animals were then lassoed and led behind the wagons for several days until they lost their wildness and fear of human beings, as buffalo calves very quickly did. Then men were sent back to Bellevue with the animals, having been given instructions to get their strange charges on board the first boat going to St. Louis. There, Campbell would see that they were shipped to Lord Breadalbane at Taymouth Castle. The astonishment, even consternation, these beasts must have aroused on their long journey may be imagined. This was the first shipment of Far Western animals made to Scotland by Captain Stewart—or anyone else of which there is any record—but it was far from being the last.

On June 20 the caravan was five days east of Fort Laramie. Few in the party noted the date—it was just another day's march to them—but that morning at five o'clock London time, in Kensington Palace, an eighteen-year-old girl named Alexandrina Victoria was made Queen of the United Kingdom and Ireland, to become, in later years, also Empress of India. Captain Stewart had a new monarch, though it was months before the news of the event reached him.

About five weeks out of Westport—Fitzpatrick's usual time, the train reached Fort Laramie. There was a great to-do of shouting and back-slapping, and exchange of news on the meadow between the fort and the Laramie River. Greetings over, the engagés began to unpack bales of goods brought to replenish the fort's stock of merchandise. Lucien Fontenelle, in charge of the establishment, shook hands with the head man of the caravan. Fontenelle, a well-educated man, had come, it was said, from a wealthy, perhaps noble, French family of New Orleans, of which he never spoke. He had made several improvements in the fort, having enlarged the horse corral and hung several framed engravings in the main room—one showing Saladin, Sultan of Egypt and Turkey, battling infidels in the Holy Land. There were a few books here, too: volumes of classical literature such as Captain Stewart had seen in Dr. McLoughlin's residence at Fort Vancouver. This occasional sharp contrast of the crude wildness of the Far West with the refinements of cultured city life, to which by this time Stewart was accustomed, came to Miller as fresh impressions that startled and at the same time charmed him.

While Fitzpatrick and Stewart readied the caravan for the long march to the rendezvous, Miller painted two pictures of Fort Laramie. The exterior view from the meadow on which the building faced shows the great log walls, with bastions at diagonally opposed corners, the blockhouse over the main entrance, and an American flag floating from a tall pole planted in the inner courtyard. Indian tepees stand in the foreground; the little plain is dotted with white men and Indians on horseback.

Fort Laramie had been built only three years. Later, the part of the logs making up the stockade that extended into the ground rotted, and the fort was rebuilt of adobes. The new building resembled Bent's Fort on the Arkansas. Miller's paintings show it to us as it was in its days of greatest glory, when the fur trade, though beginning to decline, was still a mighty industry and a great adventure.

The interior view, as depicted by Miller, is even more interesting to lovers of the Old West than the one seen from the meadow. This painting is the only source we have of knowledge regarding the interior of Fort Laramie. Not until the Miller pictures were brought to light nearly a hundred years after they were painted was anyone living aware that an open stairway led from the courtyard to the blockhouse over the zaguan gate, or that there was a small raised balcony at the rear, from which a narrow door led to the horse corral.

Here at the fort, Lucien Fontenelle wined and dined the important men of the train with the best the country afforded and that could be transported from St. Louis. Most deeply appreciated by the travelers were fresh butter and an abundance of cow's milk served from great crocks.

On June 25 the great caravan again took up its march. The rendezvous this year was once more to be on Green River, near the mouth of Horse Creek. Miles to the south, New Fork flowed into the Green from a northeasterly direction. The mountains where New Fork had its source were precipitous and lovely, sheltering small beautiful valleys replete with game. This region was Captain Stewart's favorite place in all the Far West.

Fontenelle went with the train, leaving Fort Laramie in the care of a trusted employee.

CHAPTER XVII

Chief Ma-wo-ma
and the Indian Parade

ᕗ When Stewart and Antoine were out on a hunting expedition in the vicinity of Independence Rock, they came upon two starving trappers, their ammunition exhausted, horses gone, so weak they could travel no farther. When discovered they were roasting the flesh of a rattlesnake they had managed to capture by means of a forked stick. Captain Stewart was so shocked by their provender that he impulsively expressed his disgust. They might well have replied in the words Old Hugh Glass is purported to have said when he found himself in similar circumstances: "Meat's meat when thar's hard doin's!"

Stewart and Antoine assisted the men into camp, where they were given soup and shortly afterward food of a more substantial nature. The two men accompanied the train until they had recovered their strength and were ready to go on their way as before. Captain Stewart then presented each of them with a horse, powder and shot, a blanket, and several beaver traps. They had, of course, lost theirs. As they said good-by, the men thanked him profusely, declaring that they were now better outfitted than they had been before misfortune overtook them.

Weather along the Platte, even in June, was soundly cursed by every traveler who passed that way. In spite of the fact that summer was approaching, there were frequent days of wind and rain, with only now and then a stretch of sunshine that made the wayfarer forget his miseries. One cold, wet day, Miller, to whom dampness brought twinges of rheumatism and who, like many artists, was sensitive to gloom, was riding along, head bowed, obviously depressed. Stewart reproved him in the following words, which Miller apparently took much to heart, for he wrote them down in his journal.

"Mr. Miller," Stewart said on that occasion, "you should not be downcast by inclement weather. On days of rain I am more exhilarated, if possible, than when the day is clear. There is something to contend against." After that, there were no more complaints from Miller, regardless of what the days brought of heat, cold, wind or water.

Miller also recorded the fact that he liked best to go sketching in Antoine's company, for the half-breed hunter could hit a buffalo's head with one of the twelve-gauge balls from his heavy Manton rifle in such a way that the animal would be stunned and stand still while Miller sketched him. The buffalo, having sustained only a superficial wound, would soon recover his faculties and scamper off, virtually unhurt, to join his fellows. Even a twelve-gauge ball could make little impression on a buffalo's skull.

Miller put down in his journal the details of another occurrence that happened while they were in the vicinity of Independence Rock. He had become so engrossed in sketching the great stone formation that he was entirely oblivious of everything else. Suddenly the artist felt strong hands press his head forward and down until it was against his knees. *Indian!* he thought, and gave himself up as lost. Determined to die bravely, he made no outcry. Several agonizing moments passed with no further movement on the part of the "Indian," who, of course, was Captain Stewart. Finally he released his pressure on Miller's head, allowing the artist to sit upright once more. Stewart then gave the young man a stern lecture on the dangers inherent in not keeping a sharp eye about him at all times when traveling through Indian country.

Buffaloes were plentiful now, so the hunters brought into

camp only the choicest parts of the great animals, leaving the rest
to be devoured by wolves. The usual way of butchering was to turn
the slain buffalo on its belly, cut the hide from head to tail, peel
it off, then take however much meat they desired. If the hunter
wanted the skin for a robe, he turned the animal on its back and
removed the thick, furry hide in one piece.

One day Captain Stewart went out with a party of hunters.
Combining their efforts, they rounded up seven magnificent buffaloes, four males and three females. This exploit was not as dangerous as it sounds, but required considerable skill. If approached
quietly, slowly, and in full view, buffaloes seldom become frightened or belligerent, and are fairly easy to domesticate. These great
brutes, one of the males probably weighing close to 2000 pounds,
were dispatched to St. Louis, there to be shipped to Captain
Stewart's friend, Lord Breadalbane.

Along the way great rocky formations rose, abruptly thrusting
their rugged heights aloft. On their precipitous sides the men sometimes glimpsed Argali, those great, unbelievably surefooted mountain goats, poised on all but invisible ledges. These stately animals
abounded most on the wildest peaks of the Rocky Mountains, but
some came down this far in the spring and early summer to feast
on the lush grass of the prairie. Warned by their lookouts that intruders approached, they would spring up the almost perpendicular
sides of these escarpments. There, standing beyond gun range,
they would arrogantly watch the caravan go by.

Their attitude became an intolerable challenge to Stewart.
One day he and Antoine, riding far ahead of the train looking for
just such an opportunity, managed to surprise several of the handsome creatures on the plain and shot one before he could escape
to his rocky fortress. His three-foot-long horns, curled in convolu-
tions as perfectly proportioned as those to be found decorating a
Greek temple, measured twenty inches around their base. Later,
Captain Stewart presented this fine set of horns to Major Lorenzo
Lewis, close relative of General George Washington who resided
at Mount Vernon.

Reaching the Sweetwater, they turned sharply westward along
the stream—and came to a prodigal bounty of ripe wild plums, filled
to bursting with sweet, purple juice. Every traveler who passed that

way in early summer accorded them lyrical praise. Small wonder, after weeks of eating an almost unbroken diet of meat.

At Independence Rock herds of antelope tempted Captain Stewart to hunt that fleet and graceful animal. There was the usual troublesome detour around Devil's Gate, then far to the left the cleft mountain known as Cut Rock, with Miller painting water-color sketches all the way. Never enough to satisfy his employer: one day Stewart suggested bluntly that Miller was letting many interesting scenes go by without getting them down on paper. Miller replied tartly, "I would be glad to paint more sketches—if I had six pairs of hands." No more complaints along that line seem to have been expressed by Captain Stewart.

At last the caravan came to the high, bare, desolate stretch of tableland known as the Continental Divide. Here, for a whole day's march, there was no water. Middle-of-the-day July heat was excessive, but the mountain men and trappers refused to carry water, considering it a sign of effeminacy. This custom was more or less localized. The men along the Arkansas and in the Santa Fe trade tolerated no such nonsense. They would have died like flies on the Southwestern deserts and they knew it. But here, farther to the north, conditions were different. No man would die of thirst crossing the Continental Divide in summer; he would merely suffer a little.

The day wore on; by mid afternoon the going was rough for both men and beasts. Most of the men were smoking now, as that seemed to relieve thirst. At least, it distracted attention from their discomfort. The animals plodded on doggedly, obviously suffering. Captain Stewart dismounted to ease his horse, walking beside the sweating mount. Two hours went by. Then the animals in the vanguard of the train smelled water. They took off over the rough ground, their drivers and riders making ineffectual efforts to check their headlong rush to a safer pace. Stewart let his horse go but would not so much as accelerate his stride to the water's edge. This self-control did not go unremarked by the men, and it brought him a full measure of their respect. For all his position, possessions, and money, he could take adversity as well as they could, if not better.

Next day, still more than twenty-four hours away from the

rendezvous, the caravan was met by a party of eight or ten trappers who had ridden out to give them a rousing welcome. There was the usual shooting, yelling, back-slapping—all the joys of old *companeros* meeting after a long separation. Making camp, Captain Stewart gathered the visitors before his tent to provide the self-appointed committee of greeters a feast of buffalo tongues and hump ribs and tender portions of broiled antelope, plus generous potations of brandy and wine the like of which his guests had probably never tasted before.

The yarning that went on around the campfire that night must have been extra special. Miller says that throughout the journey the inevitable evening tales of the trappers were interspersed with stories told by Captain Stewart of his travels and adventures in the cities of Europe and Asia, stories in which he never "put himself forward," yet held the engrossed attention of men to whom the scenes he described were as strange and alien as the dark side of the moon.

Next morning before sunrise the men were seated around the breakfast fire, eating the same kinds of food that had been served the night before. Captain Stewart decided to offer them a taste of something special. Opening a can of his precious sardines, he handed it to the man seated next to him. The trapper took one look.

"Fish!" he exclaimed delightedly, and emptied the entire contents of the can onto the piece of bark that served as his plate. Unhesitatingly, Stewart brought a can of sardines for each of the other men seated around the campfire. This action practically wiped out his stock of the delicacy, but no matter: the Stewart family tradition of hospitality had been maintained. That same day the train arrived at Horse Creek in the valley of the Green. Fitzpatrick was late, July 18. But there was plenty of trade left for him and a brisk demand for the contents of his nineteen carts.

A list of the men at the rendezvous that year sounds like a Who's Who of the Far West. Stewart had met nearly all of them before, some many times. There were Kit Carson, Jim Bridger, Joe Walker, Drips, McLeod, Black Harris, William H. Gray, Lajeunesse, Fontenelle—it is impossible to name them all. There was the usual assortment of Indians—Utes, Bannocks, Flatheads, and Nez Percés.

The Snakes, who usually showed up at the rendezvous in large numbers, had not arrived. There was considerable speculation as to possible reasons for this and Fitzpatrick may well have felt a little uneasy. They were excellent customers for the white man's goods and usually brought many beaver plews for purposes of trade.

Several hours of daylight remaining, Fitzpatrick and the engagés set up trading headquarters. Stewart rode through the miles-long encampment, greeting friends of other years, with either red skins or white. Miller, riding with him, felt profound amazement and equally profound delight in the colorful scenes that met his eyes in the open, grassy meadows that spread on either side of the Green. Captain Stewart noted the presence of a few Chinooks, from the lower Columbia River region, camping with the amiable Nez Percés. Before white men confined them to reservations, Indians—with few exceptions—were a remarkably fluid people, ready at a moment's notice to start off with their whole village for a destination hundreds of miles away.

Before starting on this brief tour of the rendezvous, Stewart had released from discipline all the men of Fitzpatrick's train, except those chosen to help with the trading and a smaller number appointed as night guards. The men thus freed joined wholeheartedly in the saturnalia: gambling, getting drunk on metheglin or raw whisky, fighting, flirting with the Indian girls, playing rough practical jokes on each other.

Finally the sun set behind the great jagged peaks of the Rockies, bare of snow this late in summer. Twilight came; then darkness, softened only by starlight, prevailed in the Valley of the Green. Campfires glowed for miles along the stream. Sounds of talk, laughter, and howls of drunken glee came from the camps of the white men; high-pitched singing and the boom of drums from the Indian villages where warriors danced around scalps stretched on frames at the end of willow wands, counting their coups. After a while silence took over, broken only by the occasional bark of a dog or howl of a distant wolf.

Next morning trading was brisk at Fitzpatrick's establishment. Trappers, fuzzy-minded from their over-indulgence the night before, exchanged beaver, marten, and buffalo robes, for traps, capotes, molds and lead for making bullets, Green River knives and other necessary adjuncts to their hard calling—which none of them would have left for the softest job in the settlements. Others bought foofaraw aimed to please the Indian girls: ribbons, gaudy kerchiefs, a few yards of bright calico, beads, hawk's bells, and that greatest treasure of all, small mirrors.

Indians came for guns made especially for trading to the red men ($9.40 St. Louis, three times that in the mountains), vermilion at $4.00 an ounce, blankets $20.00 each, tobacco $2.00 a pound, alcohol $4.00 a pint and watered at that, common shirts $5.00 apiece. Mountain men and Indians alike were paid $3.50 to $4.00 a pound for beaver.

Shortly before noon a young Snake galloped into camp, to stop before Fitzpatrick's trading tent. Sitting erect on his horse, proud of his ability to speak a little English, he delivered a message from Ma-wo-ma, great chief of the Snakes. A large village of his people, he said, was only a few miles away. Word had come to the chief that Captain Stewart was at the rendezvous. He wished to honor his old friend with a procession he would lead himself, on his way to the Snake camping grounds.

This announcement was received with proper formality and the messenger rewarded with lavish presents. A great stir ensued. The Indians loved spectacles of this kind, but they were not often possible on such a grand scale as this one promised to be. The Snakes were a large tribe and rich by every prairie and mountain standard. Plentifully supplied with horses, they wore handsome garments, beautiful and elaborate jewelry, lived in a district where hunting was excellent, and their lodges were marvels of whitened and painted buffalo hide.

Word of the impending entertainment spread quickly up and down the river. White men gathered from the traders' encampments. Women who could commandeer a horse rode up, wearing their best clothes and astride saddles with two-foot pommels, one front, one back, embroidered with dyed porcupine quills and many-colored beads. Braves appeared, scorning the use of saddles, riding

William Drummond Stewart in dress uniform—portrait found in an
abandoned church in Scotland

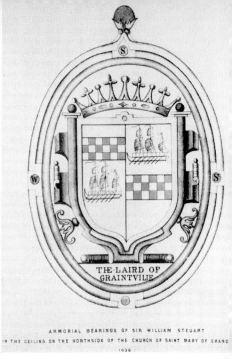

ARMORIAL BEARINGS OF SIR WILLIAM STEUART
IN THE CEILING ON THE NORTHSIDE OF THE CHURCH OF SAINT MARY OF GRAND
1636

THE·LAIRD·OF
GRAINTVILIE

Sir William Drummond Stewart, portrait
painted in 1844 *by Henry Inman*

Stewart armorial bearings

Grandtully Castle

Antoine Clement (Stewart's chief hunter), *by Alfred Jacob Miller*

Lord Stewart, *by Alfred Jacob Miller*

Lady Stewart—the beautiful laundress

Fort Laramie on Sublette Fork—near Nebraska or Platte River,
by Alfred Jacob Miller

The Cavalcade (Sir William mounted on White Horse),
by Alfred Jacob Miller

Lake Scene, Wind River Mountains, *by Alfred Jacob Miller*

Preparing for a Buffalo Hunt—Lord Stewart, Antoine and Auguste,
by Alfred Jacob Miller

Encampment of Indians near the Rocky Mountains,
by Alfred Jacob Miller

Campfire at Night—Trapper Relating an Adventure,
by Alfred Jacob Miller . Sir. Wm. in pale buckskin .

Jim Bridger in a Suit of English Armour, *by Alfred Jacob Miller*

on pieces of buffalo hide folded with the long curly hair outside. The French *voyageurs*, first along the beaver streams, had called this bit of horse gear an *a-pish-a-maux*, a word the American trapper immediately changed to apishamore, which soon came to mean any kind of horse blanket.

Captain Stewart, riding the splendid white horse on which Miller invariably shows him, stationed himself at an advantageous point for observing the wild pageant about to appear. A contingent of mounted white men grouped themselves about him as a sort of combination greeting committee and guard of honor. No doubt Fitzpatrick, himself a good hand with Indians, was one. Probably Fontenelle, Miller, and Bridger were there, too. The vanguard of the procession headed by Chief Ma-wo-ma came in sight. The leader of the Snakes was six feet tall, a man of noble appearance. Miller shows him riding a horse no less white and no less handsome than Captain Stewart's. A war bonnet of eagle feathers adorned his head, and around his neck hung that mark of ultimate valor, a necklace of grizzly-bear claws. Immediately behind the chief rode his son, Si-roc-u-an-tua, only twenty-two years old but already a warrior of high standing, having taken scalps and, like his father, entitled to wear a bear-claw necklace. His square-cut bangs extended almost to his eyebrows, the rest of his hair being drawn back and plaited in a long queue ornamented with large brass rings; had he been on foot, the queue would have extended to his knees.

Following Ma-wo-ma and his son came about 250 warriors, all on fine horses, carrying feather-decked lances eight or ten feet long and painted shields made of bull-buffalo hide. Scorning the use of bridles, as did all Indians, they controlled their spirited mounts by means of small ropes made of plaited buffalo hide looped around the lower jaws of their horses. As the braves passed Captain Stewart and his companions, they held their lances and shields at salute, rode grandly by, flaunting their pride before the assembled company at the same time they honored their friend from the far-off island.

After the warriors came the medicine men, clad in bizarre outfits, shaking rattles, flourishing snakeskins, wolf skulls and similar unpleasant objects, chanting as they advanced. Close on their heels came the rest of the Snake village: horses, women, old men, children, dogs. Dust billowed up from the dragging travois loaded with buffalo skins for the tepees, blankets, spare clothing—all the household and ceremonial gear of two thousand people. Dogs barked, women yelled at each other, at horses, at their children. The procession swept by, to proceed to the Snakes' camping ground. Reaching that large, grassy meadow, the village broke ranks and the women took charge. They erected tepees, watered horses, hung their lords' medicine bags and other insignia of rank and prowess on willow wands outside their lodges, and began to prepare food for the evening meal. During these proceedings the men of the tribe reclined on buffalo robes or strolled about idly, visiting with their equally carefree friends.

At a previous meeting between Chief Ma-wo-ma and Captain Stewart during an earlier rendezvous, the stately old man had helped to recover a number of horses stolen from the Scot by a band of young Snakes who were feeling their oats. Ma-wo-ma returned the horses, at the same time reproving Stewart, saying that if the Scotsman had put himself and his property under Ma-wo-ma's protection, his horses would have been safe.

As soon as the excitement of the Snake procession had died, Stewart had his two servants bring the mysteriously heavy box, transported by wagon all the way from St. Louis, and place it in front of his tent. He then summoned a group of his friends, making sure Jim Bridger was one. A small crowd gathered to see what was afoot. Curious Indians came to watch.

Gravely, Captain Stewart opened the box and lifted out the polished steel cuirass and helmet of the Life Guards, a British *corps d'élite* whose history extends back into the mists of centuries past. A long plume of white horsehair depended from the crest of the helmet. Stewart had not thought it necessary—or had found it impossible—to procure the scarlet tunic, white pantaloons, and black knee-boots worn by the Life Guards when on duty. Perhaps it was just as well. The cuirass and helmet alone were an even stranger sight on the banks of the Green than were buffaloes on the banks of the Tay.

Men, red and white alike, stared in astonishment as Captain Stewart formally presented the armor to Jim Bridger. That seasoned mountain man had signed on with Ashley in the early days of the fur trade and was called Old Gabe, though he was only thirty-four. First, there was wonder, then loud laughter and much knee-slapping when the nature of this gift to Bridger was explained to the white spectators. The Indians remained impassive, putting the whole performance down to the incomprehensibility of white men and their ways.

The presentation of this armor to Bridger must have been the culmination of one of those gigantic spoofs in which mountain men delighted to indulge. What that joke was we do not know, but it must have been one worthy of Paul Bunyan himself to have caused Captain Stewart to send to England for something so alien to Rocky Mountain experience as a Life Guard cuirass and helmet.

Old Gabe, game for anything, buckled on the cuirass over his antelope-skin shirt, settled the helmet on his shaggy, untrimmed hair, and mounted a horse. Miller painted two sketches of Bridger in this outfit. One shows Old Gabe riding into a shallow river, horsehair plume dangling to his shoulders. The other depicts Bridger among a group of mounted Indians in front of their tepees.

This fine steel armor would present considerable resistance to the destructive forces of time. It would not have been easy to carry away and could have had no significance anywhere else. We never hear of it again in mountain literature. If it was left there in the Rocky Mountains, someone may yet stumble on the rust-pocked remains of a Life Guard's proud accouterments in the Green River Valley between New Fork and Horse Creek.

Social life was of considerable importance at this—or any other —rendezvous. There was much visiting back and forth among the camps of the white men. Captain Stewart gave several *al fresco* dinner parties, made notable by the exotic foods that accompanied the ever-present hump ribs and antelope steak, and the fine wines and brandies with which he regaled his guests.

A special effort appears to have been made by the white men to keep Gray's easily ruffled feelings smooth and in good order— though why they troubled themselves it is hard to say; obviously the task was an impossible one. Miller called on him twice, but if he made a portrait of him it does not survive. As usual, Gray saw no good anywhere. Sin was unbearably rampant up and down the Green. He could not endure the proximity of so much evil. Against the advice of everyone, he refused to wait a few weeks for Fitzpatrick's train, gathered together a small party of equally impatient—though not necessarily as pious—souls and headed east toward distant Boston and his Missionary Board. Here he hoped to get financial backing and return, a full-fledged missionary such as Whitman and Spalding, whom he regarded with almost equal parts of envy and hatred.

Arriving at his destination without having lost either his hair or his property—a major miracle which he took to be only his due —he was promised the necessary cash for his projected enterprise. But there was a catch to it. No single man could be appointed to a missionary post among the heathen tribes of the West. Gray tried to dissuade his superiors from this point of view and allow him to proceed without the burden of a female tied to him by the holy bonds of matrimony. He failed in the effort, the Board firmly adhering to its stand—no marriage, no mission.

Whereupon—and this was doubly miraculous—Gray found a woman whom he did not dislike too much to marry and who was willing to take him as her husband. Her name was Mary Augusta Dixon. He met her on February 19 and they were married on February 26. It seems safe to conclude that the union was based on mutual love for the heathen rather than love for each other. *Au revoir* to Gray and his bride; we shall glimpse them again at the rendezvous in 1839.

Chief Ma-wo-ma invited Captain Stewart and Miller to a council of the Snake chiefs called to plan a foray on a Sioux village at some distance from the rendezvous. The Sioux encampment on the Green was, of course, inviolate by the ground rules of the game, but the Snakes felt an irresistible urge to take a few scalps from their immemorial enemies.

The assemblage of Ma-wo-ma's head men was too large to be accommodated in the chief's tepee, so it gathered in front of his elaborately painted lodge. A half-circle of participants squatted around the campfire that lighted the scene with fitful, dancing tongues of flame. Close behind the crouching, dusky forms, others on horseback sat their mounts, almost as immovable as statues.

All wore formal attire, consisting of multi-colored strings of beads, feather hair ornaments, brilliant circles and zigzags of paint, and not much else. There was the inevitable dancing as each warrior in turn counted his coups, accompanied by highly imaginative boasting. Even the great Ma-wo-ma, as a courtesy to Captain Stewart and to Miller, rose and counted a few coups.

Next day Ma-wo-ma came to Miller's tent and asked if he might use a paint brush and paints to show one of his coups. Miller gladly produced the needed articles, and Ma-wo-ma went to work. Never having seen a paint brush before, he used the stick end. Miller said nothing, feeling that it was not in his province to correct a great chief. The result of Ma-wo-ma's efforts was curious. The chief, his feather headdress, and his war horse were shown as more than king-size, his enemies as mere pygmies. Having no idea of perspective, all four legs of his horse were on one side of the animal. Fifteen arrows above the heads of his enemies showed that he had killed that many of them. Nowhere did he indicate that he had any help in the slaughter, or that he sustained any losses. The sketch finished, he graciously presented it to Miller, as a gift from one artist to another. While at the rendezvous, Miller painted excellent portraits of Ma-wo-ma and also of his son, Si-roc-u-an-tua.

One day Captain Stewart sat before his tent, smoking the curious and beautiful pipe that had been designed and made to his specifications in St. Louis. A handsome young Crow approached and stood for a few moments admiring its carved red sandstone bowl, its silver-ornamented stem, and most of all, its sharp steel tomahawk, an ideal instrument for scalping. Finally, he asked Stewart to give him the pipe. Stewart refused this request politely but firmly, saying he wanted it for his own use.

The disappointed Crow advised him to guard the pipe well, as he intended to steal it. Stewart took every precaution against this threat being carried out, but three days later the pipe could not be found. Knowing well the workings of the Indian mind, Stewart made no effort to recover it. The Crow, he said, had acted correctly according to his code—he had given fair warning of what he planned to do. Therefore, the incident was closed.

A few days after Gray's precipitate departure from the rendezvous, fleeing the tents of the wicked, Lucien Fontenelle, heading a trapping brigade of 110 men with a commensurate number of horses, started for the Blackfoot country. Jim Bridger went with him as guide and consultant regarding strategy. On reaching their destination, the party would separate into small bands of four or five and go their different ways. Working in this manner, they would cover a great deal of territory as they hunted beaver along the larger streams as well as creeks so small they had no name.

At this point Miller painted a picture of his commander smoking the pipe of peace and friendship with a half-dozen chiefs preparatory to giving them presents. Wishing to add an impressive note to the occasion, Stewart had spread a large Oriental rug for his guests to sit on and directed his servants to rig a canopy from the overhanging branches of a tree to shade them from the rays of the sun.

The pipe was the usual ornate affair, with a bowl of carved red Catlinite and a long stem decorated with feathers, beads and amulets. The presents were, we may be sure, more than adequate. A distant view of an Indian encampment is shown in the painting, and beyond that, the great peaks of the Rockies thrusting upward to the sky.

Among the sketches Miller made at the rendezvous were two especially notable ones of Joseph Reddeford Walker, thirty-nine years old, straight as an Indian lance and over six feet in height. Brown-haired, blue-eyed, with strong yet regular features, he possessed to an unusual degree the many and varied skills necessary for survival in the hard environment of the Far West. He knew the trails from Independence, on the Missouri, to Monterey, on the Pacific Ocean, better than any other man, his feet having been the first to tread many of them.

Miller painted this famous bourgeois riding in to the rendezvous, followed at a respectful distance by his squaw. The gap between the two was prescribed by mountain etiquette, which neither would have considered breaking. The second and more important sketch Miller made of Walker has not been found. But it certainly existed, for when the artist returned to his studio in New Orleans, he painted an incomparable portrait of Walker in oils measuring about eighteen by twenty-four inches. The colors of this picture are as warm and brilliant today as they were more than a hundred years ago when Miller first brushed them on canvas. The mountain man and the artist, though their backgrounds were a world apart, became friends. Before they separated Walker presented Miller with a dozen pairs of moccasins, fashioned and embroidered with porcupine quills by Walker's squaw.

A few days more and Captain Stewart had exhausted the delights of the encampment on the Green—for a time, at least. He decided to take a brief hunting trip with friends into the Wind River Mountains.

CHAPTER XVIII

Strange Vow on the Big Horn

૪꙳ Miller and Antoine went with Captain Stewart on this trip into the Wind River Mountains, but who his other guests were we do not know. They were probably chosen from the brigade leaders still in camp on the Green. Fontenelle and Bridger had already taken their departure for the Big Horn and Yellowstone, so they can be ruled out. Fitzpatrick is almost certain to have gone along, Drips and Provost also. Including a cook, three engagés to look after the pack horses, and Stewart's two servants, the party probably numbered around twelve.

They set off, the engagés urging along the pack horses laden with potted meats, rare cheeses, preserved fruits, as well as mere comforts such as coffee, sugar, bacon, blankets, tents and the like. Mention is made of ten gallons of brandy, which seems an overly generous amount for a stay of not over ten days, one gallon of port, and about the same allowance of whisky.

It wasn't long until Stewart became aware that a band of fifteen or twenty mounted Indians were skulking along behind them. This boded no good, as the whites were outnumbered, though not seriously so. Stewart was puzzled by the situation, since he was on good terms with the chiefs and sub-chiefs at the rendezvous. Finally, one of the engagés confessed that the Indians were seeking revenge on him; he had incurred the animosity of their leader by some peccadillo, and they would like nothing better than to take his scalp, and his life along with it.

Stewart knew that Indians out for revenge would not be averse to taking other scalps along with that of the engagé, once a fight started. He ordered the cavalcade to close ranks and avoiding narrow canyons and defiles, kept to open parks or on top of ridges. Camping places were carefully chosen and the night horse guard doubled. The Indians continued to stay in the white men's vicinity for several days, but Stewart's vigilance finally discouraged them and they turned back. The members of the small caravan relaxed.

Their journey brought them to an exceptionally beautiful mountain lake about twelve miles long, its northern shores guarded by impressive peaks characteristic of the Wind River Range. Some one in the party named this body of water Stewart Lake in honor of their host, and it was so labeled on early maps.

Several years later, John Charles Frémont came through this same country on one of his "pathfinding" trips, which bore a curious resemblance to guided tours. This time he had Kit Carson with him. Frémont "discovered" this lake and named it for himself. To this day it remains Frémont Lake, but the fact is that the traveling Scotsman and his party were the first white men known to have walked on its shore and given it a name.

They camped there several days, some of the men hunting and fishing, Miller deliriously painting view after view, declaring that each vista was more picturesque than anything the mountains of Switzerland or Italy had to offer. No one had thought to bring fish hooks, but small pieces of bent wire sufficed to catch the "noble" but "unsophisticated" trout.

At night when the men gathered around the campfire, they entertained each other, as was mountain custom, with tales of their adventures. Considering the lives they led, the stories must have rivaled those of Scheherazade. No one wrote them down, a matter for lasting regret. Miller mentions casually that Captain Stewart's contribution to this symposium was accounts of the "antiquities" he had seen and legends connected with them. Imagine if you can, the Parthenon sharing honors with an account of a Crow scalping party, the story of the Sphinx following a tale concerning a hand-to-hand encounter with a grizzly b'ar. No one present could have been more aware of the contrasting elements of these fireside chats than Stewart himself, a man at home in both worlds.

After a few days spent in this idyllic spot, the party moved on, still deeper into the Wind River Range. There they came upon a small, quiet stream, icy cold, with mint growing luxuriantly in its shallows. They stopped there for mint juleps, a drink Stewart had learned to concoct in accordance with the most critical Southern taste. Who can doubt that exactly the correct amounts of bourbon and water went into this beverage, or that it tasted no less delectable because of being quaffed from battered tin cups instead of crystal goblets?

One day Miller was riding with Stewart somewhat in advance of the others. They came to a wide, turbulent stream flowing at a slight angle to the course they were following. Miller, somewhat fearfully, asked the captain if he intended to cross the torrent. Though there was no necessity for him to do so, his firm reply was "Yes." He turned his horse and plunged into the racing water, calling to Miller to follow him. Miller, though frightened out of his wits, obeyed. An almost perpendicular bank on the opposite side offered no foothold for the horses. Fortunately, the racing current carried them downstream to where gently sloping banks provided a landing place.

Water streaming from his clothes, Captain Stewart turned imperturbably to his shivering companion. "You swim, don't you?" he asked. "No!" Miller declared, his teeth chattering. "Well," Captain Stewart replied, "neither do I. Experiences like that will teach you self-reliance. You know not what you can do until you've tried."

Impulsive and impetuous, the stream had offered him challenge and opposition. As was his nature, he had accepted the first, conquered the second. Why he felt it necessary that Miller embark on the same rash course is one of the enigmas of the Stewart character.

Antoine shared this trait of his employer's, and the fact may, to some degree at least, explain the feeling of equality that existed between them. Antoine appeared to love danger for its own sake and was always ready to engage in a daring exploit, whether the situation called for it or not.

One day when Antoine and Miller went away from the camp together, the half-breed to hunt, the artist to sketch, Antoine wounded a large bull buffalo, though apparently not seriously. Antoine leaped from his horse, raced to where the buffalo stood, wrapped the huge brute's tail around his hands and gave it a powerful jerk. The buffalo, roused to fury, twisted and turned, trying to gore his tormentor, sometimes swinging Antoine off his feet. The half-breed hung on until the enormous beast fell dead, as much from exhaustion as from the wound that had been inflicted on him. Antoine came back to the horrified artist laughing heartily, having thoroughly enjoyed his exploit.

At some time during this trip Miller, much to his astonishment and even uneasiness, was the unhappy witness to a violent quarrel between Stewart and Antoine. The three men were in an open valley of considerable extent, Miller sketching the distant peaks, while his commander and Antoine sat their horses near by. Stewart took the half-breed to task for failing to attend to some duty that had been assigned to him. Antoine hotly defended himself. Tempers flared higher and higher with each breath. Soon both men were shouting at each other as if they were equals, instead of one being the untutored offspring of a Canadian trapper and an Indian squaw, the other of noble blood and ancient lineage.

Miller became deeply concerned, fearing they would shoot each other. Part of his alarm was due to the fact that they were at least twelve miles from camp and Miller, who wisely made no attempt to learn mountain skills, had no idea how to get back there. Just when the whole situation seemed hopeless, the contenders, apparently at the same moment, glimpsed a small herd of buffalo some distance across the valley. The altercation broke off in midsentence. Away the two men went, all their thoughts on securing roast buffalo for supper. In a short time they returned to Miller with their booty, laughing and talking, their quarrel forgotten.

Mid-August brought chill nights. In the hours just before dawn spears of ice formed along the banks of small streams. Captain Stewart knew it was time to break camp and turn their faces toward the Green. Arriving at the site of the rendezvous, they

found only ragged remnants of the great encampment remaining.
Indian villages were moving out, accompanied by the usual confusion, noise and dust. The camps of the white men were breaking
up. Word had gone out, even before Fontenelle and Bridger left,
that next year's rendezvous would be held here on the Green, between Horse Creek and New Fork. True, there hadn't been as
many pelts brought in this year as last and the price of beaver
was down, but with the optimism of their breed, everyone felt confident that, come next year, all would be as usual.

Fitzpatrick started for Fort Laramie, taking the wagons with
him. Captain Stewart's engagés and servants packed on the backs
of horses what was left of his exotic foods—which couldn't have
been much by this time, considering his lavish generosity with
them—also the usual necessities of travel in this wild country. He
evidently made up his mind to have one more adventure before
returning to St. Louis and New Orleans. He and his party set off
in a generally northeasterly direction.

Details of this trip are scarce and we are not sure, except for
Miller and Antoine, who went with him. Of course there were
his engagés and servants, but he could hardly have gone into the
regions he did without a larger number of guns than we can
count. First, traveling fast, they went to the Big Horn, and from
there to the Yellowstone, turning west to the Rosebud and beyond
that to Cross Creek.

Somewhere on the way he met Fontenelle and Bridger and,
it is said, lost some of his horses to the Crows but recovered them.
At Cross Creek he caught up with the irrepressible Joe Meek and
also Markhead. Both of these boys were continually turning up in
the most unexpected places. It is here that Joe had his famous
fight with a bear. No story of the year 1837 in the Far West is
complete without it.

Joe was out hunting with two companions. They sighted a female grizzly. Always seeking trouble, Meek left his horse, stalked
the unsuspecting bear until he was within gunshot of her, cocked
his rifle and pulled the trigger. The cap popped—and that was all.
The bear, hearing the sound, whirled to face Joe. Snarling as only
a grizzly can, she charged. Meek ran at full speed back toward his
horse, yelling frenzied appeals to his friends that they cover his

retreat. The rapid approach of the grizzly was too much for the horses. They took off, two of them carrying Joe's companions with them. This left Joe alone with the bear, who had all but caught up with him by this time. He turned and faced her, rammed the muzzle of his gun into her gaping red mouth with its fine assortment of sharp, white teeth all ready to go to work on him.

In spite of the stress of the moment, Joe managed to set the double triggers of his gun, but just as he fired, she swung about, knocking the gun to one side. The bullet inflicted a painful flesh wound, but one that didn't even slow her down. In fact, it increased her rage. At that moment the bear's two cubs appeared, which did nothing to calm her furious determination to annihilate Joe at once. She closed in, arms extended to grasp him. Meek snatched a knife from his belt and tried to stab the bear behind her ear, but she struck the weapon from his hand with one hairy paw. The cubs started squawling. This distracted her attention, giving Meek a few seconds to jerk a hatchet from his belt. Joe struck one desperate blow, felt the steel blade crunch through her skull. She fell dead, splattering him with blood.

This episode established three things for all time: Joe's astounding foolhardiness . . . Joe's indomitable courage . . . Joe's built-in good luck.

Whether or not Stewart came up in time to witness this wild battle is not known. But the record has it that Joe gave the captain the bear's hide, which was afterward mounted and shown at a St. Louis museum.

From Cross Creek Captain Stewart went into the Tetons, those incomparable mountains in northwest Wyoming. That he did so is attested to by several of Miller's sketches which could have been made nowhere else.

At some time during this trip in the fall of 1837, Captain Stewart had a strange and brief experience that resulted in his following a course of action not easily reconciled with the man as he showed himself to the world. Considered evaluation of his complex character, motivations, and lines of heredity far back into the past would be necessary before a valid explanation could be arrived at.

The known facts of what happened at this time are few. He

was suddenly stricken with a very nearly fatal illness, the nature of which remains obscure. An itinerant Jesuit friar, probably a medical missionary, sojourning in a neighboring Indian encampment, heard of his plight and came to offer his services. Captain Stewart made a vow to this priest that if he recovered, he would return to the church of his fathers, restore the chapels at Murthly and Grandtully castles to their former glory, put resident priests in charge of them, and employ Catholics on his estate wherever possible. The vow was entirely characteristic of him: it went the whole way, held nothing back.

Those who find it possible to conclude that Stewart made these far-reaching commitments at the solicitation of the Jesuit friar are free to do so. But at no other time of his life did he embark on a course of action that he himself did not initiate. It does not seem likely that he acted otherwise in this instance.

Whether due to the friar's prayers or his medical ministrations, or to the course of nature, the captain recovered his usual good health quickly and completely. It seems likely that he swore Miller to secrecy, for nowhere in the artist's notes does he reveal that his commander suffered from any indisposition whatever. That we know anything about this incident is due to a recent revelation made by a member of the Stewart family. The story came to her by word of mouth from her grandfather, who had it directly from Captain Stewart himself.

Leaving the Tetons, the party turned eastward to Fort Laramie. From there the Scotsman, Miller and Antoine returned to the States with the company caravan led by Andrew Drips. Before the middle of October they arrived at St. Louis. Miller went on to New Orleans, taking his sketches with him, under instructions from his commander to begin making oil paintings from the water colors, for the walls of Murthly. Stewart established Antoine in lodgings and again occupied rooms in the Mansion House.

Several interesting letters awaited Stewart here in St. Louis, where he maintained a permanent address throughout his years in America. One of these letters, possibly from mild, artless brother George, brought tidings of the demise of Lady Harriet Drummond, one of the spinster sisters of their mother. Furthermore, Lady Harriet had left to Captain Stewart the very comfortable sum of £10,000. But, George went on to state, their estimable but cautious aunt had placed the money in the hands of brother John for transmission to William, since at the time of her death Captain Stewart's exact whereabouts was not known. It would seem that the captain was entitled to one of his better rages at this disclosure. For John had not communicated with him in any way, not even to the extent of sending two overdue payments on William's annuity from his father.

Though he most certainly knew that the present Lord of Murthly and Grandtully Castles was not long for this world, Stewart was too fundamentally honest to entertain, or even pretend to, the slightest false sentimentality on that account. He immediately dispatched the following legal notice to his attorney in Perth:

> Know all men by these presents that I, William Stewart, late of Grandtully in Scotland, now at St. Louis, Missouri, have appointed John Stewart, of Marshall Place, Perth, Scotland, my lawful attorney, to ask and demand, sue and receive, all such sums of money, debts and demands which shall be due, owing, and payable to me, especially all rights from the estate of the late Lady Harriet Drummond, deceased, of Logiealmond, and also, for me, to demand annuities coming from Sir John Drummond Stewart, Baronet of Grandtully, of Scotland.

At least one letter from faithful Christina would have told him details of their son's growth, health, and progress in school. That he wrote to her now and then can be taken for granted, though none of these communications survive. If she kept them, they would have been in her possession when she died and would not have passed into the hands of the Stewart family.

A week or so after the Scotsman arrived in St. Louis, he received a letter from his friend and business associate, John Crawford, the British Consul in New Orleans. In this communication, dated October 18, obviously a reply to a recent letter Stewart had written to him, Crawford says he has seen Miller, who is looking well. The consul is uneasy that Stewart may be short of funds, and if so, to draw on him. He has heard from Vernunfft, their mysterious partner, who is very comfortably lodged in (of all places) Windsor Castle (selling American railroad stocks to Prince Albert? It seems unlikely, but so does everything else that a man named Vernunfft might be doing while "comfortably lodged" in the same palace with royalty). Crawford goes on to say that there is a little yellow fever in New Orleans, but they have had a frost, so no danger from that quarter is expected. If Captain Stewart decides to come, his old quarters are at his service. It ends, "Believe me, my dear sir, Yours sincerely, John Crawford."

Stewart was in no hurry to leave St. Louis. He spent a few weeks seeing his many friends in the city, among them William Sublette and Robert Campbell. He called several times on General Clark at his office and museum, attended the usual round of social affairs, and took the preliminary steps toward fulfilling his vow, given months before to the Jesuit friar.

The St. Louis Cathedral, where two bishops conducted the simple but impressive ceremony that marked his return to the church, was a handsome stone building of which the city was justly proud. It stood on a tree-lined street not far from the river. Four Doric columns supported the entablature of an imposing Greek portico. In its tall steeple, surmounted by a shining gold cross, hung fine, mellow-toned bells that rang at sunrise, noon, and sunset. A young French artist of some renown had been brought from France to paint the glowing frescoes depicting scenes from the life of Christ.

In the archives of this cathedral there may still be seen the following notice, written in the frail, elaborate script of the time:

> On the 25th of November, 1837, we the undersigned Bishops of St. Louis, have baptized William Stewart, of Grandtully in Scotland, second son of Sir George and Lady Catherine Drummond Stewart, forty-two years old, who has returned to the faith of his illustrious ancestors. The Godfather has been the right Reverend Dr. Simon Bruté, Bishop of Vincennes.
>
> JOSEPH ANTHONY LUTZ, Bishop of St. Louis
> SIMON G. BRUTÉ, Bishop
> J. N. NICALLET
> Jos. H. LUTZ, Priest Sec.

When news of this event reached Scotland, everything Captain Stewart had previously done to make clear his independence and defiance of his family's domination over him must have seemed small and comparatively unimportant. But William was an ocean and half a continent away and there was nothing they could do about it, any more than they had been able to do anything about his marriage to Christina seven years before. Furious letters must have been dispatched, demanding to know why? why? why?—as if any explanation would decrease their sense of outrage, even though he replied to these diatribes.

Archibald, judging by his actions at a much later date, was most deeply and lastingly infuriated by William's return to the church. His venom increased rather than lessened as the years passed. With the exception of the always benevolent George, the Stewart men of that generation appear to have had an unusual capacity for hate, and in this field Archibald undoubtedly excelled both John and William. What is more, if he possessed any likable qualities, man or boy, they were never mentioned by his family, nor in the legends still told of him by the villagers of Dunkeld. A remarkable man was this Archibald, in his own consistently offensive way.

After a while Stewart took his departure for New Orleans, leaving Antoine in St. Louis, with only Campbell near at hand to keep the exuberant half-breed out of trouble where gin, gambling and women were all readily available to this fair-skinned, handsome man of the wilderness. Comfortably, even luxuriously ensconced in the St. Charles Hotel, the captain called on Mr. Nichols to see how the cotton-buying business prospered; more particularly, how much money was immediately available to him from that source. There apparently was none, seemingly because accrued profits were in transit from England, since the business connection continued between the two men along with a steadfast friendship.

Captain Stewart remained in New Orleans during the winter of 1837–38. He was kept occupied attending to his business concerns involved with Crawford and Vernunfft and buying cotton through E. B. Nichols for the insatiable looms of England. In March he boarded a steamer for St. Louis, joined Antoine there, and prepared to return once more to his beloved mountains.

CHAPTER XIX

Momentous News

꿈 Pratte, Chouteau, and Company faced the hard fact that the fur trade was dwindling. Casting about for ways to economize, they decided not to send the yearly caravan to the Green River. Instead, they would hold the rendezvous where the Popo Agie and the Wind River joined their waters to become the Big Horn. This plan would save them more than a hundred miles of travel, much of it in the mountains.

Because the trappers and Indians expected to meet them on the Green, they would send a messenger ahead to post a notice of the change at the old familiar grounds between Horse Creek and New Fork. The shift in location would cost their customers some inconvenience, but they would come on to the new site anyway.

Andrew Drips headed the American Fur Company's caravan that year; Fitzpatrick, usually chosen for the task after Sublette became a city man, was off somewhere on business of his own. In late March of 1838 Drips went to Lexington, there readied his train, buying supplies at Aull's store, horses and mules from Jem Hicklin, as was customary. Captain Stewart and Antoine were there helping him. So was Black Harris, a man with little education but great wisdom and five highly trained senses. He as willingly, and apparently as safely, traveled alone as with a party. He entertained the profound conviction that the Indian didn't live who was smart enough to "lift his ha'r."

Stewart took only one wagon, with four mules to pull it. Perhaps the fact that he had received none of the money due him from John restrained him to some extent. Or perhaps Drips suggested that one wagon was enough for carrying what was, strictly speaking, unnecessary baggage. Drips loaded twenty carts, known as charettes, each carrying from eight to nine hundred pounds of merchandise and supplies, and drawn by two horses, hitched in tandem fashion for easier traveling on the way. Thirty or forty extra horses with as many men completed the train.

To the consternation of the old hands, a group of oddly assorted missionaries presented themselves, asking to go with the caravan as far as the rendezvous, their ultimate destination being somewhere on the Columbia River. It was the policy of the fur companies to take on the responsibility for missionary parties traveling to the Indian country as a kind of public service, without regard to their religious affiliations.

Drips eyed the party dubiously. For reasons already made clear, it was difficult for caravan leaders and missionaries to achieve a meeting of the minds, and this outfit appeared to be especially unpromising. However, he could hardly refuse their request.

There was W. H. Gray, with whom no one could agree for long, and his dedicated bride, Mary Augusta. While in the East on this trip, Gray had attended a three-months medical lecture course and now called himself Dr. Gray, but as soon as he reached the Columbia, Dr. Whitman forbade him to use the spurious title. Captain Stewart had seen a good deal of Gray both on the trail and at the rendezvous of '36 and '37, and had at that time taken the measure of his shriveled, acrimonious soul.

Then, in order of authority, came Elkanah Walker and his helpmeet, also named Mary, as was Gray's wife. At first these two appeared to have more common sense, along with the milk of human kindness, than the others, but this proved to be a mistake. Cushing Eells and his wife Myra consistently found fault with all other members of their group, thus easily achieving a feeling of superiority. Asa and Sarah Smith monotonously followed the common pattern of mutual dislike and recrimination. Last, like a very

short tail to a very large kite, was twenty-two-year-old Cornelius
Rogers, a volunteer with the humble status of helper, who at least
kept quiet.

Another and quite different addition to the party presented
himself a few days before the departure from Lexington. This was a
personable man of thirty-six, practically broke, but with charming
Continental manners, an attractive foreign accent, and unlimited
imagination regarding his family antecedents and past achievements. For one thing, he declared he had been a captain in the
Swiss Guards.

In fact, he had left the shores of Europe surreptitiously to
avoid being jailed for debt, the small draper's shop he owned
having gone bankrupt. After confused wanderings he had taken up
his residence with the kindly but impoverished Delaware Indians
along the west side of the Missouri. He soon realized there was no
future in that and decided to go west—all the way to California.
His name was Johann Augustus Sutter.

This heterogeneous company left Westport some time during the first week in April and struck out into the greening prairie.
After a few days the missionaries became so vocal in their quarrels,
brought so many complaints to Drips that he asked them to
travel by themselves. It would have been impossible. Greenhorns
that they were, and foolish besides, they would have lost their
property, scalps, and even lives before reaching Fort Laramie.
Drips, a sensible man, relented, but the episode did nothing to
improve relations between the two groups. To Drips's credit, his
behavior toward the missionaries from that time on was punc-
tiliously correct.

A few days farther along the trail, the caravan leader, accompanied by Stewart, the urbane "Captain" Sutter and Black Harris,
made a formal call on the missionaries, taking them a gift of pork.
Mary Walker, wife of Elkanah, took the trouble to write in her
journal before she went to bed that these gentlemen were very
courteous, but Mr. Asa Smith acted "rather hoggish," a mild
epithet for her and one not intended humorously, even though it
did concern division of the pork.

Captain Stewart and "Captain" Sutter called on the missionaries several times while en route to the rendezvous, present-

ing the ladies with small luxuries from the Scotsman's wagon. On one of these occasions Mary Walker served biscuits and cheese to her guests. So were social amenities observed on the prairie.

Three weeks out from Westport Stewart's wagon tipped over as it was being driven down a steep bank. Much was spilled, a few jars of sweetmeats broken. Finally all was made right again, and no serious damage done—except perhaps to Captain Stewart's equanimity. Such mishaps were, in his book, certain indications of carelessness or poor judgment, either his or that of someone else. In either case, he put the blame squarely where it belonged.

They reached the haven of Fort Laramie about May 25, having been thirty-eight days on the road, slightly longer than the journey usually required. Fontenelle, in charge that year, welcomed them heartily. Drips decided to remain there for several days to rest the horses. The four missionary women rushed about, relieving their long pent-up desire to wash, bake bread, air clothes. They also visited with the Indian wives of the fort's head men. Even Gray had the good sense not to tell them that the marriages were entirely without benefit of clergy. No use spoiling their pleasure. They would have little enough feminine companionship, white or red, from now on.

Gray, remembering the almost super-human effort Dr. Whitman had expended struggling with the Dearborn beyond Fort Laramie two years before, packed the contents of the missionary wagon on mules and left the cumbersome vehicle behind. Stewart, knowing the trail would be less difficult than in '36, because more pack trains and more wheels had passed over it, took his own wagon on. Anyway, he was only going as far as the Popo Agie, which was east of the Rockies, while Gray was going on to the Columbia.

While they were still at Fort Laramie, Black Harris set out on his lonely journey to last year's place of rendezvous on the Green. When he reached the spot he posted a sign on the door of a tumble-down log shelter built there several years ago. The message, which he had composed himself and laboriously printed on a scrap of paper, read: *Come on to the Popoasie. Plenty of whiskey and white women.*

Maybe he lacked formal education but he knew the basic

principles of selling as well as any advertiser of today. Every trapper or partisan who read that sign would hurry post haste toward the delights that awaited them on the Popo Agie. If they hoped that there might be another Narcissa among the "plenty of white women," however, disappointment awaited them.

Three days after Black Harris left the fort, the caravan again set out. Up the Platte and to the Sweetwater, the way now as familiar to Captain Stewart as was the road from Murthly to Grandtully, but fascinating at every turn because of its wildness, its almost continuous challenge to his ingenuity and courage and endurance. Nor did the always-varying beauty of prairie, mountain, stream and crag ever lose its compelling charm for him.

The train camped at Independence Rock, but it is doubtful if the endlessly bickering missionaries gave it more than a fleeting glance. It is certain that neither Stewart nor the amiable "Captain" Sutter carved the names of the missionary ladies on its side, as the Scotsman and Major Joshua Pilcher had done for Narcissa Whitman—and Eliza Spalding, too, of course.

Leaving the Sweetwater, the train headed toward the Popo Agie. Arriving there about the first of July, they encamped in an extensive, tree-bordered meadow that formed a triangle between the two streams where they came together. Black Harris, along with a company of trappers, awaited their coming. Indian villages and partisans with their men began to arrive, bringing clouds of dust, much noise, and loud hilarity with them. While the numbers were smaller than in former years, it was still a wild, uproarious gathering, full of fun and frolic as well as hard-headed business.

A few days went by and Francis Ermatinger, trusted employee of the Hudson's Bay Company, appeared with a small party that included Jason Lee of the Willamette Valley. Successful as a colonizer, Jason was on his way east to recite his truly impressive achievements to the missionary board, ask for more money, more missionaries, more settlers. Being a firm believer in adages such as "Nothing succeeds like success," and "Them that has, gits," he confidently expected to receive everything he planned to ask for— and did. Also in Ermatinger's party were the two young half-breed sons of John McLeod, whom their father was sending east to school.

Ermatinger observed the half-hearted efforts of Drips to sign up trappers for next year's hunt, cocked his ears to the rumors that the American Fur Company would send no more caravans west. Then he went ahead, openly contracting trappers to work for the Hudson's Bay Company, which ethically he was not supposed to do. However, ethics at no time cramped the style of any fur company, so no great blame attaches to Ermatinger for his actions. He only did what Drips would have done had their positions been reversed. The fur trade of the Rocky Mountains was shot, and everybody knew it. Beaver had been slaughtered until there weren't enough of them left to make trapping worth while. After the Americans were out of the way—as they soon were—the English company instituted a conservation program under which the number of beavers taken in any given territory in one year was strictly limited. In this way they kept their own fur trade going for a long time.

At this rendezvous—the last Captain Stewart was ever to attend, though it was not his last trip west—he saw many old friends of other years: Jim Bridger, that grand mountain man, of course; and Joe Meek, roistering, boasting, full of amazing lies that were really fantasies and never meant to be believed. Then there was Joe Walker with his Indian wife. The missionary women especially approved of her because, as Elkanah Walker's wife, Mary, wrote, she acted with such modesty and propriety. Joe must have appreciated her, for she, as well as her horse, was decked out in all the foofaraw of bells, ribbons, beads, rings, and gay calico that even she could desire. Report has it that her features were "more comely than was usual among squaws"—count on Joe to pick one of the best.

That year Joe Walker was not at the rendezvous with furs, but was just passing through the country driving a hundred or so California horses to the States where he could sell them at a good profit. Some said he had stolen them, but that seems hardly likely, since those two wealthy and honorable men of Los Angeles, Don Juan Bandini and Don Abel Sterns, were his agents.

July saw the last of the Indian villages streaming away and the departure of the white men. Ermatinger took the missionaries with him to the Columbia. John McLeod's boys went eastward with the fur caravan, headed by whom we do not know, because Drips went somewhere else—probably on a hunting trip with Captain Stewart and Antoine. They may have gone to the Crow country, or with Bridger to the haunts of the Blackfeet, or even to the territory of the Snakes. Most likely of all, the three men with a few engagés to look after their pack horses, went a few hours' journey northwestward into the Wind River Mountains and there sojourned a while at Stewart's Lake.

Wherever they went, by early August they had left the Rockies and were making their way down past the familiar sights along the Sweetwater and the Platte. The journey was fairly pleasant, since it was too early for the rigorous storms of wind, rain and sleet that beset this country in the fall.

Somewhere on the journey down the Missouri with Antoine, Stewart received via the river grapevine, or maybe a note from Sublette, the momentous news of his brother John's death on May 20, in Paris. That was the day, Captain Stewart remembered, when he had crossed the South Platte on his outward journey almost three months before.

With sudden and somewhat uncharacteristic caution, he did not take for granted that he was now undeniably Sir William Stewart, Nineteenth Lord of Grandtully and Seventh Baronet of the line. Instead, he sent a letter off to Scotland post haste, addressed to James Gillespie Graham, an architect and a close friend, who appears to have had charge of his family affairs. In this letter he asked an important question, to which he could not possibly get an answer in less than two months.

He and Antoine arrived in St. Louis to find interesting letters awaiting Captain Stewart. One was from John Crawford, the British Consul at New Orleans, dated May 25. It contained the news that the money Captain Stewart had ordered had arrived. This money was the small annuity he had demanded of John months before. The £10,000 from Aunt Harriet's legacy was not available until much later, when John's personal affairs were settled.

There was also a letter from Lord Breadalbane, dated May 25, addressed to Sublette and Campbell, saying that he would be greatly obliged to them if they would apprise Captain Stewart of the death of his brother John in Paris, on May 20. Brother George wrote that he had attended to the sealing of the papers and rooms on the death of John, and was living with their sisters, Frances Marie and Elizabeth, at Logiealmond. Keys to Murthly Castle had been turned over to him. He expected and hoped that William would return by the next packet. (No chance.)

On a lighter note, Lord MacKenzie of Scone Palace invited Captain Stewart for the shooting and curling, and remarked that it had been a long time since their last meeting. It was some seven years, in fact. He, like brother George, expected the captain to rush home, eager to embrace the life of a Scottish nobleman, but the traveler from those shores had other plans. Competent overseers were in charge of the estates. All that could wait.

It was, of course, a matter for profound regret to Captain Stewart that he arrived in St. Louis too late to greet his friend, General William Clark. That venerable and highly respected gentleman had died on September 2, at the age of sixty-eight. He was accorded a full military funeral. Six black-plumed white horses, each animal led by a Negro wearing black livery, drew the hearse through streets lined with people gathered to do him honor. The obsequies were held at the home of his son, Lewis Clark. Everyone deeply mourned the passing of this great and good man who had done so much for his country. Shortly after his demise, Major Joshua Pilcher was appointed to the office of Superintendent of Indian Affairs for the West, which General Clark had held with distinction for sixteen years.

About mid-October a letter came from John Crawford, acknowledging the receipt of one from Captain Stewart. He was pleased that his friend had returned safe from the mountains, as there must be some danger among the Indians. He forwarded letters from various people announcing John's death, which he knew Captain Stewart already had heard about. He would have forwarded them sooner to Sublette and Campbell, but did not expect Captain Stewart to return so early in the year. He gave a somber report on "poor Vernunfft," who did little good by his trip to Europe and hoped Vernunfft had learned by experience. He would explain everything when they saw each other, Crawford said.

So the tantalizing mystery of Vernunfft and his doings re-

mains in the realm of the unknown. Crawford's letter went on
to say that "we" were now waiting for some fortunate event to en-
able "us" to commence again. Whether he meant to refer here
to himself and Captain Stewart alone or to include "poor Vernunfft," one cannot be sure. Crawford had seen Miller, who with
his pictures, was in his old quarters on Chartres Street. He did
not know what progress Miller had made, but feared not much;
the man seemed lazy.

Apparently Miller could never paint fast enough to satisfy
anyone, though nobody seems to have found fault with the quality
of his work.

After a week or two, Stewart went to New Orleans and established his residence at 46 Bourbon Street. Here he picked up the
threads of his business—and friendship as well—with E. B.
Nichols. He received a formal invitation from one Samuel Wright
for dinner at his home at 13 Bourbon Street, no doubt one of many
such invitations.

The crowded social and business life in New Orleans may
have helped to distract his mind from the fact that he as yet had
received no reply to the question he had asked of James Gillespie
Graham. But in early December the anxiously awaited letter arrived. In it Graham assured Captain Stewart that Lady Jane,
John's widow, "*is not with child.*"

At this point the recipient of the letter must have paused for
a moment, even drawn a long breath of relief. He had not been
certain until now that he really had become Sir William Drummond Stewart, owner of the estates of Murthly, Grandtully,
Logiealmond, and several other odd bits of real estate with a combined value of well over two million pounds. From now on we
shall accord him the title that had in fact become his some six
months before.

Graham had more news. Lord Breadalbane was making splendid improvements at Taymouth Castle; he had recently greatly
enlarged the library. George had "kicked out" his late brother's
trustees and formed a new Trust. (What? *George?*) After John's
funeral it was intimated by Lady Jane's agent that shortly before
his death John had executed a will in Paris, leaving her everything
heritable and movable belonging to him. But George had said that

the Parisian deed would not be allowed. The one made the year
before was the true one. In consequence, Lady Jane had gone to
reside in London on an annuity of £2000.

All this sounds suspiciously as if Graham had put George
up to all this high-handed business. George was certainly incapable
of carrying it through by himself, or even thinking of being so
forceful and belligerent.

Though Sir William now felt sure of his position, he still did
not return to Scotland at once. He did begin to make plans to do
so, as a letter to Sublette, dated September 17, clearly indicates:

> Dear Sublette: I suppose Campbell has already started
> for the East. I do not therefore write him on the subject of
> Crawford and Vernunfft. . . . I remain here longer in hopes
> those canny Scots [his relatives in Perthshire?] may favor me
> with some communication which I hope you will forward in
> case it should arrive before the month of February is past. I
> wish you'd be good enough to send for Antoine and tell him
> I wish him to get some gourds of the best form for dippers,
> also some red birds and keep them in cages as I wish to take
> them to England. I expect him to be ready by March. I trust
> you can procure me some tame deer. I may have to draw
> on you for seven hundred [dollars?] before long, which I shall
> advise you of. I am sorry for it, as I would rather have left it
> in your hands, but I think that will do me. . . . Remember
> me to your sister.
>
> WILLIAM D. STEWART

In early January another letter from John Gillespie Graham
brought further news. He had evidently been busy carrying out
instructions sent him by Sir William. He, Graham, had brought
Christina and George (Sir William's son), now eight years old, to
Edinburgh, and placed the boy in a school in the Royal Circus
where gentlemen sent boys of his age until they were ready for
High School. The boy was stout and healthy and applied himself
well. He (Graham) had procured a nice and cheap flat near Inver-
leith, which was in both town and country; it had a small parlor,
bedroom, and a bed-closet in which the boy slept. There were an excellent kitchen and water closet and it was comfortably furnished,

chiefly with furniture Christina had brought from Perth. She was conducting herself with the greatest propriety and was contented. She had no complaints or needs beyond her allowance.

Judging from these modest arrangements made for Christina, it might appear that Sir William was being more than a bit tight with his wife, now Lady Stewart. It should be kept in mind, however, that the choice was almost certainly Christina's. At no time desirous of being a great lady, Christina had a level head on her beautiful shoulders and never tried to be anything but what came naturally: a loyal wife, helpful to the limits of her capacity, and a good mother to her son. As for young George, he was sent to a school suitable to his high station. A more fitting or sensible arrangement hardly could have been worked out.

Sir William's bankers in Perth appear to have taken over the estate's business management. They informed him that they had rented out the shooting privileges of Grandtully for £100 to Lord Mesborough. Game was plentiful, especially wild geese, and they were sure he would be more than satisfied.

Sometime in April Sir William took leave of his friends in New Orleans, and of Miller in Chartres Street, painting oils for Murthly. Joining Antoine in St. Louis, he appeared to have gathered together whatever he could of the Far West to take with him back to Scotland. Antoine helped him in this undertaking. There were the red birds, of course, and the gourds that he had instructed Antoine to secure. Crawford was called in to help, also. Two buffaloes from somewhere on the Platte arrived in New Orleans aboard the steamship *Vandalia*, along with a grizzly bear. Crawford had the job of getting them aboard the British ship *Actress*, whose commander, Captain Toole, would superintend their transportation to Liverpool. Crawford reported that the male buffalo, though young, showed evidence that when grown he would have a good-sized hump. The female was thin, probably because traveling worried her. The bear was "a most noble fellow," not full grown but possessing a well-developed head and claws. He still retained a "plentiful supply of the savage."

The expenses for getting these animals to Liverpool were itemized for Sir William as follows: Passage to Liverpool from New Orleans, $100.00. Building a shelter on shipboard, $25.00.

Hay, $7.50. Cost of freight from St. Louis to New Orleans, $20.00. Expense before shipping, $14.00. Cost of three dozen bottles of port, $36.00.

The last item makes the account a swindle sheet, style of 1839. It seems fairly certain that neither the two buffaloes nor the grizzly bear ever saw the port.

Miller had at no time been enamored of the hardships or even the discomforts that were an inescapable part of his excursion into the West. Now, in retrospect, he was becoming sentimental about them, and so expressed himself in a letter to Sir William as follows:

> I find recollections of our wanderings growing dear, and in addition to being restored to health, I am the envy of everyone who speaks to me.

Miller was premature when he said that he was "restored to health." Harsh weather and exposure in the mountains had resulted in an attack of rheumatism. He occasionally suffered from this disability for the rest of his life.

While Sir William was in St. Louis busily collecting animals, plants, seeds, and so on for transportation to Murthly, Miller received an invitation from the Apollo Gallery in New York to exhibit a group of his oil paintings of scenes in the Far West. The showing would continue for two weeks: from June 9 to June 22.

Miller felt deeply gratified, as a request such as this from the famous gallery was a very great honor indeed, and especially so for an artist as young as Miller, who was only twenty-nine. While Sir William was absent the previous year, Miller had informally exhibited a few Western pictures in Baltimore, where they won the highest acclaim from critics as well as the public. It was this success in Baltimore that had led to the present invitation.

Miller wrote to Sir William for permission to accept the invitation, and this was immediately forthcoming. He then packed eighteen of his oil paintings and shipped them to New York by the packet *Vicksburg*. Arrangements were made that Miller and Sir William should meet in New York prior to the opening of the exhibit.

Sir William left St. Louis by boat during the second week

in April for the first part of his journey home. When taking leave
of Sublette, Campbell and his many other friends in the city,
there was no finality in their parting, and therefore no sadness.
He had informed them of his plan to return in '40. Then he would
undertake a journey into the Rockies that would—in some respects—do justice to the imagination of a modern Kubla Khan.
As it turned out, he didn't get back to America until three years
had passed, but except for the delay, his expectations and dreams
remained unchanged.

Antoine went with Sir William to New York, as did two Indians, who couldn't be shipped to Liverpool as the buffaloes, the
bear and all the rest of the Western flora and fauna had been.
The difficulties and problems of getting these untutored savages
of mountains and prairie from the Far West to Murthly Castle
must have been considerable. Of course, Antoine was a help. Presumably he could talk to them and so calm their fears, curb their
exuberances, and repress their unpredictable emotions.

Arriving in New York, the party went at once to the home of
Sir William's good friend, J. Watson Webb, himself an experienced Western traveler. The Indians could be quartered in the
upper story of the carriage house, where their uncouth ways would
trouble no one. Antoine presented no difficulties: he talked better
than passable English, was familiar with city life, and had been
taken by his patron into many fashionable homes in St. Louis. He
wore conventional clothing with the ease of one long accustomed
to it. Miller probably joined Sir William and Antoine as a guest
in Webb's spacious and hospitable home.

When at last the 9th of June came and with it the opening
of Miller's exhibit, everyone was astonished by the enthusiasm
with which the paintings were received. Visitors crowded the gallery, politely pushing and crowding to get a closer look at "Hunting the Buffalo," "An Arickara Squaw," "Greeting the Snake
Indians," and all the rest. The critics gave the exhibit rave notices.
They praised the originality, boldness, accuracy of drawing, and
perspective of the artist, and commented on his great talent.

Most of the newspaper stories carried a good word for Miller's
patron as well. One writer went so far as to say, "Of Sir William
himself, the originator, the traveler and the subject of the pic-

turesque and the grand, we hardly know how to speak. The romance of his taste and the enthusiasm of his character, in spending seven years around and about the Rocky Mountains, are without parallel in these days of steamboats and railroads. We hear that he is on his way to the interior of Persia via England and the Mediterranean. God go with him and protect him."

A bit on the florid side, perhaps, it stated the case accurately, nonetheless. Between them, Sir William Drummond Stewart and Alfred Jacob Miller preserved much of the Old West in all its beauty and strangeness and color for us and countless generations to come, a service which has placed the civilized world forever in their debt.

Days passed. Crowds at the Apollo Gallery increased, in spite of the fact that it was no free show, an admission fee being charged. The chairman of the Apollo Gallery board wrote a letter to Sir William in which he said:

> The paintings lent to our Association and exhibited one week have brought receipts more than double any former week. I thank you and say we would like to continue the showing until the close of July.

Sir William was happy to oblige. The group of Miller pictures remained on exhibition for seven weeks instead of two weeks as originally planned, drawing admiring crowds every day. Miller went back to New Orleans long before the closing date. Before he left, there was an agreement made between him and Sir William that the artist would come to Murthly the following year and paint much larger canvases than any he had so far done, pictures that in size and scope would make suitable embellishments for the great halls of the castle.

On the 25th of May, 1839, Sir William sailed for Perthshire. Antoine and the two "red men" went with him. To J. Watson Webb was left the responsibility of seeing that the canvases at the Apollo Gallery were packed and shipped to Murthly.

CHAPTER XX

Sir William Returns to Murthly

৪৯ Sir William disembarked at Glasgow with his protegés, Antoine and the two Indians. Their appearance in the staid old city evoked considerable speculation. During Antoine's intermittent visits to St. Louis, his patron had induced the fair-skinned half-breed to have his red hair cut in the fashion of the day, and to wear suits of conventional style; but the Indians refused flatly to make any sartorial changes. They clung to their buckskin shirts, leggings, and moccasins and let their black hair stream over the three-point Hudson Bay blankets in which they impassively wrapped themselves against the chill Scottish air.

From the great port city they traveled to Perth by railway. Here a family carriage awaited to take them over the intervening sixteen miles to Murthly. Nearing the great stone pile that had been the home of Stewarts for centuries, Sir William came in sight of New Murthly. There it stood, topped by glittering turrets and domes, its brash newness outlined against the dark Birnam hills.

The building looked finished, but he knew, because of reports from George, that much remained to be done within its walls. Work on it had been stopped at John's death. As he looked at the ornate structure, Sir William must have made another irrevocable

vow: to let the monstrosity stand as a monument to the extravagance, envy and bad taste of his older brother, and never expend
another farthing of Stewart money on the garish building. At any
rate, that is what he did.

It was not yet noon when the coachman drove up the long
tree-bordered avenue and stopped at the entrance to Murthly. Sir
William alighted, preceded his charges up the short, curved flight
of steps leading to the front door. He stepped inside the great hall
hung with banners and crowded with trophies brought home from
time immemorial by the lords of Murthly. The servants and
workers attached to the castle had gathered there to welcome him,
all smiling, some struggling to hold back tears of joy. Many of the
faces were familiar to him, some from as long ago as his childhood.

There was Ryder, Sir William's servant at Waterloo, old now
and so feeble he was allowed to do only the lightest tasks. Jamie,
the dwarf, hopped about on his huge, spraddled feet, grinning
and bowing. Many more were there who had been at Murthly
long before Sir William had gone away to that dangerous country, the United States. Now he was safely back again, and their
lord, instead of Sir John, whom they had never liked. Sir William,
now, there was a lad who was kind and had a bit of feelin' for a
body, though to be sure his temper was hot and quick.

A large room above the stone tool house in the garden had
been made into an apartment for Antoine and the Indians. A man-
servant took the alert half-breed and the dead-pan savages in tow,
showed them down a stately tree-bordered walk to the tool house,
and waved them up an outside stairway to what would be their
dwelling-place for several years.

The housekeeper took Sir William to the second story of the
castle where rooms had been prepared for him. They were the
same quarters that had been his when he was a young man and
looked almost the same as when he had left them long ago.
There was the great carved tester bed, its canopy of green velvet
encrusted with gold embroidery, satin coverlid sweeping the floor,
Persian carpet underfoot; in the sitting room, Gothic chairs fit for
a bishop, somber paintings of classical scenes in enormous gold
frames. Counterpoint to thoughts of buffalo robes spread by the
campfire at Stewart's Lake, the log walls of Fort Laramie, the

bower made of willow withes and brush that he had shared with poor Holmes in the Valley of the Green.

The housekeeper waited hopefully for words of appreciation from the new lord of the castle. He gave them to her unstintedly, and then explained that he would occupy these rooms in the daytime, but for the present he would sleep at Dalpowie. This, it will be remembered, was the spacious lodge that stood in the garden at some distance from the castle.

Baffled, she returned to the servants' quarters with this curious information. Tongues wagged as the older retainers dredged up from their memories details of the terrible quarrel between the two brothers, and what William had said to John about his never sleeping under the roof of Murthly again. Shaking her head, the housekeeper went to prepare a room for his lordship at Dalpowie. Fortunately, no one was renting it at the time.

For a while after Sir William's return, his days were crowded with matters connected with the estate. John had not been content with spending his excess income from the lands of Murthly, Grandtully and even Logiealmond, on New Murthly in a futile effort to out-shine Lord Breadalbane, but had gone deeply into debt. And while Thomas, the overseer at Murthly, was a good man, he needed supervision. During John's long illness, every plan, every decision, had been left to Thomas. As a result, there had been appalling mismanagement and waste.

As soon as Sir William's tangled affairs were straightened out, at least to some extent, he went to Edinburgh to see Christina. He must have felt pride in his small son, grown so tall for his age, doing well in school, eagerly begging to hear about his father's adventures in the Far West. Christina's beauty, her devotion and sweetness, which seemed to increase rather than grow less with the years, must have moved Sir William deeply. They were two people enmeshed in a strange situation. He could not enter her world, she could not enter his. Yet the bond between them remained strong and warm until it was broken by death.

Returning to Murthly, he resumed his manifold duties there, not the least of them being to extend hospitality to his neighbors, from whose good company he had been absent for so long, and to friends from Perth, Edinburgh, and even as far away as London. These people, not always titled, not always rich, but invariably interesting, made the castle a lively place.

The boxes and bales filled with plants, seeds, animals, mementoes of many types that he had shipped from St. Louis, began to arrive. Among the array were several hundred small trees—fir, oak, ash and the like—that had been packed on muleback to the city on the Missouri from points as far away as the Rocky Mountains. Gangs of workmen were assigned the task of planting these saplings on Birnam Hill, long denuded except for two examples, of its noble trees, to satisfy the greed of a rapacious owner long ago. Once more Birnam Hill would wear its crown of green, now a diadem from across the ocean.

This effort made by Sir William to combine the worlds he loved began to emerge as a recurrent pattern of his life. On the harsh Western trail, he took what luxuries he could command, for fine living was in his blood. Now he was trying by every means in his power to bring all that he could of the Far West to Murthly, his ancestral home. The birds, the seeds, Miller and his paintings, even Antoine and the Indians, were all significant of a deep-seated, powerful drive, of which he may have been only dimly aware.

Sir William had been at home for scarcely a month when one day a messenger brought a bulky document to the castle. It was an invitation to a dinner in his honor from the fifty-eight tenant farmers on the estate. Each man, as he signed his name, had also given the location of his land. The dinner would be held in Birnam Inn, a first-class hostelry in Birnam Village, a short distance south of the castle, the date to be in accord with the convenience of his lordship. This mark of liking and respect from his tenants did not go unappreciated by Sir William, and the dinner inevitably proved a joyous occasion for all.

In spite of the busy life he led with its many distractions, pleasant and otherwise, restlessness began to assail Sir William, a yearning for new scenes and fresh experiences; but so many things needed his guiding hand. Besides, his very good friend, Lord Glenlyon, was going to be married, come October, to beautiful Ann Home, daughter of one of the great families living to the east of Murthly. Many would take it ill if he did not attend the festivities.

Lord Glenlyon's seat was the castle of Blair-Atholl, a few hours' ride to the north on the River Till, a stream that dashed in wild abandon through the Scottish Highlands. Murthly and Dunkeld were about halfway between these two estates.

On the twenth-ninth of October the widely heralded wedding took place with pomp and ceremony. Sir William arranged that as the bride and groom rode through Dunkeld the villagers would serenade them with bagpipe music and set off fireworks in their honor.

Following Lord Glenlyon's marriage, Sir William decided to travel for a few months, revisit places he had last seen before the long interlude in America. Thomas, the overseer, was given explicit instructions concerning every conceivable situation that might arise during his absence. George came over from Logiealmond, where he was living with the two maiden sisters, promising to stay for the duration of Sir William's projected trip. He would keep the large household running smoothly and dispense hospitality to the constant stream of guests.

Sir William then departed for London, taking Antoine with him, but wisely leaving the two Indians in George's somewhat timorous care. He stayed briefly at the family town house, renewing old friendships interrupted eight years before and making arrangements for a tour of Egypt and Turkey.

While he was in London he received a letter from Robert Campbell, dated August 29, 1839, saying that he would endeavor to send to Sir William in the fall, roots of the buffalo berry, also of wild currants and gooseberries from the upper Platte. In addition, his friend might expect a dozen buffalo tongues that Sublette had packed in salt, and the missive closed with news that the Missouri was low.

Late in November, while still in London, Sir William wrote to Sublette regarding a number of things he planned to send to his friend in the spring. These included two pedigreed calves to improve the herd on Sublette's farm. When the colts were sold, which would be in April or May of the following year, he would send a fine young horse. The letter went on:

I must inform you that I have not yet done with the U.S. and if it pleases God, I shall be in New York in the fall of 1840 with a view of going to the mountains in the spring, if I can get a party to join me of sufficient strength. Remember me to Andrew Drips and let him, or any other of my friends, know that I am in life and health, and shall be on the Susquadee in July, 1841.

Susquadee, Seeds-kee-dee and Sis-ka-dee were all variations of an Indian word meaning "sage hen," which the wild tribes applied to Green River. The white men pronounced and spelled it any way they saw fit. As for Sir William's plans to be on the Green in 1841, he was due for an instance of the Scottish poet's "best-laid plans of mice . . ." He did not get there until two years after that date.

Sitting in his drawing room, the noises of London all about him, he must have remembered with a pang of nostalgia that he had been a part of the colorful pageantry that was the fur trade, now forever gone. Nor could he have been unmindful of the fact that the water color sketches he had commissioned Miller to paint that summer of 1837 were the only pictorial record made of the trail up the Platte and the people and scenes of the rendezvous on the Green in that climactic year.

While business affairs detained Sir William in London, word had gotten around to interested people in Perthshire that he had in mind to do something about the crumbling chapels at Grandtully and Murthly. He received a stern communication from William MacLaven, overseer of Grandtully, reminding him that the chapel there was in an unusable condition and that "the priests," names not given, hoped it would soon be repaired. Reprovingly, MacLaven went on, now that Sir William was in the faith again, he should make the chapel safe for the tenantry.

This reminder of his duty was followed in a day or two by a letter from Bishop Gillis (perhaps of Dunkeld Cathedral?) saying he was looking for a chaplain for Murthly, but that it was difficult to find one, there being no congregation. Only old men were willing to consider the post, and Sir William had said he wanted one of quality. The Bishop inquired bluntly as to the

salary, desired to know whether the chaplain would be expected
to live in the castle, or would he have a house of his own? The
epistle closed with brusque command that Sir William *must repair
the chapel.*

Both the overseer and the Bishop struck a note in their letters
that would get them nowhere with Sir William. He obeyed commands with good grace when issued by constituted authority, as
past events in his life clearly showed, but neither of these men
possessed any such authority over him. He had every intention
of fulfilling his vow made to the Jesuit friar somewhere on the
Big Horn, and of fulfilling it handsomely, but no one was going
to tell him when or how. So for the present the repairs on the two
chapels remained in abeyance.

A few days later he and Antoine set off for Constantinople.
No record of their itinerary or activities has been discovered. One
letter received by Sir William while en route has been preserved.
It is from Lord Breadalbane and only one item in it is of interest
to us now: "I have given orders to have the long wool plucked
from the buffaloes and yarn spun from it. The yarn shall be
knitted into socks for the donor of these interesting beasts by the
time you return."

No doubt the owner of Taymouth Castle thought it a good
idea at the time, but we hear no more about buffalo-wool socks.
Whether the bottleneck occurred when he asked someone to
pluck the wool, or when he proposed to a cottager that she spin the
yarn and knit it into socks, is not known. The Indians made stout
ropes of buffalo wool, but . . .

While Sir William and Antoine were gone, a momentous
event occurred. On February 10 Queen Victoria was married to
Prince Albert, son of the Duke of Saxe-Coburg-Gotha. At that time
the young Queen was having trouble of a political nature with
her restive, stubborn subjects in Scotland, so it was decided that
she and her bridegroom would honeymoon in that country. This
gesture was expected to quiet the recalcitrant citizenry of Bonnie
Scotland and curiously enough, it did.

This was the first visit Victoria ever made to the northern-
most country of her island kingdom. It planted there the seeds of
Scottish loyalty to the throne that burgeoned into great and last-

ing growth. As for Victoria, it was the beginning of her long love affair with Scotland that continued until her death more than sixty years later.

All the great families sent invitations to the royal couple, requesting the honor of a visit. As Sir William was away, introducing Antoine to Karnak, or the Mosque of St. Sophia, or perhaps the Casbah, he did not join in this flutter of obeisance to royalty. However, the prestige of the country was adequately upheld by Lord and Lady Breadalbane. Their invitation to visit Taymouth Castle was one which the Queen and her consort graciously accepted on their grand tour of the moors and highlands.

Since the court entourage would pass through Dunkeld on its way to Taymouth Castle, Lord Breadalbane saw to it that arches of greenery were erected at strategic points and that the pretty village streets were lined with smiling cottagers who tossed flowers under the horses' feet. During Victoria's and Albert's stay at the vast and truly impressive Taymouth Castle, the Queen noted in her journal that she saw in the deer park there "those strange hump-backed creatures from America," Sir William's gift to Lord Breadalbane.

Sir William and Antoine were back in London at the proper time to buy the two pedigreed calves and fine young horse that the baronet had promised to send Sublette; then they went on to Murthly. At once Sir William became deeply immersed in plans for an ambitious building program, only a small part of which could be started because sufficient funds were not available. Also, there was the matter of John's debts to plague him. Some way out must be found. As a small beginning he determined to build a new hunting lodge that could be rented to wealthy sportsmen at a good price. Murthly's expanse of wooded hills abounded in deer, squirrels, rabbits, brilliantly colored pheasants and brown capercaillies almost as large as wild turkeys.

He named the new villa Rohallion, after an immensely old castle that once had stood on the site. All that remained of this structure was a bit of crumbling wall, part of a tower ante-dating the Roman occupation. The place he selected for Rohallion was on the shore of a tiny lake about two miles from the castle, east of Birnam Hill. These storied slopes were now showing faintly green, as the trees from America unfolded their first leaves in the alien air.

When finished, Rohallion's drawing-room windows would overlook the quiet beauty of the lake and its surrounding banks where young oaks and rhododendron shrubs had been planted. In superintending this work Sir William had the help of his overseer, but every day he walked the two miles to Rohallion checking on the progress being made. That progress was slow, probably for two reasons: Sir William's demand for perfection in every detail, and the difficulty of getting good workmen. From the time Rohallion was started until it was finished years later, the beautiful two-story villa seemed to have a special place in his affections.

Sir William broke the tedium of his days by visiting friends living on near-by estates, and with brief trips to London for conferences with architects, artists, stained-glass makers, and so on. His plans were taking definite shape for the restoration, rather than mere repair, of St. Mary's Chapel at Grandtully, where his ancestors slept in their lead coffins under its stone floor. At the same time the preliminary steps were being taken for bringing back its original beauty to the burial chapel at Murthly and adding a wing that would house the new chapel for the priests who would one day be established on the estate.

Where the money for all this was to come from, he was not yet sure. But a daring idea was beginning to take form in his mind which, if carried through, would solve all his financial problems, take care of John's debts, pay for the improvements at Grandtully and Murthly, and leave more than enough for him to take a really bang-up trip to the Rockies in a style to which until then he had not let his imagination soar.

What a row the family would raise when they were told! Archibald's acidulous fury, Thomas the churchman's aloof, cutting scorn, George's fluttering objections—he could hear them all. Well, he had met family storms before. This one would be no worse than the turmoil of thunder, lightning, and pelting hail he had many times encountered on the Platte. Sir William went steadily ahead, keeping his own counsel, while the will to carry through his plan hardened to steel-like rigidity. The time to put it into effect had not yet come.

Miller was expected in September to begin his enormous canvases for the walls of Murthly. Sir William wanted to have the final word in selecting the subjects for these paintings. So he bided his time, gave up the idea of returning that fall to the United States. But his objectives remained unchanged.

CHAPTER XXI

Lords and Ladies, Buffaloes and Indians

෫ Miller, complete with much paint and endless yards of canvas
—though, as it turned out, not enough of either—arrived at Perth
during the first week of September. There a Stewart carriage was
waiting to take him the rest of the way. Though exhausted by the
long journey from New Orleans, he was enchanted by his ride to
the castle through the lovely rolling Perthshire countryside. Much
of the road followed the gently curving Tay, as different from the
wild, turbulent streams of the Rockies as it was from the muddy,
slow-moving rivers Miller was more accustomed to.

As Miller came in sight of the grounds of Murthly, the first
building he saw was the castle erected by John. Later, he wrote
of it to his sister in Baltimore and his remarks are worthy of note,
for he was deeply impressed by the glitter and glory that burst
upon his astonished eyes. It was, he said, of Elizabethan architecture, confusing the Virgin Queen with somebody else. There were
towers surmounted by gilded spires. There were lofty turrets. A
tower larger than the others rose from the center of the roof, with
a rampant lion at each corner. Surrounding this tower were nine
domed turrets, each topped with a golden spire—all this mélange
interspersed with ornamental chimneys more beautiful than any
he had ever seen.

We are much indebted to the Miller letters, none of which

have previously been published, for most of our knowledge regarding Old Murthly, its grounds, the appearance of the castle itself and of its interior as they were during Sir William's time. As Miller approached the ancient castle he marveled at the terrace bordering the Tay, thirty feet wide and over a mile long, "with the appearance of rich green baize." He afterward discovered that the effect was achieved by means of moss growing amid the grass, the whole expanse being mowed every third day.

The coachman turned into the stately tree-bordered avenue leading to Murthly itself. There, Sir William being briefly absent from the castle, George cordially welcomed the artist and escorted him into the great hall. This was an impressive room with its vast stretch of floor, its high vaulted ceiling. Miller saw rusty pikes, helmets, gauntlets, tattered banners, while on massive tables lay sabers, pistols, stilettos, spurs with six-inch rowels, Scottish knives, their solid gold handles set with jewels. In the drawing room Miller stared, his eyes on paintings by Corregio, Leonardo da Vinci, Raphael, and other artists only slightly less famous. All this was a jumbled impression at the time, but he later confirmed the details and wrote a long account of them to his sister. Miller, an essentially modest man, must have been startled to discover that his work was destined to hang "cheek by jowl" with pictures executed by the Old Masters.

After the preliminary amenities were taken care of, the housekeeper showed Miller to his room. Furnished in the rich elegance of the Tudor period, it looked magnificent to the young American. His window overlooked the formal garden, and beyond that he could see a wide, shadowed path leading directly to St. Anthony the Eremite's low-roofed chapel. Later he learned the name of this somber path overhung by gloomy trees. It was called the Dead Walk. By long-established custom, only the feet of those carrying the departed Stewarts to their last resting place ever disturbed its carpeting of brown pine needles.

Before an hour had passed, Sir William returned to the castle, sought Miller out, and welcomed him to Murthly in a most cordial manner, while noting with regret that his guest limped so badly. This limp, Miller explained, was the result of an attack of his old enemy, rheumatism. Sir William insisted on putting the artist in the care of the baronet's own London physician, Dr. Liston, the worthy doctor to make a diagnosis and prescribe treatment by remote control. Miller gratefully assented to this plan.

Within a day or two Miller was given a pony phaeton for his own use and a spacious, well-lighted studio. Nothing that could add to his comfort or pleasure was overlooked. He was most agreeably surprised, remembering how strict Sir William had been with him throughout the trip to the Rockies. Of course, in the mountains he had been a member of the company under Sir William's command and hence was accorded no preferred treatment. Here he was an honored guest. Miller thoroughly enjoyed his changed status. He wrote his sister:

> I am necessarily thrown here amongst a great deal of refined company, and shall not neglect to profit by it, for although books are not to be slighted, yet possibly elegant conversation contributes to a greater degree to improve the mind, to arrest the attention, and to engage the thought.

Obviously Miller became a little overwhelmed by the unaccustomed luxury and the many titled personages to whom he was introduced on a footing of equality. In spite of his experiences on the Continent as a student, and the acclaim which had already been given him, he was still a simple Baltimore boy. The outward expression of his slight attack of awe remained one of naïveté rather than subservience, and was engaging rather than objectionable.

The "sketches," as Miller always called his water colors made on the spot in the Far West, now arrived at the castle. Sir William had them placed in a richly bound portfolio and, in Miller's words, "they became one of the chief attractions of the drawing room to his distinguished visitors who are profuse in their compliments."

Miller often drove his pony phaeton to Dunkeld, only four miles distant. "Nothing," he commented in one of his letters, "can exceed the romantic beauty of the cottages of the tenants, their fronts nearly covered with honeysuckle, and creeping ivy, their exceeding neatness and cleanliness giving them a most completely inviting appearance."

During the last week in November a great ball was held at Murthly for the servants and tenantry of the estate and others near by. In order that Antoine might attend this particular festivity and others of the same kind in proper style, Sir William had presented the half-breed with a full Highland costume, at a cost of fifty pounds. He must have cut a resplendent figure in it. When the great night arrived, Sir William was absent, so George, as the master's representative, led out one of the prettiest maids for the first dance. All the men, as Miller noted, wore Highland costumes, and Antoine made a great hit with the girls. Later, Miller wrote to his sister that the "condescension of the nobility," not only in sponsoring these balls, but actually being present and taking part in them, was most admirable.

Immediately following the servants' ball, great preparations began for a four-day visit from Lord and Lady Breadalbane. While she was at the castle, her ladyship accorded Miller two hours to paint her portrait. Of course he could not finish it in that time, but she was so enchanted by the likeness that she insisted on taking it home in her carriage. Miller was invited to Taymouth Castle for a long visit, during which he would have plenty of time to complete the portrait.

A short time after the letter concerning Miller's ill health was dispatched to Dr. Liston, a reply was received. The eminent physician directed Miller to massage the ailing leg with warm vinegar while wearing a hair glove. This regimen, meticulously followed, or the faith engendered by Dr. Liston's reputation, or a turn for the better in the raw fall weather—who can say which—brought the artist considerable relief from his affliction.

About this time Miller started a large oil painting based on the sketch, "An Attack of the Crows on the Whites at the Big Horn." It would, he said, contain about thirty figures, one-half life size, and would require the rest of the winter to complete. When tired of painting, he could retire to the extensive library, which Sir William had placed at his disposal.

In reply to an inquiry from his sister as to what Sir William's quarters in the villa were like, Miller wrote the following detailed description:

The floor is overspread with Persian prayer carpets fringed
with silk and the walls covered with crimson cloth hangings.
Along the ceiling extend brass rods from which are suspended
reminiscences of the Rocky Mountains painted by your un-
worthy brother. There are "The Death of a Panther," "Return
from Hunting," "Indian Belle Reclining," "Auguste," "Roasting the Hump Rib," etc., etc., which are all in beautiful frames
and have a fine effect.

On one side rises a cushioned divan of damask cloth extending the length of the apartment about three feet wide,
over which is spread some magnificent buffalo robes. On these
he sleeps.

A glittering tomahawk, the one worn by him in the
mountains, is placed on a small table near the divan. . . . In
one corner are numerous pipes, Indian, Turkish, and German.
A rich toilette table, richly garnished, occupies the center of
one side and the light is admitted through silk blinds which
at once subdue and soften it.

Fancy surroundings for Bill Stewart, partisan of the trail and
rendezvous. Miller thought so: "It is a doubt whether in the last
eight years he has even touched a feather bed."

The cold, gray Scottish winter settled down over the country.
Lord and Lady Glenlyon enlivened the gloom of the season by
giving a tremendous house party to celebrate the christening of
their son, now almost two months old. The festivities took place
at their family seat, Blair Castle, northward from Murthly some
thirty miles, near the River Till. The great families of the County
attended, and among them was the Glenlyons' special friend, Sir
William Drummond Stewart.

That evening a costume ball, with its sparkle of magnificent
jewels, its gleam of gold and satin and velvet, was held in the castle.
Sir William appeared in the rich ceremonial robes and insignia of
his rank, encrusted with precious stones, of a high Albanian
churchman. At the same time that "quality" enjoyed its dignified
pleasures in the ball room of the castle, twelve hundred tenants
of the estate made merry in the wooden pavilion that had been
erected the year before for the wedding dinner of Lord Glenlyon

and his beautiful lady. Sometime during all these elegant goings-on, the small heir-presumptive to the titles and estates of Blair Castle was duly christened.

Back at Murthly, Sir William dispensed hospitality with a prodigal hand. A continuous stream of guests came and went, some staying only for days, others remaining for weeks. Sir William's business took him often to Glasgow, to London, and during some of these frequent absences he went to Perth where Christina and his son now lived. That he saw Christina often is certain. A number of letters received from his friends at this time end with the request that he give the writer's regards to Lady Stewart.

When Sir William was not at home, George took over the duties of host, and when George was absent, Miller upheld the honors of the castle, presiding at the dinner table. The responsibility caused him more than a little concern, especially when it came time to carve the "joints and fowl."

Antoine, following Sir William's orders, had been given some fast coaching in the servants' quarters, after which the half-breed had been presented with a fine black suit of livery. When distinguished guests arrived, he acted as butler. This arrangement could have added little to Miller's serenity, as he was well aware of the wild, savage, mischievous streak that was part of Antoine's nature. However, he seems to have behaved with perfect decorum on all such occasions.

Sir William made a point of being at Murthly for Christmas, but left three days later for London with the expectation that he would be gone six weeks. Miller took advantage of this opportunity to accept Lord and Lady Breadalbane's invitation to visit them. Taymouth Castle and its enormous estate impressed the Baltimore artist deeply. Well it might: Taymouth was one of the largest and most richly furnished castles in Scotland. There Miller finished the portrait of Lady Breadalbane that he had begun the previous fall and also executed a picture of Lord Breadalbane. In a letter to his sister he mentions seeing seven buffaloes and two buffalo calves there in the deer park, and they seemed quite tame. As Miller later discovered, several of the beasts were Sir William's, being cared for on the Taymouth estate until a place could be prepared for them at Murthly.

Sometime in February Miller returned to the castle and resumed his work on the great canvases for its walls. Sir William preceded him by a few days. From Sublette came a large package of buffalo-grass seed and the promise of more buffalo as soon as his friend had a place to care for them. Sir William immediately ordered that work should begin on a paddock suitable for the huge animals. An enclosure was laid out not far from Rohallion measuring five or six miles in circumference. This area was enclosed by a stone fence topped by several strands of thick wire.

While this was progressing, Miller suffered a severe attack of his old enemy, rheumatism, from which he was slow in recovering. In fact, he never did regain complete use of one leg. But he was soon up, painting again. Visitors were frequent, among them Lord and Lady Glenlyon, who stayed for several days. Miller, who was by no means immune to feminine loveliness, described Lady Glenlyon to his sister with a somewhat strained nonchalance:

> What a display of diamonds at the dinner table! Such aigrettes! Ringlets and bracelets! And then, unlike Niobe, she's all smiles, all graciousness and, I was very near saying, all tongue. Lady Glenlyon is a charming woman and her laugh is bewitching and contagious.

As soon as the fence around the buffalo paddock was completed, the grass seeds from America were planted over the whole area. Spring came early in Scotland that year, so that tiny shoots soon pushed through the ground and put out the curly leaves so familiar to both Sir William and Miller.

In May the artist sent to London for a piece of canvas measuring eight by ten feet. As soon as it arrived, Miller began painting "The Trapper's Bride," taken from a water-color sketch made in the Rockies. The figures were almost life size. This picture achieved great popularity and he later made several copies of it. The painting glows with color, against which the white buckskin garb and dusky comeliness of the young Indian girl appear to great advantage.

A letter came from J. Watson Webb in New York, evidently in reply to one of Sir William's to him. He regretted that he could not come to visit his friend at Murthly. The depression, still continuing, had hit him so hard he feared he would not get to Scotland for several years. This news came as no surprise to Sir William. Before he had left the United States two years before, the country was in financial difficulties which had increased with the passage of time. Sir William had kept informed regarding conditions in America, and understood why his friend Webb could not leave his business at that time.

Miller recovered sufficiently so he could once more walk about the estate. One day he went to see "the two large trees of Birnam Wood, the only ones remaining. Truly, they are wonders! The greatest circumference of their trunks is twenty-seven feet; the least, twenty. One is oak, the other beech. No slightest sign of decay." He was working hard then in his painting room, endeavoring to complete as soon as possible the enormous canvas begun the year before, "Attack of the Crows on the Whites at the Big Horn."

Sir William spent much of his time superintending the building of Rohallion. Miller presents an especially vivid picture of the man, one showing a facet of his character we have not seen before, and a somewhat astonishing sidelight on what was then considered the simple life—from a dietary standpoint, at least.

His habits are regular and very simple. He rises about seven, breakfasts at half past on steaks and cutlets and eggs, under-done, and a bottle of claret, never touching either tea, coffee or butter. He walks out to see the improvements and returns at one to lunch and to see the letters brought by post. He reads the papers and walks out again and does not return until the dinner bell at half past six; dines heartily on the richest dishes, but takes little wine; converses or reads until nine or ten, smokes his meerschaum, and then to sleep.

However, he took time out from his building activities to visit Miller frequently in his painting room. In reporting this custom of Sir William's to his sister, the artist says, ". . . but woe to the Indian who has not sufficient dignity of expression and carriage, for out he must come. His conception of a picture, both as regards composition and coloring, is excellent."

About this time two astonishing chairs arrived that Sir William had designed and ordered made. They were placed in the

hall of the castle for everyone to see. It must be admitted that this
time his determination to bring every possible reminder of the
West to Murthly got out of hand.

The backs of these mahogany chairs were deeply carved to
represent life-sized buffalo heads, complete with glass eyes, up-
standing ears, and real horns. The front legs ended in cloven hoofs.
The effect was more than a little nightmarish and it was, of course,
impossible to sit on one with any comfort whatever. The natural
contours of a buffalo's face do not lend themselves to being leaned
against. Miller, always carefully loyal to his "noble patron," merely
states that the buffalo chairs arrived, and refrains from commenting
on them.

July ushered in the shooting season, and there was another
spate of guests at Murthly. To entertain them, Antoine was requested to appear in the drawing room wearing the full regalia of
an Indian chieftain. The restrained astonishment with which this
apparition was greeted upstairs was as nothing to the screams of
terror evoked by his appearance in the servants' hall. All of which
greatly pleased Antoine, who was always a show-off, an unmitigated
ham.

At the coming of summer, the buffalo grass in the paddock
had grown thick and lush, its curling leaves dark green. The buffaloes that Sir William had left in Lord Breadalbane's deer park
were transported to Murthly. Here they became something more
for the high-born visitors to view with wonder and some fear.
Would the fence, stout though it looked, hold these great, strong
animals in case they became restive at the barrier between them
and freedom? There was no occasion for worry. With food plentiful, the weather mild compared to their former storm-swept range
on the prairies and among the mountains, the buffaloes had settled
down to almost a bovine peacefulness.

The boredom engendered in Antoine by his quiet life at
Murthly—no hunting, no gambling worthy of the name, no ad-
venturing among the high peaks—plus more than his usual alcoholic intake, finally brought the half-breed to disgrace. One evening he and the Indians, whom he was supposed to restrain, im-
bibed too much firewater. With Antoine leading in the wild
prank, the three of them tied a large row boat onto four wagon

wheels, hitched two buffaloes to the strange vehicle and drove
through the streets of Dunkeld at a mad gallop, their warwhoops
echoing from the near-by Grampian Hills.

This experience completely shattered the nerves of the villagers. Next day they made aggrieved complaint to the lord of the
castle. No doubt Sir William had some difficulty keeping a straight
face during the recital of their woes. And, as soon as Antoine so-
bered up enough to know what was being said to him, we may
safely assume that he received a tongue-lashing couched in mountain and prairie language he could clearly understand.

Sir William began to build a spacious villa as a residence for
the two priests who would one day be established at Murthly.
This house, called Laguna, was situated at a distance of about two
miles northeast of Murthly. Sir William delegated most of the
responsibility for its construction to Thomas, his overseer. It was
not finished for a long time.

Sometime in October Miller completed "The Trapper's
Bride," but with difficulty, as he was far from well. Sir William
insisted that the artist send to Inverness for four dozen bottles of
Strathpeffer Water—a beverage strongly impregnated with sulphur
—which would surely improve his condition. Nobody mentioned
Dr. Liston, his hair glove and warm vinegar.

The Strathpeffer Water must have had a salutary effect.
Miller decided to spend some time in London before returning to
Baltimore. Sir William commissioned him to paint a large picture
to be placed in the new chapel at Murthly, when it should be
built. To be titled "Mary Magdalene Anointing the Feet of the
Savior," it would depict fourteen life-sized figures. This task could
be counted on to occupy Miller during the months of his stay in
London. Sir William planned a short trip to the Continent immediately after the first of the year. On his return, he would pick
up the finished painting and say farewell to Miller, who would then
return to America.

After Sir William and Miller left, the stream of visitors
dwindled to a casual guest now and then. George went back to
stay with his sisters at Logiealmond. Archibald came, stayed
briefly and departed, destination unknown. A shadowy figure, Archibald, coming into clear focus only when he was infuriated with

his brother William because of something he had done or proposed to do.

Reaching London, Miller took up his residence at Mount's Hotel, Grosvenor Square, and found a suitable studio at 30 Gerrard Street, Soho, near the National Gallery. He planned to spend his leisure time in that great institution, studying the paintings and other works of art that it contained. He wrote to his sister in February, telling her he was working very hard on the religious picture. Sir William was expected to arrive at any time and Miller wanted the work to be ready for his criticism. Another American artist who painted Indian subjects and scenes of the Far West, George Catlin, was in London and had called on Miller several times. Catlin had experienced the honor of exhibiting his model of Niagara Falls to Queen Victoria.

"There is, in truth," Miller wrote, "a great deal of humbug about Mr. George Catlin. He has published a book containing some extraordinary stories and luckily for him, there are but few persons who have traveled over the same ground."

Miller's criticism of his brother artist did not spring from professional jealousy. Catlin was not in the same class as Miller, either as a colorist, a draughtsman, or a portrait painter; his conclusions as to the noble character of Western Indians were often quaint indeed. However, Catlin holds a valued place as pictorial historian of the red man's customs, clothing, ornaments and weapons as they existed in the regions he visited in the early 1830's.

Sir William arrived in London late in February, as he had planned. He was entirely pleased with the religious picture. During Miller's last interview with his "noble patron," Sir William assured the artist that they would meet again in the fall of 1842. At that time the Scotsman would call on him in Baltimore.

Miller left immediately for the United States, where he was received with honor by President John Tyler and attended a reception at the White House. Returning to Baltimore, his health slowly improved. He resumed his profession, reputation greatly enhanced.

CHAPTER XXII

Once More, America!

੩ A few days after Sir William bade Miller good-by in London, he set out on his journey to Murthly. Having, presumably, stopped off at Edinburgh to see Christina and their son, he went on to Perth and several days' visit with his lifelong friend, William David Murray, Fourth Earl of Mansfield. This nobleman's family seat was the Palace of Scone, situated only a few miles from the busy port on the Firth of Tay.

The time had come for Sir William to implement the plan made long before, to acquire the large sum he needed to liquidate the debts incurred by John. Also to rebuild the chapels at Murthly and Grandtully, and finance his farewell trip to the Rocky Mountains. He told his friend, the earl, that he intended to sell the estate of Logiealmond.

"Do you want to buy it?" he asked.

"I certainly do, William!" the earl replied.

The Earl of Mansfield's lineage could be traced as far back as Sir William's, and both family trees were closely connected with several royal blood lines—a king here, a queen there. Back in 1296 the even then immemorially ancient Stone of Scone, on which Pict and Scottish kings had been crowned in the Palace of Scone for centuries, had been taken to Westminster Abbey by Edward

I, where it still rests. This move was part of Edward I's long effort
to conquer Scotland and gain its allegiance to the English crown,
a project in which he was unsuccessful.

In 1600 the estates and Palace of Scone passed to Sir David
Murray of the Tullibardine line, a direct ancestor of Sir William's
friend. New Scone Palace had been built in 1803 and, as Scottish
castles and palaces went, could be considered a modern building
with all the latest improvements. It was, after all, only forty years
old.

Immediately after Sir William arrived home, he informed
George of his intentions regarding Logiealmond. George, acting
in his usual role as news distributor for the family, spread the
shocking word that William was about to sell the property that
had belonged to generations of Drummonds; where William's
mother and sisters had been born; where Elizabeth, Marie-Frances
and George were living. The words "disloyalty!" "sinfulness!"
"outrage!" echoed through the halls of Logiealmond.

George wrote to his brother in what, for mild, amiable George,
was a towering rage. The letter said, in effect, that William should
not break up the family lands, and not only that, it was illegal
for him to do so. Of course George was wrong there: Logiealmond
belonged to Sir William and he was free to do with it as he
pleased.

Thomas, coldly disapproving, took time from his ecclesiastical
concerns in Italy to say that William would do well to consult
with members of the family before taking such a drastic step as
he appeared to contemplate. The maiden aunts refrained from
communicating with their recalcitrant nephew, but their bitter
scorn and anger grew by feeding on itself.

Sir William, who had allowed the spinsters and George to
live in the tumble-down castle at Logiealmond ever since he had
come into the estate, might well have felt that he was doing
them a favor by obliging them to move to a more comfortable
and even safer place of residence. He knew the two women had
inherited considerable means from their father, Sir John Drummond, and could well afford better surroundings than the old
castle provided. Even before the death of their father, the ancient
building had been in need of repairs. After his death, the aunts

had refused to allow a single stone of their ancestral home to be touched, even though it seemed about to tumble down on their heads. They wanted to keep everything exactly as it was, but in spite of them, time continued to have its way with beams, walks, and stairways.

During this time when Sir William was the object of his family's ire, he had at least one staunch supporter. His friend, Lord Breadalbane, wrote a long letter from Taymouth Castle, setting forth his views regarding the matter. He recommended that Sir William be patient with George, remember how helpful he had been taking care of business details after John's death, while his brother was absent in America. However, he continued, William was entirely right when it came to his selling Logiealmond. After all, some way must be found of paying John's colossal debts.

If Archibald joined in the family disapproval, which it is impossible to believe he did not, he must have come to Murthly and expressed his ire in person; no letter from him on the burning question of selling Logiealmond has shown up.

In the meantime, Robert Campbell wrote that he was offering mountain men $200 for each buffalo they captured and sent him for shipment to England, but they said the beasts were too hard to get. However, he had collected a number of other beasts for Sir William and would send them over soon.

An earlier letter from Sublette thanked Sir William for a fine cow who had a calf two months after she arrived at St. Louis. He asked for a horse of dray breed, and mentioned deer and buffalo he had sent to Murthly. The exchange of animals between Sir William and his two closest friends among the mountain men continued for a long time. The game preserves of Murthly became well stocked with strange animals—birds as well—from the Far West of America.

Months passed. Details of the sale continued under discussion by the lawyers. Neither George nor the two elderly spinsters indicated that they intended to move. The sale was finally completed, the Earl of Mansfield paying £203,000 for the property, or about a million dollars in round numbers—and what nice, round numbers they were—computed by the value of the English pound at that time.

Soon after the final legal steps were taken, the Earl of Mansfield—a kindly man who had no possible use for the decaying old castle anyway—went one day by carriage to call on the two Leddies o' Logie. He intended to tell them that they—George, too—were welcome to live there as long as they liked. A servant met him at the door, listened to his announcement that he had come to call on the Misses Drummond, and padded away. After an interval, the servant returned with the message that the ladies did not care to receive the Earl of Mansfield. His dignity unruffled, but feeling considerable inner resentment, the earl withdrew to his carriage and was driven back to Scone Palace.

Following this episode, George and his maiden aunts received a formal notice from the Earl of Mansfield's lawyer requesting them to vacate Logiealmond. This communication, couched in legal phraseology, convinced them that facts were facts and had better be faced. They lost no time in buying Braco Castle, in Perthshire not far from Murthly, and took up their residence there. George, as incapable of sustained anger as a kitten, was soon back on a friendly footing with his brother. But neither aunt ever again gave the slightest indication that she was aware of William's existence. Elizabeth, the older of the two sisters, died soon after the move to Braco, leaving Marie-Frances and George to live there alone.

The records of Sir William's life now and then contain items that rouse curiosity more than they enlighten. One such reveals that Sir William Drummond Stewart inherited from a distant relative the euphonious and romantic title of Lord of Lorn. Whether any estates came with it is not known. Probably not. All that is certain at present is that the title was one of great antiquity, having been established sometime prior to 1414, in a distant branch of the Stewart family. So far as is known, Sir William never used the title.

As soon as the money from the sale of Logiealmond was available to Sir William, he paid John's debts to the last farthing. Then he gave instructions to Thomas concerning the building of Rohallion and Laguna, the priests' house. That done, in company with Antoine and the two Indians, he set off for America. They sailed sometime in August, 1842, on the *Weston*. After an uneventful voyage, the party arrived in New York on September 7. Here they were met by J. Watson Webb and taken to his home for the duration of their stay in the city.

On the same day that Sir William arrived in America, an elaborate social affair was being given in his name at the Murthly estate. Lord and Lady Glenlyon were in charge of this momentous occasion, a luncheon held in Dunkeld for Queen Victoria and Prince Albert. The royal couple was making its second visit to Scotland, and Sir William had asked his friends at Blair Castle, Lord and Lady Glenlyon, to offer the sovereign and her consort refreshments in his name, while on their way to Lord Breadalbane's castle. Later the visitors would go to Blair Castle for a short stay.

Victoria rode under arches of heather and juniper over the bridge spanning the Tay. They reached Dunkeld at one o'clock, greeted by chimes from the cathedral bells. A gaily colored marquee, over a hundred feet long, stood on the north side of Dunkeld's ancient cathedral. From this vantage point Victoria and Albert reviewed a parade of Murthly tenants, all wearing resplendent Scottish costumes, the marchers interspersed by the best bagpipe players of the district, each exerting all his lung power to bring forth the skirling Highland tunes.

The decibels produced by the pipers would have shattered any modern microphone at close range but they came sweetly to Victoria's aching eardrums. Here was noisy proof that hers and Albert's first visit to Scotland had paid off. Her Scottish subjects had been won over to accept the rule of England, and would cause her no more trouble.

Since a real Scottish feast could not be thought of as complete without haggis, that noble dish appeared on the board as one—if not the main—delicacy served to the royal couple. Truly a product of Scotland, the basic ingredient of this concoction was oatmeal. But it is the materials added to the oatmeal, and its manner of cooking, that give haggis its distinctive flavor. Proportions were left up to the cook's discretion but the following ingredients were required: to a large pot of simmering oatmeal suitable amounts were added of coarsely chopped onions, hearts, lungs, liver and small intestines (the *boudins* of the trapper) of almost any available animal. Also, salt and pepper, of course. The cook who masterminded this operation then stuffed the mixture into a sheep's stomach, sewed it up firmly, and boiled the object for several hours.

To Scottish tastebuds, trained from infancy to appreciate haggis, it was—still is, probably—the ultimate delicacy. To people of other cultures it does not usually appear in that favorable light. If Victoria, who was English, and Albert, who was German, managed to swallow more than one mouthful, they proved their devotion to Scotland then and there.

The dessert for their sumptuous luncheon bore the euphonious name of Athole-brose. Being Scottish, it of course contained oatmeal. The only other ingredient mentioned in the contemporary account of the dish—or drink, whichever it might have been—is whisky. Queen Victoria is said to have "tasted" Athole-brose from a Neil Gow glass, one of the treasures of the Atholl family, to which Lord Glenlyon belonged. Neil Gow, a violinist, had spent most of his lifetime collecting old folk songs of the country, writing them down, and popularizing them. The Scottish people, proud of their past, burning with a sense of nationalism, revered him as more than a national hero. No greater honor could have been shown Queen Victoria than to serve to her Athole-brose in a Neil Gow glass; the significance, we may be sure, was not lost on either the queen or her politically astute consort.

Promptly at three forty-five the royal couple departed for Taymouth Castle. Here they stayed several days with Lord Breadalbane and his semi-invalid lady, then went on to visit Lord and Lady Glenlyon at Blair Castle on the Till.

Victoria wrote in her journal a brief account of that day, of which the following is an excerpt.

We saw where once stood Birnam Wood, so renowned in Macbeth. We passed a pretty shooting lodge of Sir William Drummond Stewart's, "Rohallion," nearly at the foot of Birnam. Murthly is on the right, and belongs to Sir William, and is in a fine situation with the Tay winding along under the hill. There is lovely scenery all along to Dunkeld. Approaching Taymouth Castle we drove along the banks of the Tay under fine trees and saw Lord Breadalbane's American

buffaloes. Albert rejoiced in the beauties of Nature, the mountains, the pure air.

In New York, when Sir William arrived, the effects of the
great depression were still being felt. J. Watson Webb, being a
very clever businessman, as well as having the good fortune to
belong to a family of wealth, had so far ridden out the financial
storm. He still held control of his newspapers and was at the
head of several other fairly lucrative enterprises.

However, he reported to Sir William that many of his friends
had not been so fortunate and the country, on the whole, was in
bad shape. Webb was pessimistic as to when the financial tide
would turn, since the government stubbornly refused to act. He
expressed a strong wish that Sir William would complete a novel
he had begun while in the wilds, so it could be prepared for the
press. This story was later published under the title of *Altowan*,
a fictionized and badly written account of the Scotsman's adventures in the West. This volume and a later one titled *Edward
Warren*, were written, Sir William stated, for the amusement of
the Webb children. This may have influenced Webb to take an
active interest in the publication of the two manuscripts. As a
newspaperman, he must have known they were written in a stiff,
affected style and made extremely dull reading, even though public
interest in the Far West was then at the boiling point.

Webb's gloomy outlook on business conditions in the United
States was underlined by a letter Sir William received from Sublette, one of the most experienced business and mountain men in
the entire country. Sublette wrote that he was in great need of
money, but could raise none in St. Louis. Would his friend loan
him $8000 for his firm (the partnership of Sublette and Camp-
bell?) and $4000 for himself? The money would be secured by
his personal real estate, which had never before been mortgaged.
He went on to say that he might be forced to draw on Sir William
for $5000 before a reply could be received and that he had already
drawn on his friend for $1100. To illustrate how hard money was
to come by, he related that he had become so hungry for buffalo
meat he had bought horses to go after a supply, then found he

didn't have enough available cash to make the trip. He and Sir William would eat ham the coming winter, and wait for buffalo meat until spring. As an afterthought, Sublette added that Thompson, of Old Franklin, had secured a black-tailed deer for the Scotsman.

There is no record of the reply that was sent to this almost desperate letter. But Sir William's pleasure in furnishing all the money Sublette needed was certainly deep and sincere. With the help thus afforded him, Sublette managed to steer a safe course through the financial storm and eventually recovered his former position as one of the wealthiest men in St. Louis.

Leaving New York, Sir William traveled to Baltimore, where he stayed at Barnum's hotel. While there, he and Miller talked over old times and planned for the future. During this visit the Scotsman commissioned Miller to execute two more large pictures for the new chapel, not yet built, at Murthly. The subjects of these pictures were to be "Christ's Charge to Peter" and "Jeptha's Vow." Miller promised to deliver the first one in 1846, the second in 1847, by which time the chapel would be completed. The artist was to receive $800 for one, $1000 for the other.

Sir William reached New Orleans in November. He sent Antoine and the two Indians up to St. Louis with orders to await his arrival there in the early spring. No doubt Sublette or Campbell saw to it that the three were suitably taken care of, now that General Clark was no longer alive to exert his fatherly guidance.

Sir William was welcomed in the delta city by his many friends there, among them E. B. Nichols. This gentleman had been married about three months before to a beautiful young lady named Margaret Clayton Stone, and the newly-weds were still honeymooning in the city. Nichols, bubbling over with enthusiasm and prosperity, had great plans for the future. Because of his business of selling cotton in foreign markets, the depression had scarcely touched him with its paralyzing hand, and his New Orleans wholesale drug business, in partnership with a man named Rice, continued to be gratifyingly prosperous.

Nichols had interesting news for his Scottish friend, besides that of his marriage. He had become enamored of Texas—believed that it held great potentialities for expansion and consequent profit to those who had sense enough to get in on the ground floor. This was adopting the forward look and no mistake, since at that time Texas did not belong to the United States, was an independent struggling republic, with Sam Houston as its president. Everything about it was backward, raw, undeveloped. It had declared its independence of Mexico only seven years before, following a bloody and decisive battle with General Santa Ana's troops. Mexico still did not admit the independence of the valiant little republic and continued to harass it with sporadic military forays along the southern border. But Great Britain, the United States, France and Belgium had recognized the Republic of Texas.

Hostile bands of Indians roamed about during the first years, attacking with murderous intent small settlements, adobe ranch houses, and anyone with the temerity to journey across the land except with a well-armed escort. At one time Texas currency became so debased that a dollar bill was worth only two cents. The situation in 1843 was only slightly improved.

Despite all this, Nichols's enthusiasm regarding the future of Texas blazed on unabated. His apparently unfounded infatuation caused many of his associates to consider him a wild dreamer. He and a handful of men who joined him in the 1840's talked big and spent money big. They stamped their characters and personalities on Texas and its people for all time to come.

Nichols invited his friend Sir William to accompany him and his new wife to the fine home he had built on an extensive plantation he was in the process of creating near Dickinson Bayou about twenty miles north of Galveston. It lacked several months of the time when Sir William could start for the Rockies, so he gladly accepted this opportunity to see still another part, and an almost undeveloped part, of the great continent of North America.

The party went by way of Galveston. There Sir William must have viewed with strong mental reservations the straggling huddle of shacks that constituted the town. The unprepossessing village stood on a low, almost sliverlike island with an area of about eight square miles, at the entrance of Galveston Bay. Jean Lafitte and his band of pirates had been ousted from this site a mere twenty years before. The first American settlers had been there only six years. Even when riding through the wilderness of Illinois and Indiana, Sir William had seen nothing with the look of struggle against hopeless odds that Galveston presented to the eye in the first months of 1843.

From this poor, mean-looking settlement the party traveled northward to Dickinson Bayou. Here Nichols had built a home and begun the task of converting the surrounding acres into a plantation. He called the place Nicholstone, a combination of his name and that of his wife. The gracious, southern-style mansion was furnished as handsomely and luxuriously as any home in New Orleans or St. Louis. Once inside its walls, the barren, uninhabited stretches of Texas seemed as unreal as a dream.

The two men talked long together as they rode over the plantation, or sat before the great fireplace at night, watching the flames, sipping cordials, discussing plans and political moves on which the reality of all Nichols's dreams depended. Nichols declared that it was only a matter of time—and a short time, at that—until the United States would annex Texas, peacefully, of course. There would be objections from the Mexican population, but hearty approval from American settlers in the young republic. It followed, then, that a large number of people from the United States must be induced to come to Texas with the idea of making it their permanent home.

In this patriotic and worthy endeavor Nichols intended to play a leading role, and make a fortune for himself at the same time. He had already bought large tracts of land near Galveston and Austin, and was prepared to go into the real estate business on a large scale. All kinds of improvements would follow, including railroads. Texas would become the twenty-seventh state in the Union. . . . The talk went on and on.

Before Sir William left Nicholstone he was convinced of the great future in store for Texas. It is possible that he invested money in real estate or railroad bonds. At any rate, his interest in the state and in the Nichols family continued throughout his life.

Back in New Orleans again, Sir William definitely formulated his plans for the excursion he intended to lead into the mountains as soon as spring brought sufficient grass to support the animals.

First of all, he must gather together a company large enough to make an Indian attack unlikely.

This trip, Sir William knew, would bear only a superficial resemblance to the trade caravans he knew so well and now were a thing of the past. He and his companions might travel the same routes, camp in the same places. But now the underlying spirit, the very purposes, were different. For most of the men who would go along, this tour would be one of sport, adventure, fun, not business, as the old caravans had been. There would be none of the drive to get to the rendezvous ahead of the other fellow, out-price and outtrade him when you got there, collect by fair means or foul the most beaver plews and buffalo robes to sell in St. Louis.

This would be a carefree junket, with little to guard against except some desultory horse stealing at night. There would be no trade goods or foofaraw packed along with which to buy furs from the Indians, or sell to the trappers for the adornment of their temporary dusky lady-loves. All the carts and pack horses would be laden with what it took to make the trip more comfortable, more pleasant, more enjoyable. There would, of course, be some space allotted for transporting a certain amount of cheap, colorful presents for distribution to casually met redskins along the way, as a gesture of good will. This jaunt was to be strictly for fun.

For Sir William there was the fun, of course, but also a more serious aspect. It was to be a nostalgic return, and for the last time, to scenes that he loved and where he had experienced the greatest happiness his restless spirit would ever know—release from restrictions imposed on him by his life in Scotland. Soon he would again take up that life to which he had been born and from which he could never permanently escape.

Sir William reached another decision. This was that he would take with him, with a few notable exceptions, only young men with no experience in the wonderful world to which he intended to introduce them, or in any world that had been hard, difficult or really dangerous. Furthermore, he would exert over these young men a discipline as unyielding as might have been imposed by the Iron Duke, his military hero under whom he had served in his youth. Even though conditions on the prairies and among the Rockies had changed to some extent since Sir William's earlier travels, these young, untried adventurers would come back different in character from when they set out. Maybe better, maybe worse, but different.

In fact, he determined to combine on this trip the three seemingly incompatible ways of life toward which his diverse character strongly attracted him—the world of adventure, the world of military discipline, and the world of luxury.

His plan may or may not have been a good one. Good or bad, it was sure to result in trouble for somebody.

CHAPTER XXIII

Matt Field and Company

In New Orleans Sir William kept his eyes open for suitable young men to accompany him on his excursion to the Rocky Mountains. His attention was attracted by a lively, intelligent young fellow named Matthew C. Field. Although Matt was only thirty years old, he had behind him a curiously varied experience. After finishing his education, he had opened a jewelry store. Almost at once he discovered that keeping a shop bored him. So he sold his property and became an actor. He liked the stage and soon achieved considerable success. Then someone offered him the chance to go to Santa Fe with a caravan of traders—no small adventure in the late 1830's. He accepted the opportunity without hesitation. When Sir William met him, he was assistant editor of the New Orleans *Picayune* and wrote what we would now call feature articles for that paper.

On Sir William's 1837 excursion he had taken an artist, with most gratifying results. Why not take a writer this time? Matt Field, versatile, adaptable, talented, and with a wide streak of whimsical gaiety, seemed the perfect choice. But when the matter was put up to him, he hesitated. Yes, he had traveled to Santa Fe with a wagon train and so was experienced in prairie travel. However, circumstances had changed since then. He now had a wife and baby to support.

Sir William promptly offered to assume all the expenses of Matt's trip and to make generous provisions for his little family while he was gone. The *Picayune* would, of course, pay him well for any accounts of the trip that he sent back to them, or wrote after his return.

Matt then agreed to go. He had a reason which possibly he did not confide to his patron. Matt thought he had tuberculosis, and at that time people considered a trip to the Rockies a sure cure for this disease. As a matter of fact, Matt didn't have tuberculosis at all; he had stomach ulcers. A diet of buffalo meat might not seem the best cure for this ailment, but apparently it did him no harm.

Sir William met another young man in New Orleans whom he invited to accompany him to the mountains. George Wilkins Christy, twenty-four years old, had just started practicing law. Tempted by the double lure of adventure and travel, he light-heartedly deserted his profession, promising to join Sir William in St. Louis a few weeks later. What with one thing and another, he did not return to the law until after he had distinguished himself fighting in the Civil War. Another young fellow, George E. Hepburn, was hired as a hunter.

Taking leave of New Orleans, Sir William went by steamboat to St. Louis, where there ensued a great reunion of old friends. It had been arranged long before that Bill Sublette would accompany the train as captain, but this time Sir William would be commander, not of the night guard, but of the entire expedition. Sublette was overjoyed at the prospect of returning to the mountains. Once more he would hear the creak of saddle leather, gaze on the wide expanse of prairie, look up to the sky-reaching peaks, eat pemmican, taste the unmatched flavor of hump ribs roasted on a stick before the campfire.

Now began the almost feverish activity of buying horses, charettes, and supplies of different kinds and in greater variety and amounts than had ever before been taken to the mountains; of hiring hunters, packers, cooks, and so on. Antoine was there to help Sublette with many of the details. The half-breed was an experienced mountain man in his own right, and dependable—most of the time. He made only one request, that he be permitted to bring with him his fifteen-year-old brother, François, and Sir William readily consented.

One man whom Sublette hired to drive a cart has a special claim to our interest. He was Baptiste Charbonneau, son of Sacajawea, the young, pretty Snake woman who had guided Lewis and Clark across the northern plains to the Rocky Mountains in 1805, then went with them to the Pacific Ocean. Baptiste's father was Toussaint Charbonneau, Sacajawea's husband, a French trapper and interpreter. The child had been born in a Mandan village far up the Missouri River where Lewis and Clark wintered.

Little Baptiste had become a favorite of William Clark's and when the boy was old enough to leave his mother, Clark brought him to St. Louis. Here he received a good basic education in the schools of the city, learning French, arithmetic, and—of all things —Roman history. In 1823, when Baptiste was eighteen, Prince Paul of Würtemberg, the first royal visitor to that region, came up the river. He took the boy back with him to Europe, where Baptiste stayed for six years. Prince Paul gave him a classical education, opportunity to travel, training in the etiquette of a royal court. So this young half-breed became, on the surface at least, a polished gentleman.

Returning to America, Baptiste discovered that he was neither Indian nor white, nor did he have any ambition to distinguish himself as a member of either race. Now, at the age of thirty-eight, he was content to drive a cart in an expedition that included among its members young Jeff Clark, son of the patron of his boyhood.

Long afterward someone asked Jeff if Baptiste often spoke of his famous mother. Jeff replied that most of Baptiste's talk was made up of uncomplimentary remarks concerning the stubborn mules he drove.

Sir William did not consider his luxurious jaunt to the Rocky Mountains in 1843 as entirely a pleasure excursion for himself and his guests. He definitely wanted it to have scientific significance as well. Before he left New York, and even previous to his departure from Scotland, he had begun to make arrangements to take with him—entirely at his own expense, and a sizeable expense it proved to be—a distinguished company of botanists.

While in St. Louis, Sir William received a letter from Samuel

Wade, a friend of his in New York. This gentleman heartily recommended Dr. Charles Mersch, originally of Luxemburg, as honorable, cooperative, brave, and able in his field. He would render signal service through his acquaintance with the Natural Kingdom. Wade's letter indicates that arrangements may already have been made between Sir William and Dr. Mersch. The botanist left New Orleans April 9, by steamboat, arriving in St. Louis some time before the expedition's scheduled departure.

He brought with him a number of instruments needed by a botanist in the pursuit of his work, and presented the bill to his patron, which the Scotsman paid:

Nautical Almanac	3.00
Barrand's silver pocket chronometer	225.00
Sextant	90.00
Artificial horizon	12.00
Connaisance de Temps	2.50
	332.50

It puts a serious strain on the credulity to believe that three other famous botanists, from three foreign countries, just happened to be in St. Louis that spring and that Sir William was suddenly moved to take them with him. Very probably they were there as the result of considerable previous correspondence. These men who joined him and Dr. Mersch were Friederich G. L. Luders and Charles A. G. Geyer, both of Germany, and Alexander Gordon of Scotland. Together, they made an imposing company of distinguished naturalists. Botanists all over the world were deeply interested in the many new plants that awaited discovery in the Far West. In taking these highly trained men with him, Sir William performed a valuable service to the science of botany.

At the same time, the world-famous naturalist, John James Audubon, waited in St. Louis for spring to produce the mild weather that would make possible his traveling into the wilds in search of further knowledge. He had recently completed his monumental work, *The Birds of America*, with 435 hand-colored plates and over a thousand life-size drawings of birds. Sir William offered to assume all the expense of Mr. Audubon's proposed trip and furnish him with a wagon, if the great man would join his party.

However, Audubon had already made arrangements to travel far up the Missouri in a boat belonging to the American Fur Company, and so could not accept.

Sir William invited another man to join his party, a professional rather than scientific gentleman, Dr. Steadman Tilghman, recently graduated from Baltimore Medical College. He was listed as official surgeon for the caravan.

In St. Louis that spring history was on the march, spearheaded by Lieutenant John Charles Frémont, who was getting ready for his second surveying trip west for the topographical engineers of the War Department. There is some indication that Sir William knew the young surveyor well, had probably been a frequent guest in his home. The Scotsman's interest in military and political affairs was such that he hardly could have been unaware that Frémont's mission had a more far-reaching significance than met the eye.

The year before, Frémont had accomplished two important objectives—surveyed a route from Independence to South Pass in the Rockies, and married Jessie Benton, eighteen-year-old daughter of Senator Thomas Hart Benton. It is hard to tell which achievement exerted the greater influence over the future course of his life.

This year Frémont had been ordered to survey a route westward from the Rocky Mountains to the Oregon settlements on the Columbia River. He was taking with him the finest and most complete set of surveying instruments that it was possible to assemble, in a wagon especially fitted up to carry them. His expedition would number some thirty-nine men, with the necessary pack animals, extra horses and supplies. The War Department wanted to know the most feasible route all the way to the Pacific Coast and they had entrusted to Lieutenant Frémont the task of ascertaining what that route was.

Though his outfit was a lavish one, Frémont coveted one thing the War Department had not seen fit to give him—a small cannon. Its possession would make his expedition into an armed party, which could have serious implications. He afterward said that he wanted the cannon to scare off Indians, and also that he took it to encourage Oregon settlers to make the trip with wagons, disregarding the facts that the previous year forty emigrant wagons had made the trip across by way of the South Pass with outstanding success and, even as he waited in St. Louis, 200 wagons were gathering at Westport to make the same westward journey.

Whatever Frémont's reason may have been for wanting the cannon, he prevailed on his friend, Colonel Stephen Watts Kearny, then commanding Jefferson Barracks, to let him have a twelve-pound howitzer, an accomplishment which must have required all of Frémont's persuasiveness and Jessie's charm. At about the same time these arrangements were completed, Thomas Fitzpatrick was secured to guide the expedition.

Sir William must have been aware of all these developments, and of their significance. Since no infraction of national boundaries could occur east of the Rocky Mountains, the Scotsman invited Frémont to join forces with him that far. But the army man planned to take the southern route across the plains, through the valley of the Kansas River, and so declined. The two men parted, agreeing to meet at Westport a few weeks hence.

What yardstick Sir William used to measure the suitability of the young men who were to accompany him as his guests on the proposed "hunting frolic" it is hard to determine. Some of those whom he invited belonged to old, wealthy St. Louis families. A few were impecunious but engaging privates and lieutenants from Jefferson Barracks who tossed away possible careers in the army for the chance to shoot buffalo on the Platte, camp amidst the fabled peaks of the Rocky Mountains, and take a look at completely uncivilized Indians. One young fellow proved to be wanted as a forger. Others were temperamentally unfitted to endure the rigors of the trail, and should never have been allowed to start. A few, though without previous experience in the mountains, were prepared to take everything that came with cheerfulness and fortitude. It seems not to have entered Sir William's mind that these disparate temperaments would certainly clash among themselves; and when they came in contact with his Wellingtonian ideas of discipline, real trouble was inevitable.

Fortunately, we have a rather detailed account of how two young gentlemen, each bearing proud old St. Louis names, came to join Sir William's expedition. They were Jefferson Kennerly

Clark, son of the famous William Clark, and his cousin, Clark Kennerly. Both were about eighteen years of age. Jeff Clark's mother had died when he was quite young. He had been taken into the Kennerly household, where he and Clark Kennerly were reared as brothers. Jeff had inherited the red hair and rounded facial contours of his father, in sharp contrast to Clark Kennerly's black hair and slim face.

One evening Sir William was dining at the Kennerly home. After the elaborate meal was over, the ladies retired to the drawing room. Then a Negro servant brought in a large crystal bowl of apple toddy and several homemade cordials for the gentlemen's enjoyment. In response to questions, Sir William related several of his western adventures. The two boys, unable to restrain their excited interest, begged for more, and before the evening was over, Sir William invited them to join his excursion. The consent of their parents and guardians was not easy to obtain, but they finally succeeded and made preparations to go. A colored servant accompanied each of these boys to take care of their horses and look after them generally. Other "young gentlemen" of means who later joined the train also took servants.

Among others from the old families of St. Louis who joined the expedition were Edmund Francis Xavier Chouteau, of the great Chouteau fur dynasty, known to his friends as Guesso; Cyprien Menard, son of Governor Pierre Menard, of Illinois; and John Bradford, son of Dr. Bradford and Harriet Kennerly, his wife.

Naturally, as a member of the Roman Catholic faith, Sir William went to pay his respects to Father Jean Pierre de Smet, S.J., a native of Belgium, who among many other achievements had helped to found that Jesuit educational institution, the University of St. Louis. In 1843 he was a member of the faculty and also head of all the Jesuit missionary work in the United States and Canada. The Scottish nobleman was received even more warmly than he had expected, for Father de Smet really needed him. Two years before, the Catholic dignitary and several other priests had journeyed to the Flatheads and established a mission which they named St. Mary's. It was situated not far from the Columbia, about 500 miles upstream from Fort Vancouver.

Once the mission was well started and substantial log buildings constructed, Father de Smet returned to St. Louis, promising to send reinforcements the following year. The priest had not been able to keep that pledge because there had been no fur caravans to act as escort for a missionary party. Sir William's expedition was, the priest felt, an answer to a prayer. The missionary party was organized, ready to go, and only awaited this heaven-sent opportunity. If Sir William would see them to the Rockies, they would take a chance on getting the rest of the way by themselves.

Sir William was happy to be of service. Father de Smet could not go himself, much to his regret. He was scheduled to make a fund-raising tour of Europe that summer. He would, however, accompany the party as far as the flourishing Catholic Mission in the country of the Shawnees, several miles out in the prairie from Westport.

The missionary party that accompanied Sir William included Father Peter de Vos, Belgian-born as was Father de Smet; Father Adrian Hoecken; two lay helpers, Brother John Baptiste MacGean and Brother Eneas, the latter a young Iroquois convert; and Solomon Sublette, guide.

As the time drew near to start for Westport, Sir William applied for and got a permit to transport liquor into the Rocky Mountains. Never before had so many kinds of fine alcoholic beverages been taken into the Far West. There would be no diluted whisky for *his* guests, nor would their metheglin be made on a base of raw alcohol. There would be no drunkenness either, except when the commander of the train gave his permission.

He took a hand in buying supplies, making sure there were lavish amounts of sugar, coffee, white flour, and so on. Charettes were packed with hams, tinned meats, preserved fruits, pickles, many varieties of cheese, condiments, even spices. Regulation canvas tents were provided for hired hands and "young gentlemen" alike. William Sublette may have looked on all this orgy of buying with disapproval; more likely, it was with tolerant amusement. After all, this trip was for fun, not business, except for the scientists and priests, of course.

One of the curious items that Sir William bought was a newfangled contraption called an "electrifying machine." It consisted of a box somewhat over a foot square containing a strong electric battery. A cord several feet long extended from each side, ending in a smooth metal handle that could be grasped in the hand. One person could use it, or a number of people simultaneously, if they all joined hands and the two at the ends gripped the handles firmly. When the electricity was turned on by means of a switch on the top of the box, a powerful current shot through those who had subjected themselves to the test, of sufficient strength to shake them up considerably and tighten their grip on the handles so they couldn't let go. Sir William thought this machine would be a fine thing with which to amaze and amuse the Indians.

His characteristic impulse to combine widely separated ways of living operated more strongly at this time than at any other period of his life. He would take his party west under a form of military discipline. He would experience the adventure of the trails, the rivers, the mountains, and mingle with savage people amidst the wildest scenes of nature. And he would do all this surrounded by luxury of which only he—or an Eastern potentate—could dream. What he achieved was little short of fantasy and fable, which was no doubt what he aimed to do. Sir William Stewart had no lack of originality and imagination.

He had made for himself a splendorous crimson tent, fourteen feet square, stout enough to stand against the worst that prairie or mountain could do in the way of wind, sleet, rain, or hail. Several folded buffalo robes formed his bed. Dozens of fine Irish linen sheets and towels occupied space in his wagon. Instead of blankets, there was a coverlid of Russian sable. Skins of leopard and otter made regal thrones out of packing boxes.

Of course his carved ivory toilette set would accompany him, along with the silver whisky flask engraved with the Stewart coat of arms and his traveling clock in its red leather case. A jewel-colored Persian carpet was provided to serve as a floor for the crimson tent. A king-size brass incense burner, intricately patterned, which he had picked up on one of his visits to Turkey, created the final exotic touch. Three servants went with him: Corbie, his Scottish valet; Adrian, a quarter-breed; and Tom, a boy from the Murthly estate.

At last, all was in readiness. The charettes, the wagons, goods, horses and hired hands went overland. Sir William, the "young gentlemen" to the number of about thirty, and the missionaries boarded the steamer *Weston,* and sailed upstream, destination Westport. It was the second of May.

One afternoon the boat halted and tied up at the bank, probably to take on wood for the insatiable boilers. Members of the Stewart party went on shore for a stroll. When they returned the *Weston* had burned to the water's edge. Since everything except clothing required for the few days on the river had been dispatched overland, their losses were not overwhelming. Most articles could be replaced in Independence. The party boarded the next steamer that came along and arrived at Westport several days ahead of the land party.

As soon as a few final arrangements could be completed, Sir William led his reunited company two miles out into the prairie, where they encamped in a grove of wild crab-apple trees, then in full bloom. Tents were set up, horses picketed, men on foot and on horseback moved about attending to the necessary tasks. The Methodist Shawnee Mission could be seen in the distance, and close by it a village of the Shawnee Indians. The Catholic missionary party did not stop here, but went to the Catholic Mission, about twelve miles farther on.

Some distance away Sir William could see the great assemblage of covered wagons belonging to the Oregon Emigration party, the vehicles numbering close to 200 now, with more than 900 men, women, and children encamped about them.

He had ridden over every mile they would travel to their destination on the Columbia. He had been a part of more than one fur caravan whose passing had beaten out the trail over which their wagon wheels could now roll. Reining his horse to a standstill, he must have looked at the scene before him for a long time, thinking, perhaps, of all it presaged: the eventual ownership of all the Oregon territory by the United States, soon the easy acquisition of California. These Oregon emigrants would suffer much on their journey, their agonies the growing pains of a nation destined for greatness.

Gray clouds advanced from the west, casting a shadow over the prairie. Sir William stirred in his saddle. He had old acquaintances in that wagon train. Tomorrow he would ride over and call on them. Rain began to fall. He turned his horse's head toward the crimson tent among the crab-apple trees.

The downpour that began that first afternoon continued almost without cessation for a full week. A dreary time. Mud everywhere, damp firewood, nothing to do but play cards and write letters home—with no interesting developments to write about. Already some of the more sensitive souls among the "young gentlemen" were beginning to grumble. What kind of pleasure excursion was this, anyway? Why this business of having to ask Sir William for permission to ride into Independence? Or even to the Shawnee Village? Intolerable. They'd go anyway. But they didn't. Sir William had learned from the Iron Duke how to command obedience and no spoiled, petulant youngster would have the temerity to disobey him. The sensible, level-headed men of the party understood without explanation their leader's reasons for the restrictions imposed on them, and accepted orders with no complaint.

Matt Field named the assemblage of tents in the crab-apple grove Camp William. Here they must wait until the grass, now only a green film over the prairie, became thick enough to nourish their horses. On the second day Sir William rode over to the emigrant camp and sought out the two missionaries he had met in other years. There was Reverend Jason Lee, returning to his flourishing settlement on the Willamette, with much to say about his successful trip east, his plans for the future.

No doubt Sir William found his visit with Dr. Marcus Whitman more pleasant than listening to Jason Lee. Marcus was on his way back to Waiilatpu, bringing with him supplies and farm tools needed at his growing establishment not far from Fort Walla Walla. He was enthusiastic, full of talk about the outlook for expanding his work. Sir William felt a deep satisfaction in the doctor's success. He sent his warmest regards to Narcissa. Both men were mercifully unaware that only four years later, Marcus and Narcissa would die at the hands of the treacherous Cayuse Indians, all the work of their well-intentioned, unselfish lives brought to a tragic end.

The rain ceased at last, temporarily. Sunshine brought increased cheerfulness to those encamped on the prairie, but waiting

for grass to grow was a tedious business. To break the monotony
of Camp William, Matt—the old Shakesperean actor—recruited
helpers and put on a scene from *Romeo and Juliet*. "Juliet," a
young man named Powers, played the balcony scene from a wagon
while "Romeo" (Matt Field, who else?) declaimed his passionate
lines in the pale light of a tin-lantern moon. This somewhat du-
bious entertainment was followed by a song entitled, "The Little
Pigs," rendered by Dr. Tilghman. Except for such theatricals, and
attending a Shawnee dance or two, the boys had little to amuse
them.

On Sunday, May 14, Sir William, Matt Field, and several
others of the party, rode over to the Catholic Mission and attended mass there. The service was held in a rough log chapel
only large enough to accommodate about sixty people. Father de
Smet officiated. The following day De Smet set out on his return
journey to St. Louis. This man, not only a priest but an educator
and organizer, was the most successful missionary the Far West
ever saw. The reasons are not hard to discern. He loved the Indians as persons, not merely as souls to be saved from hellfire. He
felt compassion for them. They were Stone Age people and he
accepted them as such, having no desire to make them over into
white men. His attitude, in direct contrast to that of the Protestant
missionaries in the same field, can best be shown by quotations
from his writings: "The morals of this savage race can scarcely be
termed corrupt, considering their very limited means of enlightenment." And: "Laxity of morals [among the tribes] is far short of
what it might be supposed inevitable in their rude, uneducated
state."

No wonder the priests he trained and the missions he founded
were beloved by the red men.

Then one day Lieutenant Frémont's party arrived, consisting
of thirty men, ten or twelve carts, a wagon, and the howitzer.
They halted a mile or so away from Camp William. The Scotsman and Sublette rode over at once to visit their old friend, Fitzpatrick, and talk for a while with Frémont. The army man told
them he had a number of matters to take care of in Independence and might not get away for ten days or so. Sir William expected to leave sooner than that, for the grass was growing rapidly

now. He would go northward toward the Platte, while Frémont planned to continue west along the Kansas River.

One morning excitement swirled among the tents of Camp William. Two officers of the law rode up, dismounted, and arrested a man named Watson who had joined the party, at Sir William's invitation, before they left St. Louis. Watson was charged with stealing and altering United States bonds, several months earlier, in New Orleans. He was taken to Independence and put in jail. The Stewart party saw young Watson no more, though Matt and one or two companions rode into Independence and visited the young miscreant there, perhaps more because they were curious to see the inside of the jail than anything else.

Every day the grass thickened and grew taller. The Oregon Emigrant party, too large to make traveling in one body practical, split into sections of fifty or sixty wagons each. One section pulled out into the prairie and disappeared into the vast distance. A day or so later another group started.

Sometime during the last week in May—those who were there, including Matt Field and William Sublette, disagree as to the exact day—Sir William struck camp and the party began their march across the lush green prairie, already dotted with countless wild flowers. They would join the priests' party, captained by Solomon Sublette, late that afternoon on the banks of a small stream named Muddy Creek.

William Sublette's view of the caravan as it started out that morning was perhaps somewhat sardonic. Writing about it in his journal, he said, "Some of the armey. Some professional gentlemen. Some on a trip for pleasure. Some for health, etc., etc. So we have Doctors, Lawyers, botanists, Bugg Ketchers, Hunters and men of nearly all professions, etc., etc."

But Sublette was on the way to his beloved haunts in the Rockies and his old friend—in spite of all the fancy fixin's—was still Bill Stewart, the mountain man. It really made little difference to him who marched behind them.

CHAPTER XXIV

A Touch of Crimson

&v After leaving Camp William, the Stewart caravan traveled until midafternoon, when they came up with the missionaries, waiting for them on the banks of Muddy Creek. Both groups passed without difficulty through the shallow water, as brown and frothy as a chocolate sundae, and encamped together on the farther side. Servants erected the crimson tent and spread the Persian carpet, a ritual that was enacted each evening until, on the return trip, an accident put a stop to it. The other men chose to sleep under the charettes and wagons as being more adventurous. For most of the "young gentlemen" it was the first night of their lives spent in the open, without sheltering walls.

Next morning as soon as breakfast was over, the long caravan stretched itself out and moved across the prairie. At its head rode Sir William and Sublette on their fine mounts. Next came the two-horse wagon and ten carts belonging to the commander, their crimson-painted tops brave and gay against the bright green of the prairie grass. The "young gentlemen" on horseback with their eight or ten carts, servants and wagon came next, then the hired hands of the party, numbering some thirty or thirty-five. The priests had six carts, one two-horse wagon, and a vehicle which Sublette, writing in his journal, sometimes called a "carriol" and sometimes a "berouche"—a carry-all or barouche being a light, four-wheeled covered carriage. Included in the priests' outfit were about twenty men, a coop full of squawking, frightened chickens, and an indeterminate number of loose cows, oxen, and horses.

Strung out in single file, the long train of charettes, wagons and horsemen made a splendid sight as it wound sinuously along in the bright spring weather. Viewed from a distance, it might almost have been a caravan of centuries past, bringing carved ivory and jade from Mongolia to old Peking. On closer approach, any such impression would have been rudely shattered by the language of the men who drove the tandem-hitched mules pulling the charettes.

A few days' easy travel brought the party over the softly undulating, treeless prairie to where they could see ahead of them the heavily wooded banks of the Kansas River. Here, while still on the open prairie, the whole of the Oregon Emigration had reassembled. Halting the train, Sir William rode over to see what was up. It appeared that dissatisfaction with the leaders had arisen and the emigrants were holding an election in an effort to select others whom they hoped would have more acceptable ideas of how a wagon train should be managed. The candidates stood at different spots on the prairie. As each candidate's name was called out, the men of the train who wished to vote for him joined a line that formed a queue in his rear. This done, the candidates for office marched their henchmen here and there, around and around, until the "votes" had been counted. Sir William wished them well, returned to his own party, and went on, leaving the emigrants behind. No one in Sir William's train saw them again.

The many fine trees of oak, black walnut, and other varieties of hardwood that grew along the river afforded welcome relief after the monotony of the prairie expanse. But here they met real difficulty. Their carts and wagons could not be driven across the deep, swift, 200-yard-wide river, swollen by the unusually heavy rains. There was a ferry of sorts, operated by two brothers, Joseph and Louis Papin. The "ferry boat" consisted of a wooden platform resting on three large dugout canoes, the unwieldly contraption being propelled by men with long poles.

After many anxious trips, the vehicles were safely transported to the other bank. Then came real trouble. The stock, rejecting the idea of swimming across the cold, turbulent river, had to be coerced individually into entering the stream. One mule got his head wedged under a low-hanging tree-branch and was almost drowned before he could be extricated. Sir William and Sublette dismounted, pushed, pulled, swore with the others. It was one of those nightmarish experiences that make amusing stories, long afterward, when told in safe, comfortable surroundings.

Everything was in order and on the trail again. Wind and sun quickly dried their clothes. Some distance away, three Indians appeared, riding toward them. The savages proved to be Pawnees, curiously subdued and acting like frightened jack rabbits. Their spokesman explained to Sir William in barely understandable English, interspersed with sign language, that they had become separated from their companions two days before. Knowing they were in the country of the Osages, their mortal enemies, they were plenty scared. Would the white man let them join his train until they came to the territory of their own race on the Platte?

Sir William agreed to this, and the three Pawnees dropped back to the rear of the cavalcade.

During the morning of June 5, the party came to the Vermillion River. No ferry here, but the water was not deep. The horses could have hauled the charettes and wagons through without difficulty. But, perhaps remembering the Kansas, they refused even to try. The vehicles had to be dragged across by sweating, cursing manpower, and the horses led to the other side.

Beyond the Vermillion they had their first brush with hostile Indians. A party of trigger-happy Osages to the number of about seventy rode up, circled the caravan at full gallop, yelling and waving lances, from a few of which fresh scalps dangled. In spite of their threatening attitude, Sir William did not think they would attack, since his force outnumbered their own. But savages were always unpredictable, and especially so if excited by the possession of newly taken scalps.

As a precautionary measure, he ordered the train into close formation. The three Pawnees, recognizing the new arrivals on the scene as Osages, were so panicked that they dismounted from their horses and ran toward the priests' wagon, intending to crawl inside. The Osages saw the three fugitives, grabbed them, took possession of the poor wretches' blankets and weapons, tied their hands behind their backs and were hustling them away, when Sir William galloped onto the scene. Gun drawn, he ordered the Osages to free their prisoners. Father de Vos and Father Hoecken hurried to Sir William's assistance and backed him up with commands and exhortations. Several men from the caravan advanced and forcibly released the prisoners from the grasp of their captors. Sir William ordered the caravan to resume its march.

The Osages, furious but afraid to attack such a large and resolute party, once more circled the train at full speed, yelling threats. Watchful, but showing no fear, the cavalcade advanced. The Indians kept up their attentions until evening, when they became discouraged and rode away, to the white men's relief.

There already had been several brief but violent prairie storms which the men had taken more or less in their stride. Now came a storm that showed what nature could do here when she put her mind to it. One afternoon a great wind blew, bringing with it dark gray clouds that fired stinging arrows of rain, then bullet-like hailstones as large as marbles. The animals turned their rumps to the wind, put their heads down, and refused to move. The men, wet, cold, and miserable, waited out the furious onslaught with what endurance they could muster. Finally the wind fell from hurricane velocity to gale proportions; the animals were induced once more to take to the trail. Light faded early, shut off by clouds. Rain continued to fall. Sir William's tent was set up with much difficulty. The rank and file put up their tents for the first time. No chance for campfires. Cold and hungry, the members of the company waited out the night in utter discomfort.

Next morning dawned bright and clear. The men soon recovered their good humor. Several days passed uneventfully. The greenhorns began to voice complaints because there were no buffalo. Old hands knew that any expectation of seeing buffalo until they were well up the Platte was nonsense. One day Antoine shot an antelope and they had their first taste of fresh meat since leaving Camp William.

At last they reached the Platte and started up that river, following along on its southern bank. Here another storm hit them, worse than the one they had experienced the week before. Matt Field reported that water stood three inches deep inside his tent and that he and the members of his mess stood up all night, indicating that neither he nor his companions were sufficiently trail-wise to circle the tent with a ditch to carry off excess water. Their supper that night consisted of whisky and crackers, well enough in themselves, at suitable times and places, but leaving something to to be desired when substituting for a square meal.

While the gloomy mood in Matt's tent was at its darkest, a fight started outside. Everyone rushed for his gun. One young man, conceded to be the wit of the party, called a halt to the proceedings both in and out of the tent by declaring that if there was any shooting to be done, he would like to hire himself out to be shot, for a small remuneration. In the shout of laughter that followed, everybody forgot what had started the fight.

Good weather returned. At last, well up the Platte beyond its confluence with the Loup, Antoine, who had ridden ahead to scout for game, suddenly galloped into camp to exchange his mule for a fast horse. He yelled that buffalo were ahead. Fourteen men, most of them greenhorns, jumped on their horses, and accompanied Antoine as he returned to the chase. One, however, was Joe Pourier, a professional hunter whose reputation was second only to Antoine's. After much galloping, chasing and shooting, two of the great beasts were brought low. Antoine and Joe applied themselves to the task of butchering the animals, sending the rest of the men back to camp for sumpter mules to transport the meat.

Arriving at the South Fork of the Platte, the party crossed the river without much trouble and camped on the other side. Next morning they headed toward the North Platte, more than a day's journey away. The country was barren of vegetation except for an occasional clump of dwarfed sagebrush, struggling to keep alive. Heat quivered up from the ground, enveloping them like the blast from a steel furnace. Following the unwritten dictum of the mountain and prairie that only the western equivalent of sissies carried water on their journeys, they were without any means of quenching their thirst. By midafternoon, animals as well as men were thoroughly uncomfortable, though by trail standards they were not yet really suffering for lack of a drink.

When reaching the country where hostile Indians might be expected, their leader had issued strict orders that only the official hunters and a few other experienced men were to leave the close proximity of the train without permission. This restriction was especially galling to the greenhorns of the party and stirred up hot resentment among them.

At one side of the trail, perhaps a half mile away, one or two young men saw a small canyon debouching on the plain, with a suspicion of green at its mouth that promised water. Knowing that asking permission from their commander to investigate was useless, one rider, then another, wheeled out of the line of march and headed for the canyon, until the recalcitrant ones numbered about fifteen. Unnoticed by either Sir William or Sublette, they rode into the green coolness of the canyon. There they found a grove of ash trees and a trickling stream of almost icy water. Whooping with joy, they flung themselves from their horses, drank deeply and long from the small pool among the rocks.

The damp, almost chilly air of this sheltered spot brought great relief from the heat of the plain. Lying on the grass, the young men yielded to the apparently irresistible impulse that overpowered most western travelers of that time: the urge to apply a name to every place that seemed at all notable. With complete lack of originality, they decided to call this idyllic spot Ash Hollow.

Later, they found out that the little canyon had been known as Ash Hollow to most travelers along the Platte since the earliest days of the fur trade. Probably Sir William and certainly Sublette were aware of its existence. They passed it by on this occasion because they were anxious to reach a good camping place they knew of farther along on a small tributary of the Platte.

After a while returning sanity brought to the young men a realization of their situation—a small party far from the caravan that, while they dallied here, had been advancing steadily in the direction of the North Platte, with no one in authority aware of their absence. Springing to their horses, they lost no time making their way back to the hot plain. The caravan was out of sight. At a considerable distance one solitary horseman could be seen, his back toward them. They decided he must be one of their party and set up a chorus of warwhoops to attract his attention. The

rider disappeared, and though they searched for him, he could not
be found. Riding hard, they caught up with the train as soon as
possible and told their story to Sir William.

Sir William's anger at the disobedience of his orders had to
be swallowed for the nonce. First, who was missing? It proved to
be Cyprien Menard. The next necessity was to get his train to
water for some of the animals were showing their distress. By the
time that was accomplished, night made search for their absent
companion impossible. Many lay awake through the hours of
darkness, waiting, hoping, listening, for young Menard's return.
Morning dawned: no Cyprien. They went on to the Platte, hoping
to find the missing young man waiting for them there. But only
silence and emptiness greeted them.

Sir William immediately dispatched search parties, but met
with no success. Anxiety increased. A second day went by spent
in the same fruitless efforts. Gloom filled the camp. Everyone
gave young Cyprien up for dead, either from thirst or an Indian's
tomahawk. Next morning the march was resumed, following along
the banks of the Platte. It wasn't long until Sublette's alert eyes
saw a weather-whitened buffalo skull with curious black marks on
it lying close beside the trail. He picked it up. Written on the
skull with a charred stick were the words:

> June 28—Evening. I have lost my horse, my feet are
> bare and sore, I am hungry and tired, my ammunition is gone,
> assist me soon or I perish.
>
> MENARD

A party of young men, accompanied by the intrepid Father
Hoecken, hastily put food in their pockets and set off at a brisk
pace ahead of the train. Five or six miles farther they found another buffalo skull bearing the words:

> June 29—Menard is still on the Platte and will continue
> so. Please hasten to me, as my feet are so sore I can go no
> farther.

He did go farther, however, because of his mistaken notion
that the train was ahead of him. The search party hurried forward.
Evening was almost upon them when they found Menard on the

bank of the Platte, crouching over a small fire cooking four terrapins he had managed to catch. It was indeed a glad reunion. Matt's
comment was that Cyprien "looked dreadful" but "showed brave
heart and spirit." He had been absent from the train for four
days. His friends produced what food they had and he devoured
it, abandoning the half-cooked terrapins.

As soon as the exhausted young man had recovered, at least
to some extent, he told his story. The realistic yells of his friends
at Ash Hollow had convinced him they were Indians after his
scalp. He had quickly hidden himself among the rocks and stayed
there for hours, afraid to move. When darkness came he picketed
his horse and using his saddle for a pillow, went to sleep. During
the night his horse escaped. Next morning he crossed the intervening miles to the Platte, reaching that stream at a point ahead of
the caravan, and went on while they lingered, sending out search
parties to look for him somewhere behind them. Cyprien struggled
on toward Fort Laramie, knowing that if he could stay alive that
long, he would find help there. The buffalo-skull messages had
been left in the forlorn hope that a band of wandering trappers,
of which there were still a few, might find them and hurry to his
assistance.

The rescued and rescuers waited for the caravan to catch up
with them, which it soon did. Sir William provided Cyprien with
a horse and the train moved on. What punishment was meted out
to the greenhorns who caused all the trouble is not known. Almost
the only punishment that could have been inflicted under the
circumstances was to "ground" the men for several days, making
them walk and lead their horses. This was a humiliating experience, as well as a tiring, even painful one.

Now that the anxiety about Cyprien was happily over, plans
began to be formulated for a suitable Fourth of July celebration.
The United States was only sixty-seven years old and its people
had not lost their excited awareness of their country's natal day.
The occasion was always marked, in remote regions as well as settled communities, with ceremonies as elaborate as could possibly
be arranged.

Since the Stewart party was too large to partake of dinner
together, four messes decided they would hold their feast by them-

selves. Sir William invited the rest of the men to have dinner at his "board" (both food and guests would rest on the ground). A little Englishman named Storer offered to make not one, but two, plum puddings, a graceful gesture of international good will. He began three days before the event, working every evening preparing and mixing the materials for his masterpiece; all the ingredients came, of course, from Sir William's private stores of fruit, white flour, spices, and so on, except buffalo marrow, which took the place of suet. That was by courtesy of Antoine and Joe Pourier.

Employing considerable ingenuity, three or four of the "young gentlemen" constructed a flag, using two red silk handkerchiefs from a pack containing presents for the Indians, quite a lot of Dr. Tilghman's material for making bandages, blue calico, and several gold-wire hat tassels patriotically sacrificed for the occasion. A very creditable flag resulted. Matt, the literary man of the party, went to work on several flowery and sonorous stanzas which he titled, "An Ode to the Fourth of July," and also another set of verses called "God Save the Brave." This last was to be sung—in honor of Sir William—to the tune of "God Save the King."

At sunrise a committee of three fired a salute of twenty-six guns in honor of the twenty-six states of the Union. This burst of noise woke the rest of the camp with a jerk, sure they were being attacked by a war party of Sioux. The Stars and Stripes, so laboriously constructed, floated from a tall flagpole in the morning sunlight.

After breakfast Sir William issued an "order of the day," to the effect that one-half the men of the train would remain sober and be alert in case of a surprise attack. This edict caused considerable discontent among the men of the "dry" contingent, but all unpleasantness soon disappeared in the warming rays of patriotic enthusiasm engendered by the day.

When dinner time came, two of the largest tents were joined together to accommodate Sir William's guests. A long strip of oil cloth, laid on the ground down the middle, represented the table. Guests seated themselves about it on the grass. The main part of the feast consisted of various cuts of buffalo, cooked in the manner best suited to each. Interspersed among these viands appeared choice items from Sir William's wagon. Drinks of various kinds were passed around: juleps, fine hock, and twenty-four bottles of Rhine wine.

Sir William gallantly proposed a toast to the Union. Matt's "Ode to the Fourth of July" was recited, with gestures, and Sir William joined in the song, "God Save the Brave." The rest of the Glorious Fourth passed in hilarious fun, helped by frequent potations, all on the house.

Next day the caravan traveled eighteen miles and camped that night on Laramie River, near the point at which it flows into the Platte. On the following day, Sir William, the two Sublette brothers, and several other men rode over to visit Fort Laramie. The building, although the same size and constructed along almost exactly the same lines, was not the structure that Sublette had erected there ten years before. The logs forming the stockade of old Fort Laramie had rotted where their ends had been buried in the ground. The new fort, built almost on the site of the old one, was made of adobes, the same material the Bents had used for their great establishment on the Arkansas. A Sioux village consisting of some thirty lodges was encamped on the meadow beside the fort. As soon as the newcomers were recognized, the chiefs came forward, giving Sir William and Sublette a warm but dignified welcome.

Before returning to their camp across the Laramie, the Sublette brothers, accompanied by Sir William, visited Milton Sublette's burial place in the graveyard near by. Storms or straying cattle had toppled the rude cross that marked Milton's resting place. Before the train left, all damage had been repaired and everything was in order again.

Sir William and the two Sublettes tarried there for several days. The fort and its vicinity held many memories for them. When Jeff Clark rode over with several companions, the older chiefs of the Sioux were astonished by his red hair and facial contours, so like those of his father, General Clark, whom many of the Indians at the fort had seen long ago.

When assured that Jeff was General Clark's son, they invited him and his half-dozen companions to a feast. At this, the young men became more excited than the chiefs had been. An Indian feast! What tales they would have to tell around the dinner tables at home!

That night the guests assembled in one of the largest tepees. Jeff and his friends were deeply impressed to discover that the only Indians present were chiefs and head men. Young boiled dog and a kind of soup made of chokeberries and dried roots, the greatest of delicacies, were served. At the conclusion of this feast, a handsomely decorated stone pipe of peace was smoked with all due ceremony. Then Jeff distributed presents, knives, tobacco, envelopes of vermilion, and fine red woolen cloth.

On the morning of July 7, Brother Eneas of the missionary party, and Mr. Asa Lovejoy, an experienced mountain traveler who happened to be at the fort, were sent on an express—meaning they would travel light, fast and dangerously—to the Flatheads, carrying word that the missionaries were on their way and asking that an escort party be dispatched from that tribe to the appointed place of rendezvous in the Wind River Mountains. Then the reverend fathers might proceed safely to St. Mary's Mission, hundreds of miles farther on.

About the ninth of July, Sir William's caravan left Fort Laramie behind. Traveling up the Platte, the botanists became more entranced than ever by the many plants, new to science, which they discovered. Alexander Gordon, discarding both caution and common sense in his frenzied botanizing, abandoned his horse and walked all the rest of the way, scarcely lifting his eyes from the ground, fearful that he might miss something. At times he ranged as much as five or ten miles away from the train. No amount of expostulation from Sir William had the slightest effect on him. He was the only man of the party who quietly defied the commander's orders, apparently oblivious of them. Sir William could hardly discipline a distinguished scientist, especially one who became totally deaf when anything was said that he didn't want to hear. By the greatest good luck, the man missed being killed and scalped by some wandering band of Indians. Charles Geyer, no less enchanted by the plants of the region than Gordon, but with more western experience—he had been with an earlier expedition of Frémont's—sometimes walked for a while, but never without first looping the reins of his horse's bridle over one arm.

Here on the North Platte the company suffered its first and only tragedy. François, young brother of Antoine Clement, dragged a double-barreled rifle from under a tent, muzzle first. The trigger caught on an obstruction and fired a bullet into the boy's left lung, where it severed an artery. Dr. Tilghman did what he could, but there was no chance of saving François's life. Father de Vos performed the services of his faith for the dying. At nine o'clock that evening the boy drew his last breath. Matt Field sat up most of the night composing a poem about the sad event.

Next morning the body of the boy they had come to regard with affection lay in a tent, surrounded by a profusion of wild flowers the botanists had gathered. Father de Vos said mass for the soul of the departed and Matt read his poem which Joe Pourier said "makes me hurt." Then they laid François's body in his grave and the caravan moved on.

Days passed, broken only by hunting forays. Finally they were on the Sweetwater, pausing long enough at Independence Rock to carve their names beside the many others inscribed there. Then to Devil's Gate, only a short distance away.

On the 26th of July Sir William detached a small party that included Joe Pourier and Guesso Chouteau, sending them to contact the Snakes in the neighborhood of Fort Bridger, built the year before on Black's Fork, a tributary of the Green. The party carried an invitation from Sir William for a delegation of the Snakes to visit him at Stewart's Lake, northeast of the old rendezvous grounds on Green River where he had last seen them.

Farther along on the trail, Asa Lovejoy and Brother Eneas returned with disturbing news. They had been unable to find the Flatheads, so no escort would be waiting for the priests.

Turning away from the Sweetwater, Sir William led his train to Sandy Creek, a tributary of the Green. Here the missionary party, with Solomon Sublette in charge, left the protection of the caravan to set out on their long, dangerous journey. With them went Charles Geyer, carrying a letter of introduction from Sir William to Dr. McLoughlin at Fort Vancouver. The botanist's plan was to board a ship at the mouth of the Columbia, sail around the Horn, and visit Sir William at Murthly the following year.

In the Rockies, even during the first part of August, nights may be cold. One morning the men found ice in their water buckets. That afternoon they reached the edge of Stewart's Lake, gazed at the beauty of its curving shore and blue surface that reflected the rim of protecting peaks shouldering toward the sky. For a while, the men sat their horses in trancelike silence.

Then the travelers dismounted, tents were pitched in a green meadow, and crimson-covered charettes were arranged among the great trees fringing the blue lake. Here was the climax of the whole journey: scenery beautiful beyond imagining, clear blue and gold days, invigorating air, incomparable hunting and fishing—and visitors expected. Joe Pourier and Guesso Chouteau had returned with a message from the Snakes, Sir William's greatest friends among the Indians, saying that they would journey swiftly to make talk and smoke the pipe of peace and friendship.

Sir William inflated the rubber boat and rowed a party of his friends over the crystal waters of the lake. A few days passed in exploring the delights of this idyllic spot. Hunting parties went into the surrounding mountains, bringing back deer, mountain sheep, elk.

Then with yells and shooting off of guns, the Snakes arrived, a party of thirty or forty riders. The Indians wore their richest costumes, brought their wives to do the work and pretty girls to gladden the white men's hearts.

Sir William relaxed the iron hand of discipline. The men could come and go as they pleased. Only a skeleton guard was maintained, in case a roving band of Bannocks or Blackfeet might happen along and try to steal some of their horses.

A course for horse racing and one for foot racing were marked off. Indians won in these contests more often than the whites. Then there was the game of "hand" where the white man did better. The Snakes had brought a fortune—by white men's standards—of buffalo robes, bearskins, otter pelts and beaver plews, purely for betting purposes. Against these rich trophies of the chase, men of Stewart's party wagered the usual trade goods:

colored beads, mirrors, ostrich feathers, brass rings, fish hooks, mirrors, and knives.

The whites were not cheating the Indians in these transactions. The palefaces' goods were as treasures to these Stone Age savages, incomparable for decoration or for practical use in getting food, infinitely more valuable than anything they parted with to get them. They doubtless had many a good laugh over their own campfires at the gullible white men who would give them a large knife for a small beaver plew, half a dozen fish hooks for a pair of beaded moccasins, and even bet two whole strings of blue beads against a buffalo robe. These whites must have been eating loco weed!

Feasting, hunting, and gambling went on simultaneously. It was a small but vivid approximation of the fur rendezvous Sir William and Sublette had known so well, though lacking some of the less pleasant features, such as sudden, brutal, eye-gouging fights, excessive drunkenness, and the hard pressure of business that bore down on the fur traders. This was good, clean—well, fairly clean—fun, and a great time was had by all.

Several skilled seamstresses of the Snake tribe came with their lords and masters, no doubt with a shrewd eye to picking up a little business. A number of white men availed themselves of the opportunity to acquire a fringed and porcupine-quill-embroidered suit of buckskin and several pairs of beaded moccasins. The women were delighted to receive payment in figured calico, tinkling hawk's bells, and the other foofaraw that they loved so well.

Days were crowded with hunting, feasting, games. Evenings were given over to entertainment. Men of the Stewart party lounged around campfires telling stories, singing old songs of home, love, and beauty, or watching Indian dances, their strange rhythms accented by drums, rattles, grunts, and yells. The "young gentlemen," all of whom had received classical educations, recited bits from Homer, Milton, Shakespeare, or the romantic poets. Not many could do what Matt did at the drop of a hat—compose verses of doubtful value. Matt seems to have had an enthusiastic audience for his cadenced output.

Sublette related hair-raising adventures with grizzlies and Indians. Sir William spoke casually of what happened to him in

Tashkent, that strange vast Russian city that few people in the Western world had ever heard of. Rolling out from the opened flap of Sir William's crimson tent came waves of incense from the faintly glowing Turkish burner resting on a leopard skin, the heavy sweet odor losing itself at last in the clean Rocky Mountain air. Evenings were never dull at Stewart's Lake.

The nights grew colder. Even at midday the air had a slight nip. Sir William knew that their departure could be delayed no longer. As it was, winter would catch up with them on the Platte. On the 16th of August, he ordered the charettes packed with what was left of their supplies, clothing, and furs won from the Indians. That same afternoon the tepees of the Snakes came down amidst the usual screaming and turmoil. Travois were loaded and the visitors streamed away.

Next morning at sunrise Sir William gave the orders for his party to fall in line and move out of the little valley that he loved. This was the moment of farewell to a place and a way of life that had fulfilled some deep need within him, and he knew that he would never see or experience either again. Sublette, riding grim-faced beside him, must have felt much the same. After this, the mountains which had been so much a part of his life would see him no more. The "young gentlemen" were full of gleeful quips and pranks; they were starting home. The hired hands were joyful. But the two leaders at the head of the train rode silent and aloof, reliving a thousand memories.

On to Sandy Creek, then down the Sweetwater they went, retracing their steps. Discipline, relaxed during the rendezvous, went into effect again. Each night guards were posted against the danger of horse thieves. No straggling or dashing off in pursuit of individual adventures were permitted. The days' marches were shorter than on the outbound trip, another source of resentment. The young men were in a hurry to get home, but Sir William imperturbably continued to order camp made each day at midafternoon. He knew how unwise it would be to overwork the now tired horses or unduly shorten their grazing time. It probably did not occur to him that a simple explanation of the reason for his actions might soothe the ruffled feelings of the men in his party.

Explanations were no part of the military way of doing things. As a result, friction began to build up.

Soon after they reached the Platte, something happened that fanned the smoldering anger of some of the hotheads until it was almost ready to burst into the flames of open rebellion. On the night of August 24, the woman of Henry, one of the hunters, gave birth to a baby girl. Ordinarily, an occurrence of this kind would have been of no moment whatever to the members of the caravan. Almost without exception, Indian women bore their children easily, and were ready to travel or put up a tepee an hour afterward. But this time something went wrong.

When morning came Sir William announced tersely that the caravan would not move for two days, because of the arrival of the little half-breed the night before. To the already restive members of the train, chafing at any delay, this was incredible. Wait two days because a squaw had a brat? There was furious, just-under-the-breath grumbling. A deep sense of injury pervaded the camp. Even loyal Matt was goaded into referring to Sir William as "His Omnipotence." No further word came from the crimson tent; a tactical error, perhaps, but a natural one in view of Sir William's character and military training.

The facts were that the woman had been unable to give birth to the baby in a normal manner. Henry, her husband, believing she was about to die, came to Sir William with his grief and fear. The commander immediately sent for Dr. Tilghman and instructed him to render whatever assistance he could. After several hours the baby was born and the woman's life saved. However, she was in no condition to travel immediately. Probably not a man in the train would have objected had he known the reason for the delay. So much for Wellingtonian methods applied to young American men on the Platte.

A brief sidelight on the above circumstance: among the Stewart papers in the Edinburgh Archives now rests a yellowed scrap of paper on which is written in fading ink: "For delivering Henry's squaw, $14.00. DR. TILGHMAN."

The caravan resumed its march. One night a little before daybreak, yellow flames suddenly raced up one side of the crimson tent. The light woke Sir William and others who slept near by. Springing up, they quickly beat out the fire, but not before several square yards of canvas had been destroyed. Fortunately, most of the luxurious furnishings escaped damage. Whoever was responsible for the blaze, all suffered its consequences. Sir William ordered the train to remain encamped at that spot while a sufficient number of antelope skins was secured for the construction of a lodge to replace the crimson tent.

It was not until September 10 that the train reached Fort Laramie. Sir William and his party camped across the river. Eleven only moderately distinguished head men—meaning they could count only a few coups—belonging to a near-by village of Brûlé Sioux came to visit. These Indians were invited to return that evening for a Soldiers' Feast—that is, a feast which only warriors of their tribe, and their white hosts, would attend.

There was much speech-making that night in Sir William's antelope-skin lodge on the banks of the Laramie, both sides outdoing themselves in the field of oratory. What viands they feasted upon is not known—probably boiled or roasted buffalo, with perhaps a little choice pemmican with dried chokeberries added, from the store Sublette would certainly be taking back to St. Louis with him. And coffee, of course, with judicious amounts of sugar, if there was enough of that precious commodity left to divide with the red men. When all were filled to repletion, the red sandstone pipe of peace made its rounds with stately ceremony.

Then Sir William distributed presents, and very handsome ones they were. A young chief named Pankeska Marza, who had recently taken eleven Pawnee scalps, received an unusually fine horse. Others received generous quantities of ammunition, tobacco, blankets, and so on. Great goodfellowship prevailed. No one suspected what trouble this amiable entertainment would stir up.

About midafternoon of the day following the Soldiers' Feast, eight haughty Sioux chiefs came riding into camp at breakneck speed. They were highly indignant with Sir William. The night before they had expected that the Scotsman, accompanied by a number of his men, would visit them at their village about ten miles away. Their women had prepared a great feast, spread buffalo robes. Instead, the white men had given a feast to the in-

significant Brûlés, presented them with fine gifts. Their anger grew
as they recited the wrongs that had been done them. They went
so far as to threaten they would steal all Sir William's horses.

Neither the commander of the train nor any of his men exhibited the slightest fear—whatever they may have felt. Their
demeanor remained confident, courteous, firm. The Indians could
see they were outnumbered many times, so eventually the redmen
calmed down and accepted Sir William's invitation to spend the
night. The visitors were given a plentiful supper of their favorite
food and drink—buffalo stew and coffee.

One of their number, named O-kee-ka-gha, wore a great,
heavy silver medal four inches in diameter hanging around his neck
on a massive silver chain. On one side, in high relief, appeared a
likeness of President Jefferson, and on the other, the word PEACE,
curving above a crossed tomahawk and pipe. Under the tomahawk
and pipe were two clasped hands and the word FRIENDSHIP.
O-kee-ka-gha was immensely proud of this medal, which, he declared, had been bestowed upon him as a mark of honor by General William Clark himself. When young Jeff Clark appeared,
the older chiefs showed great excitement. They were struck by his
close resemblance to his father, and immediately guessed his relationship to the famous Indian agent. The sight of young Jeff
dissolved what traces of their anger remained.

Next morning, amid an atmosphere of complete amiability,
Sir William offered them, as a special honor, a demonstration of
the electrifying machine. At first, the idea of lightning in a box
terrified them; but when Matt Field, Dr. Tilghman, and a few
others, gave a demonstration of how the "lightning" worked, they
advanced, though with obvious trepidation, to give this white
man's magic a try. When Sir William turned on the current they
were astonished beyond measure. The most amazing part of it to
them was that they all felt its effect at the same instant . . . the
black box was certainly great medicine. Finally, after expressions
of undying friendship for their white brothers, they rode away.

The delay occasioned by Sir William's entertaining his Indian friends still further incensed the young men of the party.
They wanted only one thing now—to get back with all possible
speed to the comforts and pleasures of home. September was

upon them and they experienced more than usual bad weather, which did nothing to pacify them. One night a hard wind blew up a brief fall of snow and ripped apart some of the tents. Next morning rain fell, and then the temperature dropped until ice covered everything. Sublette declared he had never seen such weather at that time of the year, except in the most elevated parts of the Rocky Mountains.

They waited a day or two, hoping the cold would abate. Sir William sent out hunters, as supplies of dried meat were low, and few, if any, buffalo could be expected below where they now were. Their commander announced that he was going to visit the largest village of the Pawnees, at a distance of about ten miles, a junket that would cause still further delay. At this, a number of the young men spoke their minds, and in no mild terms. Their words were received in silence. Matt Field did not openly identify himself with this dissident group. He confessed that he wanted to, but his curiosity to see the Pawnee village was too great and, instead, he accompanied Sir William. They were received with great honor at the village and the Scotsman saw again old friends of other days.

Returning to his own camp, he discovered that Antoine, Joe Pourier, and the other hunters had returned without meat. Sir William immediately dispatched them again for another try. Another delay. The men comprising four messes set out for Westport by themselves. Cyprien Menard, Guesso Chouteau, E. Hepburn, Clark Kennerly, and Jeff Clark were among those who left in what is sometimes referred to as "high dudgeon." Matt, older, wiser, and perhaps more understanding, remained with his patron, as did thirty or thirty-five others.

What luck, if any, the hunters had we do not know. Both parties traveled on, but at no great distance apart, visited back and forth several times. The group that included the two cousins, Clark Kennerly and Jeff Clark, finally forged ahead and arrived in St. Louis a few days in advance of Sir William's party. When they were all back in civilization, their differences seem to have been forgotten. Clark Kennerly, who had been one of the most vocal objectors, afterward said that in St. Louis "amidst much good fellowship the whole party disbanded." He added that Sir

William was a mighty hunter and a prince among sportsmen, and hoped that wherever he went he might find good hunting.

Sir William was given a farewell dinner at Persimmon Hill, home of Clark Kennerly and Jeff Clark. During the course of the evening he invited both young men to visit him at Murthly for the shooting season.

In this warm glow of friendliness, Sir William's last excursion into the Far West came to an end. A few weeks later he was in New Orleans, started on a leisurely journey that would take him back to Scotland, there to begin another, and quite different chapter of his life.

CHAPTER XXV

Sir William Keeps His Vow

৯৯ Sir William spent a busy winter in New Orleans, most of his time being occupied with the varied and often difficult tasks attendant on collecting and shipping to Scotland as many of the most interesting plants and animals of America as he could secure. Sublette wrote from St. Louis in November that he was looking for "white cranes" which, when found, he would buy for his Scottish friend.

It is a reasonable assumption that the white cranes Sublette spoke of were the great whooping cranes, now almost extinct, but which then still wintered, in countless numbers, within the boundaries of Texas and Louisiana. They were the largest birds in North America. In flight their great pinions had a spread of over seven feet. Sir William almost certainly secured a number of the great birds, for they were not difficult either to find or to capture. It is easy to imagine these beautiful snowy creatures nesting among the sedges along the banks of the Tay, or standing on their incredibly slender legs in its shallows. Their wild, resonant cries would have come with equally eerie strangeness to the ears of Dunkeld villagers and the highborn guests at Murthly Castle.

The *New Orleans Picayune* carried a brief announcement in one of its November issues: "A botanist, from England, Alexander Gordon, is with Sir William Drummond Stewart. He has made a large collection of flowers, plants and herbs, important and new to the medical profession." Later, Gordon wrote to Sir William from New York just as the botanist was about to sail for England, assuring his patron that he would deliver safely to Murthly every seed he had gathered and thanking the Scotsman for his kindness.

Sometime during the winter, Nichols prevailed on Sir William to journey with him to Nicholstone on Dickinson's Bayou in order that they might inspect the route of a railroad Nichols proposed to promote. The tracks would extend, Nichols explained, from Galveston to Houston and on to Henderson, a distance of some 350 miles, through a slowly developing but potentially rich area.

As yet, the steel rails, the locomotives, the cars, even the necessary preliminary surveys, for the Galveston, Houston and Henderson Railway, as Nichols called it, were no more than a determined and enthusiastic gleam in the industrialist-promoter's eye. However, with a man of his character and habit of success, it was not hard to forecast that the gleam would be transformed into concrete results. But, Nichols pointed out, it was not a good time to proceed with the scheme. The tiny, insecure Republic of Texas was beset with uncertainty. That it would soon be annexed by the United States was a foregone conclusion. When that came to pass, and things settled down, he would proceed with his dream.

After this trip to Texas, Sir William returned to his absorbing tasks in New Orleans. But the jaunt with Nichols had lighted in him a bright flame of interest in railroads in general, and this one in particular, that would not soon die out.

From brief references in letters, it is clear that Sir William planned to take Antoine back to Murthly with him. But the half-breed, left pretty much to his own devices in St. Louis, took the money he had been given to buy new clothes for the journey to Scotland and spent it all on a gay time in the taverns along the levee. The details are not entirely clear, but clear enough. When Sir William left New Orleans for New York during the latter part of April, he was not accompanied by the colorful and erratic mixed-blood. Antoine Clement had made his final exit from the life of Sir William Drummond Stewart.

The homeward-bound traveler stopped briefly at New York for a visit with J. Watson Webb, and obtained from him a promise to visit Murthly within the next few months. Sir William sailed for London and on June 21 he registered at Mount's Hotel in the metropolis. Not tarrying long enough to open the town house on Eaton Place, he hastened to Murthly, where Dalpowie, the lodge in the garden so well described by Miller, had been made ready for his occupancy. A crowded summer lay ahead of him. There would be many guests to entertain, and far more exciting and important, the resumption of his building plans and improvements on the Murthly estate.

Now that he was home for good, sleeping at Dalpowie, always inconvenient, became irksome. Yet Sir William felt bound by his old vow never to sleep under the roof of Murthly, even though it now belonged to him. The solution he hit upon can hardly be considered a happy one, though perhaps the only way out of the corner he had gotten himself into by his anger and impetuosity. He had an apartment built for him, its rooms attached to the outer walls of Murthly in much the same fashion as a swallow's nest is attached to the eaves of a barn. Thus honor was kept unsmirched, but at the expense of some violence to the appearance of the stately old castle.

In this apartment he had installed the latest in bathing arrangements. Folding wooden shutters, painted a lugubrious brown, enclosed a tub and shower. When his lordship desired a bath, servants brought water from the kitchen and filled the tub. A shower was achieved by pouring water into an elevated tank with holes in the bottom. These arrangements caused wonder, astonishment, and possibly envy in the minds of all who saw them. When they were completed, the master of Murthly hung his clothes in the capacious closet of his bedroom, arranged the carved ivory toilette set on the ornate walnut bureau, and slept peacefully at night, secure in the thought that he was *not under the roof of Murthly Castle.*

Perhaps it was childish. But the consistently logical and sensible man is, more often than not, also completely and boringly dull.

Even while the swallow's-nest apartment was being constructed at all possible speed, beautiful Rohallion was finished at last. Immediately other large projects were initiated. One activity that stood high on the agenda was the restoration of the two ancient burial chapels of the Stewart family: St. Mary's at Grandtully and St. Anthony the Eremite's at Murthly.

We do not know much about what was done at St. Mary's, a long, low, stone building that looked more like a dilapidated barn than a chapel. When it was built in 1533, the ceiling had been ornamented with painted medallions. Now their colors were dimmed by the passage of more than three centuries. Repairs were made, the medallions were restored to their original brilliant freshness.

The burial chapel at Murthly was also fully restored, handsomely decorated. But Sir William was not content with that. He built a new chapel—actually, an addition to the old one. Here the religious pictures Miller had been commissioned to paint would eventually hang. The cost of this comparatively small but exquisite edifice must have been enormous. The finest artists in the British Isles were commissioned to enhance its beauty with their particular genius. The noted architect, Sir Gillespie Graham, prepared the architectural details and personally superintended its construction. The well-known religious painter, Alexander Christie, produced the altar pieces. The altar itself, the altar rail, and the confessionals were carved by Charles Trotter of Edinburgh, while the renowned firm of Ballantyne and Allen designed and made the stained-glass windows. Much of the work was so detailed that the chapel was not completed until two years after it had been begun.

Archibald, who was a Mason and had his own particular brand of hatred for everything Catholic, bitterly denounced William for his mad expenditure of money on Popish fancies. Such extravagance caused penurious Archibald real anguish, and he was not one to suffer in silence. The beautiful little chapel was a sharp thorn in his side until, many years later, when at last fate allowed him to follow his natural inclinations and do something mean and vindictive and to his monetary advantage about it.

Two more hunting lodges were started, one named Dramour, the other Dalguise. The first was six miles from the castle, the other slightly nearer. They were large, plain, two-story dwellings, without the charm and grace of Rohallion, reflected in its tiny lake. These lodges were high-class "rental properties." Queen Victoria's many visits to Scotland and Prince Albert's purchase of Balmoral Castle as a royal residence had made sojourns in the land of kilts and bagpipes stylish among the wealthy élite of England, the Continent, and even America. These hunting lodges would add substantial sums to the revenues of Murthly.

Early in the summer J. Watson Webb came to the castle for his promised visit. The United States had by this time recovered from its long depression, and all of the New Yorker's enterprises were prosperous. Webb was not only able to travel where he wished, but was building a fine summer home named Pohakoe on the Hudson River. He brought with him the great American painter, Henry Inman. Sir William immediately commissioned the artist to paint his lordship's picture.

He posed for the portrait wearing a navy-blue coat with a wide collar of lustrous beaver fur—symbolic of his Western adventures, perhaps—and an apricot-colored waistcoat. His proud, imperious face looks out from the Inman canvas today, almost as if it were alive.

After his guests from America were gone, Sir William ordered a handsome frame designed and made especially for his portrait, which he intended as a gift to J. Watson Webb. For the time being it hung at Murthly, awaiting the completion of his friend's new home on the Hudson River.

As was the custom with the sons of noblemen, young George Stewart was sent to Europe with Mr. Power, a tutor, to look after him. This move left Christina with no reason to remain in Edinburgh, and as soon as Dalguise was finished she came to live there. After that, for the rest of her life, she made her home at the big, plain hunting lodge, or in grim old Grandtully.

There still exist a few letters Christina wrote to Sir William at intervals during the following years. Strictly speaking, they were not letters, but notes, probably delivered by a servant. These brief missives, written hurriedly perhaps, show more clearly the relationship between Christina and Sir William than we can gain from any other source.

In one of these notes Christina says that, owing to the death of a niece in Malaga, she must beg to be excused from participating in the festivities at Grandtully on Tuesday, as well as from the partaking of an early dinner together that day as he has suggested. But he will find the beds aired, as she has given orders to have that done. There is a large kettle, sent up from Dalguise, and wooden benches for the ladies. Also tea, sugar and candles, but little else.

This brief communication reveals a number of interesting facts. First, they are seeing a good deal of each other; she writes as an educated woman, not an ignorant serving maid; he depends on her, not only in estate matters, but in social affairs as well; there is, at the very least, a friendly comradeship between them—and a distinct implication that there might be a great deal more.

A year or so after Sir William returned from America, Charles Geyer, the distinguished botanist who had finally returned to England after having gone to the Pacific Coast, stayed for a while at Murthly. Then he returned to his native Dresden. Marie Frances, the last "leddy o' Logie," died at Braco Castle and brother George was left alone. However, Murthly was not far off, and he spent much of his time there, visiting with many distinguished guests and acting as host—a role he thoroughly enjoyed—during his brother's many absences.

In December a fire broke out in the dining room of the castle. During the ensuing excitement, many family papers, including a few records of earlier centuries, were thrown from the windows of the library. The fire was soon extinguished, doing only minor damage, but several historical documents were lost. This unfortunate occurrence brought Sir William to the realization that some orderly and permanent history of the Stewart family should be made. He secured William Fraser, a distant relative, to collect and compile the historical data of the family from earliest times. This monumental task completed, Sir William had the material printed and bound in two large volumes titled, *The Red Book of Grandtully*.

In April, 1846, E. B. Nichols wrote with exuberant joy that a second son had been born to him and his wife over a month before. They had named the baby Francis Rice Nichols. The child's brother, only a little over a year old, had been named William in honor of the baronet. The news about Nichols's latest son probably made little impression on Sir William. He was too deeply immersed in his own important problems to feel much excitement over the birth of a child in faraway Texas.

The new chapel of St. Anthony the Eremite was completed at last and the second of the pictures painted by Miller to decorate its walls arrived from Baltimore, to be placed in position. This was the painting entitled "Christ's Charge to St. Peter." Plans were made for an elaborate dedication ceremony, to which most of the great Scottish families would be invited.

Before that plan could be carried out, however, shocking news came from Rome. Thomas had been murdered at Casa Bruciate, not far from the Eternal City. He was bathing in a secluded pool, when a convict, escaped from a near-by prison, stabbed him to death, then stole the small amount of money in his clothing on the bank. Not long before this brilliant man's tragic end he had received the title of Abbé Chevalier and was well on his way to becoming a cardinal.

His body was shipped back home, coming by way of Dundee. His funeral was the first event of its kind in the new chapel of St. Anthony the Eremite, after which interment took place in the old family burial chapel, beside his ancestors. It is not known whether Archibald attended the services. Probably not. Such evidences of Catholicism as were sure to be displayed on this occasion would have been beyond the endurance of this bigoted and choleric man.

Not long after the death of Thomas, Sir William's book, *Edward Warren*, was published in New York by Harper Brothers. Webb, the devoted friend, had taken care of all the details, written a laudatory introduction, seen to it that the book received more than adequate publicity, and personally brought it to the attention of the "right" people. Public interest in the Far West was still strong and the book sold well. There were several other bits of news. Son George was in Paris with Power. The two had returned from a brief tour of Russia and Turkey. In September Lord Glenlyon succeeded to the title of Duke of Atholl and automatically his wife Ann became Lady Atholl.

Christina wrote another note to Sir William from Dalguise. In it she says she will see him before long, as she has been planning a day at Murthly for some time, but an earlier meeting has been out of her power. She is dining away, but will see him at the usual time. She wants Sir William to dine with her on Thursday at half past six, and can give him a bed. She goes on to speak of several estate matters which she appears to be supervising. On the whole, a tantalizing note, revealing little of what she and Sir William meant to each other.

In the meantime, young George was growing up. He wrote a letter to his father in French in which he told of going with Monsieur le Compte Palffy to a ball at the Russian Embassy, where there were about two hundred ladies and gentlemen. He closed his missive with the assuring words, "All conducted themselves well."

Now that George and Power were moving in high society, their expenditures increased. Power, writing to Sir William from Rome, says urgently that he must have more money. Fifty pounds a month is not enough to pay rent, servants, washing, food, clothing, library, lights, etc. George is a young man and wants eighty pounds a year, as he goes into society where his station is known. The season in Rome is beginning and they have received introductions to Prince Borghese, Mr. Sartoris, and Princess Doria.

So wrote Power, an indefatigible name dropper and complete snob. No doubt he got a larger allowance for expenses and George received the eighty pounds he desired for spending money. Sir William appears to have always been an indulgent father, and to have given Christina everything of a material nature that she wanted, or would accept.

Another note from Christina, though undated, seems to have been written about this time. She is at Dalguise and expresses a wish that he come to his quarters there. As she has no use for her carriage at present, it will be at his disposal. She has just returned from London. Signed: *Yours sincerely*, C. S. STEWART. At various times in these notes Christina mentions having been to London, or to Edinburgh, of having seen her friends there, attended concerts or visited museums with them.

During the summer Nichols and his wife came to England
on a combined business and pleasure trip. They brought Franc,
now a little over a year old, with them. During their stay in London they had a photograph taken of their child—quite a feat,
considering the long exposure required by this relatively new art.
Afterward, the Nicholses journeyed up to Perthshire for a visit
with their friend, the Lord of Murthly. Here, for the first time,
Sir William saw the child who, not many years later and then
almost by accident in the beginning, became an important factor
in his life.

In the fall of 1847, brother George died at Braco Castle. He
was buried at Murthly, though not with Catholic rites, which
irked the two priests now living at Laguna. George had not returned, as Thomas and William did, to the arms of Rome.

In the early spring of the following year J. Watson Webb
wrote that he was moving into his new home, Pokahoe. He described it proudly and at some length. Fifty feet square it was,
built of gray stone, with a wide piazza across the front and two
sides. All the woodwork on the first floor was polished black walnut. And—startling innovation—water had been piped to every
bedroom, even those on the third floor. He also informed his
friend that space had been reserved on the library wall for the
portrait Inman had painted.

The portrait was shipped to him at once. It hung at Pokahoe
until Webb's death. It then went to his son, who refused to part
with it during his long lifetime. The picture was, and is today,
considered one of the finest portraits ever painted by Inman.

In the early part of 1848, the busy Mr. Power managed to
arrange for George, now approaching eighteen, to be presented
to the Pope. It was most gratifying to some of the Stewart clan,
horrifying to others. George's future must have been of considerable concern to Sir William at this crucial time in the boy's
life. Fortunately for the tranquillity of everyone directly concerned, George chose a military career. As in Sir William's youth,
two things were required for a young man of high station to enter
one of the swank regiments: influence and money. The Earl of
Mansfield furnished the influence, Sir William the money.
George was duly enrolled in the Light Brigade of the 93rd Foot

Regiment. Sir William felt a deep satisfaction as he watched his tall, handsome son take the first steps of a military life. Power, always on hand when needed, saw to it that George's uniforms, resplendent with scarlet stripes and innumerable gold buttons, were fitted by one of the best tailors of London.

By the end of summer, all the projects included in Sir William's immediate building program were completed. He rented Murthly for a fat sum, left estate matters pretty much in Christina's capable hands, and departed. For several months thereafter he can be traced only by the datelines of letters he wrote to friends. By September he was in Russia. Several months later he stopped for a while in Piraeus, on the south coast of Greece. In the spring of the following year a cousin writes to him in Gibraltar. A month or so later, George, in a letter sent to Athens, asks if he may have Miller's picture of his father and the panther for his room. He promises faithfully to return it safely to Murthly's walls at some later date. The boy wanted to show off to his youthful companions in the barracks at Glasgow what a whale of a fellow he had for a father.

Sir William was back in Perthshire before the first spring flowers blossomed along the banks of the Tay. Since Murthly was rented, he stayed at Dalpowie. Almost at once he received a letter from J. Watson Webb, written from Vienna. The New Yorker wrote that he had been to Italy, where he hoped to get an ambassadorship, but failed, and was now on his way home. He would like to stop at Murthly if it was convenient for Sir William to receive him.

Most opportunely, George Shonley, the tenant at Murthly, informed Sir William that he found he must move quickly, as he could not live in such grandeur for under £3000 a year, and this was beyond his means. So Webb came to the castle and the two old friends had a brief visit there. Soon after that the rich Condie family of Perth rented Murthly. Once more Sir William took up his abode at Dalpowie, when he wasn't in his "own quarters" at Dalguise, Christina's home, not far distant.

In the early part of 1851, a beautiful new carriage Sir William had ordered from Naples the year before arrived at Dundee. Men from the estate were sent to bring it to Murthly. With it came a bill for £350, plus transportation costs of twenty-two pounds, seven shillings. Sir William did not become any less devoted to handsome and costly belongings as he grew older.

E. B. Nichols wrote of his ever-widening business activities and of how well they were going, now that Texas had been admitted to the Union. He was operating a fleet of twenty-two ships from his office in Galveston. He assured his Scottish friend that he had not lost interest in railroads, but the time seemed inopportune for building a line between Galveston and Henderson. Serious difference were growing up between the North and the South on the question of slavery. There was a woman in New England named Harriet Beecher Stowe who was adding fuel to the flames of this controversy by her intemperate pamphlets and speeches. It was even possible that war between the two factions would tear the United States apart. Of course it might never come to that, but he thought he would wait a while.

Sir William went traveling again on the Continent, leaving more and more responsibility for running the estates of Grandtully and Murthly to Christina. From this time on, she often stayed at Grandtully for protracted periods, though it must have been an uncomfortable old place with its nine-foot-thick stone walls and cold, dark rooms. She rented her own home, Dalguise, to a wealthy sportsman, and when duty took her to the Murthly estate she stayed at Dalpowie, the attractive lodge where Sir William displayed many of his mementoes of the West, including a number of the smaller oils painted by Miller.

During one of her sojourns at Dalpowie Christina wrote a sharp letter to an employee, a Mr. Markey, saying that when he calmed down she would discuss with him the matter of the wood. She had given him Sir William's orders. Would he be good enough to send her the key to Sir William's room (in Murthly Castle?) as he wanted something from it. The tone of the communication shows that she was no second-class citizen around there, and Mr. Markey had better step lively.

George wrote to his father from Ostend, where he was enjoying a short leave from barracks life at Glasgow. Although he had as yet seen no military service in the field he soon was to receive his lieutenancy.

Life, it seemed, was at last moving smoothly, without jar or hint of trouble, for the Lord of Murthly, his family, and his tenants.

Then suddenly Sir William came storming back home, stopping at Perth long enough to inaugurate an unprecedented legal action against Archibald and others. There were previous occasions when he had outraged members of the Stewart family by his unconventional acts, but this time he not only spread consternation among his relatives, but set tongues wagging all over England and Scotland.

CHAPTER XXVI

The Malakoff Arch

ॐ Sir William's act, so shocking to his contemporaries, was the launching of an attempt to break the sacrosanct law of entail that held the estates of Grandtully and Murthly in its iron grip. This law, which he demanded to have set aside, was an ancient statute established more than five centuries before.

The statute itself, though long, its meaning clouded by archaic verbiage, was actually quite simple. It provided that once the head of a noble family "entailed" all or part of its property, those designated holdings would then in perpetuity descend to the next male in line for succession. If the property were going from father to son, the son would have to be the "heir of his body," as the quaint phraseology ran. The "owner" held only a lifetime tenure of the property. The revenues belonged to him as long as he lived, but in every other respect his role was one of trustee only.

The whole idea of entail was a legacy from days when the overlord wanted to keep intact a group of rich and powerful families who could furnish him money and soldiers to aid him in forwarding any plan he might espouse.

In the minds of the British, whose devotion to law and order commands the respect and admiration of the world, the older a statute, the more sacred it becomes. Therefore, by the middle 1800's anyone who tried to break an entail was likely to be considered a scoundrel and a traitor to the highest ideals of his country.

The affair was the culmination of a family quarrel, as Sir William made clear. He brought suit by "raising an action against Archibald Douglas Stewart and other heirs," and issued a deed including the entire estate to a Mr. Padwick, evidently his lawyer. The deed, it was stated, would become valid as soon as the suit was decided in Sir William's favor. Mr. Padwick would, in that eventuality, deed the property back to its owner and the two estates would have become the personal property of his lordship, to manage as he pleased, even to sell, if he wished to do so.

Considerable mystery surrounds this legal procedure initiated by Sir William. Why was an "action raised" against Archibald "and *other* heirs?" So far as can be determined now, Archibald was not an heir, except perhaps in the sense of being a possible one. Son George was the heir. There is never any indication that Sir William wanted to keep George from receiving his inheritance in due time. Nor is there any discernible reason for the nobleman's desiring to sell any of the property involved. It was bringing in a princely revenue. His extensive building program was completed and presumably paid for. There was no hint of money troubles at this time.

It is possible that Archibald, taking advantage of Sir William's absence on the Continent, had made some move to block George from inheriting the estate, in case of his father's death, by bringing up the skeleton in the closet (George's birth out of wedlock) and thus establish Archibald himself next in line for succession? However, it seems unlikely. Not that Archibald wouldn't have done just that, and gladly, if he had even the slightest hope of success. From childhood he had loved the possession of money above all else. But the English law declared—and still does, in common with that of the United States—that recognition of a child as one's offspring legally establishes that child's legitimacy. And Sir William had acknowledged his parenthood of George in every possible way.

Unfortunately, the trial records of this case have been lost, so it is now only possible to surmise what actually happened and what the motives of the principals were. However, it seems an inescapable conclusion that Archibald had been up to some deviltry. Otherwise Sir William would not have come home so precipitately from the Continent and started suit to break the entail so that Archibald would never, under any circumstances, inherit the estates. Surely he felt strongly on this subject: he once said to a close friend, "I pity my poor tenants if Archibald should ever be over them."

A perhaps apocryphal story remains about something that happened while the preliminary hearing of the case was being held in Perth. The judge asked a laborer from Murthly, who was on the witness stand, if he had ever seen Sir William the worse for liquor.

"No, my lord, I have not," the fellow declared stoutly. "But I have many times seen him the better for it."

If the story isn't true, it ought to be.

The decision of the lower court was unfavorable. Realizing that the consent of both Houses of Parliament—necessary before any entail could be broken—was impossible to secure, Sir William dropped the case. The net result of the bitter controversy was to step up the animosity that already existed between the two brothers to a cold and deadly hatred.

George acquitted himself well in the army. As a lieutenant in the Light Brigade of the swank 93rd Highlanders, life was easy. There was no strenuous training. Officers took the men into the country for occasional jaunts that were supposed to have some relation to war, but which were referred to by a realistic press as "picnics." The 93rd Highlanders wore elaborate uniforms and lived a gay social life, with trips to London and Edinburgh to attend parties and balls.

Then, in 1853, a faint uneasiness stirred the air in Britain. Russia and Turkey blundered into a half-hearted war. Somehow, the French became involved. Since the British were allies of the French, they too might possibly be drawn in. But no one took it very seriously. The usual British faith in the invincibility of their troops lulled everyone's fear. Soldiers were given no more serious training than before.

Though George had seen no military service in the field, he was given a captaincy, which was gratifying to both him and his father. The promotion necessitated a whole new set of resplendent uniforms, purchased and fitted in London.

Time went along placidly.

Then, suddenly, early in 1854 the little flame of dissension between Russia on one hand and Turkey and France on the other burst into a raging conflagration. The Crimean War was on. The British joined the fray.

By September the English and French armies found themselves side by side, laying siege to Sevastopol. In the thick of things was George's regiment, the 93rd Highlanders. His immediate company, the Light Cavalry Brigade, numbered—depending on what history you are reading—from 607 to 800 men. They were encamped near a place called Balaclava, at some distance from the great redoubts of Redan and Malakoff, which were supposed to make Sevastopol impregnable.

On the morning of November 25, fighting was in progress, furious, bloody fighting. The Russian army was in position facing the English and French, with arms that extended roughly to make three sides of a square. At shortly after eleven o'clock Lord Cardigan, the commanding officer of the Light Brigade, to which George belonged, received orders to charge straight ahead. He knew the order was a stupid one, and protested it, but in true English military tradition, at the same time made preparations to carry it out.

He gave the command. The Light Brigade charged, sabers flashing above their scarlet uniforms as they yelled defiance at their foes.

A barrage of cannon fire met them from the front and from both sides. Horses and men fell wounded, dying. Those who survived dashed on, swept through the Russian lines, cutting down the gunners as they passed. On the other side, the men wheeled, galloped back between the cannons—many of them silent now —slashing at the enemy as they went.

Twenty minutes after the order to charge had been given, ninety-eight soldiers had returned to the English lines. One of them was George Stewart. He had escaped from the scene of butchery without even a minor wound. An hour later eighty men, a few of them with their horses, had straggled in. Others followed. Out of the brigade, 276 men were still alive. The action had made the Light Brigade immortal.

When Sir William heard the news his heart must have lifted with a surge of great pride in this son of his, who had shown the last measure of bravery on the field of battle. Christina, like any other devoted mother, would have thanked God that her son was alive, and prayed for peace with her whole heart.

But peace did not come for another year. The two great redoubts the Russians had built before Sevastopol were considered by them to be invincible. Because of their curious construction, these bastions could not be destroyed by cannon fire. Their enormously thick walls were formed of slender poles and tree limbs loosely held together with mud. Over their outer faces hung thick mats woven of rushes, through which protruded the mouths of their cannons. The heaviest artillery could not penetrate these defenses. Men had to climb the walls and take the fortresses from within. The Malakoff was assigned to the French, Redan to the English.

The French worked all winter and through the summer of 1855, digging trenches to within a hundred yards of the Malakoff in preparation for the attack. It was dangerous and bloody business, as the men were often under direct fire from the Russians, but the French commander declared it was better to lose men in sapping operations than during an attack. The English, before Redan, dug their trenches only up to 600 yards of the bastion, preferring to have their men charge that distance in the open, with no protection.

On the 8th of September the French attacked the Malakoff and captured it, after sickening carnage both inside and outside the redoubt. This action opened the way for the allied troops to march on Sevastopol. However, the following day English troops attacked Redan, losing so many men in crossing the open 600 yards that they had to fall back. Next day they attacked again and

were again repulsed. In this action Captain George Stewart
played his part bravely and well, but to no avail. However, the
occupants of the Redan withdrew in the night and next day the
allies marched into Sevastopol, a burning city, having been set
on fire by the Russian troops as they retreated.

The Crimean War was over. When the troops returned to
England they marched to Buckingham Palace to receive the
thanks of their queen. Crowds lined the streets, cheered them all
the way, while bands played *Home, Sweet Home* and *Auld Lange
Syne*. From a window along the route Sir William and Christina
watched their son ride by, wearing his dingy, faded uniform, in
the tragically depleted ranks of the Light Brigade. He had come
back in a splendor of military glory that matched the honor Sir
William had won at Waterloo, forty years before. George could
have given his father no greater sense of fulfillment than this.

George went back to the barracks at Glasgow and his old
life in that Scottish city. There was much talk of medals to be
given to those who had distinguished themselves by outstanding
valor in the war just finished, but time dragged on and the
government did nothing about it. Meantime, the people everywhere feted the returned heroes with lavish entertainments given
in their honor and the presentation of handsome gifts. Officers
were the recipients of solid gold boxes, jeweled dress swords,
purses full of gold coins.

The villagers of Dunkeld put on an elaborate celebration
in honor of their own hero, Captain George Stewart. Arches of
greenery spanned the streets, and a grand display of fireworks
preceded a gala dinner. As a climax to the evening they presented the youthful captain with a damascened sword, its handle
set with precious stones.

Sir William also planned a way of showing signal honor to
his son. He started to build an imposing structure spanning the
wide driveway to the castle, which he named the Malakoff Arch.
It was so large that each leg contained an apartment of three
rooms, and a spacious ballroom stretched across the top.

While the Malakoff Arch rose on the Murthly estate, Sir
William received a letter from E. B. Nichols, in which the Texan
spoke anxiously about the increasing flood of talk regarding war

between the North and South. The trouble had been aggravated
by the female named Mrs. Stowe, of whom he had written to his
friend some time before. This woman had published a book with
the ridiculous title of *Uncle Tom's Cabin*. Its contents had in-
flamed the passions of the North to such an extent that no one
knew what to expect next. He hoped that men of consequence
would be able to control the hotheads on both sides. However,
in spite of the controversy that rocked the Union, Texas was
growing so fast that he seriously considered taking out corporation
papers for the Galveston, Houston and Henderson Railroad.
Using revenue procured from the sale of stock, construction
could be started. What did his friend think? Nichols closed his
letter with glowing accounts of his three sons: William, now
eleven, Franc, ten, and Fred, a boy of eight or nine.

Sir William replied that he considered the idea of going
ahead with the railroad a good one, in spite of the threat of
sectional conflict. Perhaps it might be well for Nichols to come
to England. There was an excellent prospect of his being able to
float a good portion of his railroad stock in the British Isles.
Englishmen, on the whole, were obsessed by the idea of railroads and thoroughly convinced that as an investment they offered a chance of bonanza returns. Since the threat of war appeared to be increasing, he felt a deep anxiety about his friend's
children. Why didn't the Texan bring his sons with him to
England and leave them at Murthly until conditions became
settled in their homeland? He would be glad to undertake their
care, secure tutors for them, and at the proper time see that they
were enrolled in one of the great English public schools where
the sons of noblemen were educated.

At last the Malakoff Arch was completed and dedicated with
great pomp and ceremony before a company of distinguished
guests. Soon afterward the government got around to decorating
a select group of its heroes who had participated in the Crimean
War, with a medal individually struck for each one from a
bronze cannon captured before Sevastopol—the Victoria Cross.
This small medal, in the form of a Maltese Cross that hung from
a claret ribbon, took precedence over every other decoration and

order of the British Empire, even the Order of the Garter. Only sixty medals were awarded, but men of every rank—and of no rank at all—won them, the only qualification being that of having shown extraordinary courage on the field of battle. George traveled to London, where the ceremony took place in Buckingham Palace. There, at the hands of his queen, he received the greatest honor his country could bestow upon him.

Sir William's prideful satisfaction in George's military prowess was shadowed by Christina's fatal illness, brought on by the inroads of pulmonary consumption. While supervising a group of maids gleaning in the field of Grandtully, she was stricken by a severe hemorrhage. Her attendants carried her into the old stone castle and put her to bed.

She lingered for several weeks, slowly losing strength. A woman relative who came to attend her, suggested, "Think of your family and make a financial request." Christina is said to have replied, "I brought nothing to the estate and I will take nothing from it."

She was buried in the ancient chapel at Grandtully, among the Stewart lords and ladies of long ago. Her nobility of character and the high station of her husband, Sir William Drummond Stewart, gave her every right to be there.

Though the conditions of their marriage had been ambiguous after Christina's death Sir William felt a loneliness such as he had never known before. While he was proud of his son, and had provided every opportunity for him that wealth and high position made possible, they had never been together except for short periods of time. Now George was a man, preoccupied with his career in the army and life as a gentleman of fashion. They had little in common.

Sir William wrote again to Nichols, asking him to bring his wife and children for a visit, urging that they leave the boys with him. Nichols accepted the invitation and in a little over two months arrived in London with his family. The Galveston, Houston and Henderson Railroad was already partially financed by sales of stock in the United States. The Texas man, consulting Sir William as to the best way to proceed, sold a gratifying amount of stock in England and Scotland, part of it to Sir William.

Franc and his younger brother Fred traveled up to Murthly to see how they would like the life there. William, the oldest son, apparently rejecting the whole idea, remained in London. Franc loved everything about it from the first. Though he had been brought up in a wealthy home, the house on Dickinson Bayou was nothing like this. Young as he was, something deep in his nature responded to the background of ancient lineage, the deference accorded a great title, even to the trained, respectful servants who waited on him, so different from the help in his Texas home.

Fred, homesick for his parents and the familiar things he knew in Texas, fretted and grieved until at last he had to be sent back to his father and mother in London. When the day of final decision came, Fred gladly renounced the glories of life in a Scottish castle and returned with his parents to the United States. Franc, however, elected to remain. Fifteen years were to pass before he would see Texas again, and he went back then only because there was nowhere else for him to go.

The boy appeared to fill a great need in Sir William's life. Franc may have been for him a symbol of the America he so loved, and of the Far West where he had spent the most vivid and exciting years of his life. The boy had charm, was handsome, high-spirited and adventurous—all qualities that would endear him to Sir William.

Franc slipped easily into the life at Murthly. Tutors were engaged for him, and he appears to have been entirely amiable in all his relations with the Scottish nobleman. The only jarring note was that Franc and George were antagonistic from their first meeting—an entirely normal reaction on both sides. But George seldom came to Murthly now, and Franc was only a child, so nothing much came of their mutual dislike. Sir William may even have been unaware of it.

Like the gently gliding Tay winding among its low green Cambrian Hills, life flowed smoothly at last. For the first time in all his restless, seeking, contending years, the Lord of Grandtully and Murthly basked in the reflected glory of his son. High acclaim for military achievement had been his after Waterloo. Now it was his again, vicariously, because of George's valor in the Crimea.

It was the triumphant peak of his life. Nothing in the years to come, be they few or many, could possibly top the satisfaction he now felt—an emotion he had given form and substance in the towering Malakoff Arch.

His days of adventure were spent. Ahead lay the long slope toward the shadows of evening but now he stood in the clear, bright sunlight of fulfillment. Sometimes hard to understand, was Sir William Drummond Stewart, often rebellious against convention, but always strong and courageous.

Aftermath

ࢳ Following the building of the Malakoff Arch, and perhaps influenced by the deep satisfactions he felt because of his son's valorous military achievements as symbolized by the Arch, Sir William's restless heart quieted. No more alarums, excursions or rebellions were there, until a last violent flare-up just before his death.

He busied himself with managing the estates—alone, now, with Christina gone—looking after the welfare of his tenants, taking brief trips to London, visiting his friends, and supervising Franc's education. At long intervals, Franc's parents came from America to see him. The Civil War broke out in America. Franc was fifteen years old. Nichols received a command in the Confederate Army with the rank of general, and fought valiantly until there was no more use in fighting.

With peace established once more, Franc's parents naturally expected him to come home, but he flatly refused to do so. He liked where he was: no more Texas for him. A strong affection had grown up between Franc and his benefactor. He was being received in the great homes of Scotland and England, living a life that suited his nature and inclination. The boy refused all pleas that he come back to the United States and, at the proper

268

time, assume a part in his father's business enterprises. He declared that his decision to remain in Scotland was irrevocable, and his parents finally accepted the situation.

Soon afterward, Sir William legally adopted Franc as his son and the young Texan became Francis Nichols Stewart. His parents showed no rancor at Franc's abandonment of them, nor does it appear that they held Sir William responsible for what must have brought them bitter sorrow. Afterward, they made several visits to England, going each time to Murthly for an extended stay. There is a photograph, taken after Franc became a young man, which shows him seated in the elegant Italian carriage in front of Dalpowie. On the back of this picture, Franc wrote, *For Mrs. M. C. Nichols, Murthly, Dunkeld, Scotland.* The "M" stood for Margaret, his mother's first name.

The people of the estate and the villagers living in Dunkeld never liked Franc and their animosity toward him grew as the lord of the castle more and more accorded to this "interloper" the position of a son. The youth responded to this attitude with mischievous, annoying, and sometimes cruel retaliations which, as he grew older, became serious. As the years passed, tensions grew. George, now Major Stewart, openly sided with the villagers and finally ceased coming to Murthly except when Franc was absent. As a result, his visits were few indeed. The enmity that existed between Archibald and Franc was nothing short of virulent.

On October 19, 1868, Major George Stewart died under mysterious circumstances at Hythe, in England. One report says that he was killed in a duel, another that he lost his life because of a broken neck suffered in a fall down a flight of stairs while intoxicated. Whichever story is true—if either is—seven days later he was buried beside Christina in St. Mary's Chapel at Grandtully.

George's death opened the way for Archibald to inherit the title and estates of the Stewart line, an eventuality that Sir William had devoutly hoped would never come to pass. Archibald's sour glee must have been enormous. He was twelve years younger than his brother William, so he had a good chance of succeeding to the title. All he had to do was keep his health and wait, in the meantime planning what he would do when *he* was Lord of Murthly and Grandtully.

The following year Sir William made a will, dated October 30, 1869, leaving to "my beloved adopted son, Francis Nichols Stewart," all his "inheritable and movable property." This will was recorded in "the General Register of Sasines," on November 3 of the same year, but it did not become legally binding until confirmed by the Crown on March 2, 1870.

After George's death Sir William's health began to fail, almost imperceptibly at first. Living in the castle, with its retinue of servants and the almost constant entertaining expected of him, became a burden. He and Franc took up their residence at Dalpowie. Murthly was rented to people of wealth and fashion. The ailing nobleman went to France, where he visited a famous spa, but did not stay long. We do not know what his ailment was, or even if he had one. He seems not to have been really ill. Perhaps his disability was nothing more than the burden of years beginning to weigh heavily on his shoulders. He was seventy-three.

In the latter part of March, 1871, Sir William had a mild attack of bronchitis. The illness appears to have galvanized him into a sudden awareness that if he was ever going to thwart Archibald and insure that Franc continue to live in the manner to which Sir William had accustomed him, fast action was in order. He summoned Mr. Padwick, who came to Dalpowie post haste. All the fire and impetuosity of the years that were past, appeared to return at his command. Plans were quickly made, papers drawn up, signatures inscribed.

One of these documents was a second attempt to break the entail, which had now been in force for nearly 160 years. The effort was based on several alleged technical errors in the phrasing of the original paper. Another of Mr. Padwick's efforts was a deed to the entire estate, priced at £350,000, executed in favor of Mr. Padwick. Provision was made that this deed would not become operative until six months after the entail should be declared invalid by the House of Lords. In that eventuality, Padwick would deed the property to Francis Nichols Stewart.

These papers were no sooner in as good order as the busy

Padwick could make them, than the bronchitis attack from which Sir William suffered, developed into pneumonia. On April 28, 1871, the end came.

That was the signal for the long-pent-up hatred and contention between Archibald and Franc to burst into open battle. Within hours of his brother's death, Archibald demanded a court order for a post-mortem examination, and got it.

Archibald no doubt suspected—may even have believed—that Franc had murdered his foster father. But the doctors who conducted the post-mortem announced that the deceased had died of "congestion of the lungs." Sir William's body was then carried in solemn procession down the Dead Walk to the burial chapel of St. Anthony the Eremite, where it was interred.

Within a day or so, Sir William's lawyers demanded a second post-mortem, perhaps at Franc's instigation, though what he expected to prove by it is not apparent. The petition was granted, and so Sir William's body was disinterred and an autopsy performed by a different set of doctors, who gave the same verdict that the others had. Then the body was once more laid to rest beside that of brother Thomas and a large company of long-departed Stewarts. In spite of what would seem proof to the contrary, rumors persist in Dunkeld even to this day that Franc was instrumental in bringing about the death of the man who had done so much for him.

A rash of suits and countersuits broke out between the disputing parties. According to a detailed report in *The Scotsman*, of May 20, 1871, the more important hearings were held in the Other House of the Court of Sessions headed by Lord Mackenzie. The preliminary trials, as far as matters were to go concerning the deed and the effort aimed at breaking the entail, were heard before a gentleman named Mr. Balfour, whose keen mind probed immediately to the heart of the matter.

Mr. Balfour was of the opinion that if the paper drawn in 1717, entailing the estate in question, had been pronounced legally sound as recently as 1851, it was still operative. As for the deed to the property issued to Mr. Padwick, it was not a bonafide agreement of sale, but a pretext to "get rid of the fetters of the entail," and had no legal status whatever. Furthermore, Mr.

Balfour went on, the deed was fraudulent in that the price named for the estate was unreasonably low. The property was worth, Mr. Balfour declared, at a most conservative estimate, £150,000 more than the sum mentioned.

All the suits petered out within a month or two, sunk without a trace by the speedy justice of the British courts. It didn't take Franc long to see which way the wind blew, or as the old trappers Sir William had known would have said, "which way his stick floated." He decided to take whatever he could lay his hands on and get out. No one disputed his right to the money and property bequeathed to him in his benefactor's will, but Franc's interpretation of the word "movable" was more than a liberal one.

Acting swiftly, he removed tapestries from the great hall of Murthly that were fixed in place with moldings, screws and nails. He gathered up pictures, family jewels—including the black-diamond ring that had once belonged to Mary, Queen of Scots—furniture, hangings, a carved wainscot chimney piece, even huge vases from the garden. Presumably he would have taken "a thrashing mill at Ardoch," too, but Archibald secured a special court order restraining him from making off with it. All this loot he shipped to Edinburgh.

While this was taking place, Franc became virtually a prisoner at Dalpowie, because of the hatred felt toward him by tenantry on the estate. They declared he had made a practice of skulking through the woods at night, shooting at them when they used their ferrets to get rabbits for food. After Sir William's death Franc dared not go beyond the 300-yard long driveway that extended from Dalpowie to the main road leading to Dunkeld, for fear he would be set upon by these enraged farmers and killed. When he left Murthly for the last time, Padwick accompanied him as a sort of body-guard.

With Franc out of the way, Archibald quickly established himself in the castle, his ownership and title as 20th Lord of Grandtully and 8th Baronet of Murthly secure. One of his first acts was to carry out a plan long made and cherished. Summarily and with vindictive pleasure, he dismissed the two priests who lived in Laguna, the house Sir William had built especially for them. Next, he ordered workmen to rip out all insignia of Catholicism from the "new" chapel of St. Anthony the Eremite. Among them were the handsome confessionals, altar pieces, and ornately carved communion rail. To have injured or destroyed them would have caused him extreme pain in the pocketbook; he sold them to St. Fillan's Catholic Church at Crief, where they may be seen today.

In June, 1871, immediately following Franc's arrival in Edinburgh, several auctions were held where part of the treasures from Murthly were sold to the highest bidder, most of them at ridiculously low prices. On June 17, the pictures were offered, many of them ones painted by Miller, and brought only a little over £2000. Part of the tapestries and furniture went for a meager £1700.

Of course Archibald screamed in protest against this sacrilege, but to no avail. What Franc wanted to sell, he sold. What he wanted to keep, he shipped to Texas, box after box, crate after crate.

His business in Edinburgh concluded, he embarked for the port of Galveston, taking with him money and property amounting to more than £40,000. He was twenty-five years old. Back in Texas, he set himself up in a fine hotel as a wealthy young bachelor, which in fact he was, with Continental manners, lordly ways, and an Oxford accent.

For several years Franc, who never believed in doing things halfway, called himself Lord Stewart. When news of this effrontery finally got back to England, the House of Lords thundered at him to desist. The thunder must have been authoritative, for Franc made no further claim to being any other than plain Mr. Francis Stewart.

While still using the title he married Ella Hutchings, a girl from a prominent and wealthy family of Houston. It wasn't long until the couple were divorced. Ella later married again, but Franc remained single for the rest of his life. During his later years he gave valuable pieces of jewelry and furniture to friends and relatives.

He died of a stroke in San Antonio, November 23, 1913, at the age of sixty-seven. His body was taken to Galveston, where he had made his home, and buried there. Franc bequeathed what was left of his fortune and belongings to relatives and servants for whom he presumably felt some degree of affection or gratitude.

A few pictures, jewels, pieces of silver and furniture from Franc's collection remain in Texas. Other items may have been carried to distant places, their origin perhaps forgotten. Today, in homes scattered over the United States, there may be articles of beauty and value that once were part of the treasures of Murthly Castle in the days of its glory.

MY PATH TO SIR WILLIAM

by Mae Reed Porter

&ᴸ My path to Sir William, biographically speaking, was a de-
vious one, as over a period of twenty-three years stray bits of information concerning him came to notice.

It all began in 1935, when the secretary of a small museum in
Baltimore, occupying the home of its eminent painter, Rembrandt
Peale, brought from its storeroom one hundred water-color sketches
made in our unopened West of 1837. I was intrigued. She told of
their origin from the brush of a native son, Alfred Jacob Miller.
Hired before the days of photography to accompany a Scotsman,
Captain William Drummond Stewart, into the trapper-trader
country, he had succeeded in catching the beauty of the lakes
and mountains and activities of its aborigines, as well as those of
the intruders from civilization. His on-the-spot sketches were to
become patterns for large oils that eventually graced the walls of
Stewart's castles, while the two hundred originals remained with
the artist, eventually to be inherited by relatives. Those reposing
in the museum became mine in 1939.

Then followed six years of research upon the period portrayed,
and eventual collaboration with Bernard DeVoto on *Across the
Wide Missouri*, which, published by Houghton Mifflin in 1947,

became a Pulitzer Prize winner and, later, a film vehicle for Clark Gable.

If *Across the Wide Missouri* can be said to have a hero, Sir William Drummond Stewart is certainly of that category. During DeVoto's writing period there were a number of mysteries concerning Sir William's life that had not been solved, but since they were irrelevant to fur-trade matters, DeVoto decided to leave them to me, along with the recording of a later trip made into the West by the Scottish lord in 1843, since he had chosen to close the book with the decline of the fur trade in 1838. His conclusion that the Miller sketches were the only pictures of this brief but important period in American history, made when and where it was in progress, was to greatly enhance their importance.

Learning of the existence, in the 1843 files of the *New Orleans Picayune*, of travel accounts of a member of Stewart's party, a young actor named Matthew C. Field, I visited its reading rooms in 1940. Finding the accounts written to defray Field's travel expenses most facinating, I took copious notes. These remained untouched for seven years, when my husband decided that something must be done about Field. He secured verbatim copies of the articles and, having learned that Field's brother Joseph, an editor of the *St. Louis Reveille*, had reprinted many of them, these were checked. In time, with the death of one of Field's descendants, several of his notebooks came into the possession of the Missouri Historical Society at St. Louis.

Our findings, expertly edited by the late Kate Gregg and John Francis McDermott, were published by the University of Oklahoma Press as *Prairie and Mountain Sketches* in the spring of 1957, and so DeVoto's commission anent Stewart's expedition of 1843 was fulfilled. Sadly, death came to Bernard DeVoto shortly before the appearance of *Prairie and Mountain Sketches*.

Now for the second project—the life story of the venturesome lord of the Stewart clan. A survey of materials proved them somewhat meager, comprised as they were of a number of brief mentions in early journals of fellow travelers and in the artist Miller's notes to his sketches, made available to me by his grand-nephew, L. Vernon Miller, of Baltimore. I had received as well a gift from a friend of a book devoted to Scottish castles which had given me my first information concerning Stewart's background. Among its

illustrations were lithographs of his Murthly and Grandtully castles, accompanied by two pages of their history.

My daughter and I had spent the early spring of 1943 in Baltimore, New York, and Washington, hunting Miller and Stewart history and it had occurred to us that there might remain in New York descendants of James Watson Webb, whose friendship with Stewart had resulted in the Scotsman's two works of fiction, written to please the younger members of Webb's family. It was my good fortune to find a ninety-two-year old son, Colonel Creighton Webb, and to see upon his apartment walls a magnificent portrait of Stewart, painted by Henry Inman in 1844 at Murthly. Six years later, upon the colonel's death, it became possible to purchase it and when in 1956 we built a home in Santa Ana, California, an over-the-mantel spot was provided and from it lordly Stewart, my Laird of the Lion Heart, holds court when history lovers come to call.

There were other assets in the years of preparation for the writing of Stewart's life story. Aside from the mentions of him by his contemporaries, Matthew Field, George Ruxton, and others, and the Miller notes, there were as well, a few Stewart letters in the fur-trade files of the Missouri Historical Society of St. Louis.

Mr. Porter, after much correspondence with various Catholic libraries over the country, secured data concerning priests who traveled west with Stewart. We were especially fortunate in securing, through a professional research person in London, the military records of Stewart and his only son. *Burke's Peerage* supplied the genealogy of the family, and linked it with kings: with the Stuarts through Mary, Queen of Scots and with the earlier reigning Drummonds through Mary's cousin and husband, Lord Darnley.

I had, during the early months of collaboration with DeVoto, sent Mrs. Grace Hogarth, the London representative of Houghton Mifflin, to Sir William's native heath in Perthshire to investigate a rumor concerning his death that came to me from a Philadelphian. He had hunted grouse for many years on Murthly's moors, and having seen several pages of our Miller water-colors with mention of Sir William in the January 1944 issue of *Fortune Magazine*, he told me that the artist's patron was said to have been murdered by a Texas adventurer in 1871.

Mrs. Hogarth, after a week in Scotland, had reported the

rumor entirely unfounded. Her gleanings from files of the Edinburgh *Scotsman*, from Court Records, and from the present
owner of the Murthly estate, Steuart Fothringham, completely
exonerated the mysterious Texan, Franc Nichols, who had been
adopted by Sir William and had been a suspect unwarrantedly.

A letter of thanks to Fothringham for his kindness to my
emissary brought an invitation to visit Murthly one day. After a
Scandinavian holiday in the late summer of 1947, I stopped off
in London. From there I went to Perthshire for a week, taking
color film to carry home the beauty of the country and the ancient
ugliness of Stewart's Murthly and Grandtully castles.

My bachelor host proved a gracious guide about his domain
and placed at my disposal a handsomely illustrated tome, *The
Chapel of St. Anthony the Eremite*, giving an account of Sir William's rebuilding of the fifth-century family burial spot. We toured
Murthly's rooms and gardens and had a pleasant morning at
Rohallion, a hunting lodge built by Stewart after his succession
to the title and estates of his family.

I made the acquaintance of a grandson of Sir William's stone
mason, and the son of a gamekeeper who came to Murthly following Stewart's death, and from these gentle people came remem-
brances of stories concerning him.

The gamekeeper's son, John Keay, lent me his precious copy
of *The Red Book of Grandtully*, a two-volume family history com-
piled by Sir William himself, and gave to me from his father's
album my first photographic likeness of Stewart. Taken at Bath,
where he had gone for his gout, it pictured him of military bearing, and its face with the Wellingtonian nose closely resembled
Miller's sketches of him in his early forties. Keay became my companion for drives to Grandtully, where its caretaker served as guide,
and to Taymouth Castle, the home of Sir William's neighbor,
Lord Breadalbane. We spent a day driving to Blair Castle, the
seat of the Atholls, close friends of Sir William. It proved of special interest. Open to the public, I found on its walls, and secured
copies of, portraits of its beautiful mistress and her Duke. These
people had been guests at Murthly during Miller's stay there in
1840 through 1842. In the artist's letters to his family I had read
of Stewart's deep admiration for the enchanting young duchess.

A day in Edinburgh concluded my week and I left for London and home, feeling that although a fair start had been made, I still knew very little about Sir William.

A few weeks after my return to Kansas City, *Across the Wide Missouri* appeared, and my first gift copies went off to Murthly's owner and to John Keay in gratitude.

I filed my notes away and let three years go by—years filled with getting together the material for two books: *Ruxton of the Rockies* and *Life in the Far West*, which, edited by LeRoy R. Hafen, came to print in 1950 and 1951, from the University of Oklahoma Press.

With a cleared desk, out came the notes taken in Scotland, but they presented so meager a picture that I decided that if a book were to emerge, I must return to Scotland. After several months of listing questions and sending letters to Steuart Fothringham and John Keay, asking that they set their minds on my project, I embarked alone on the *Queen Elizabeth* in the fall of 1952 for a cold but fruitful stay in wee Birnam. Two miles from Murthly Castle the former gatehouse is maintained as a hotel. On my first visit to Murthly, Fothringham had told me of the existence of early family papers and that they had, on his father's succession, been transferred from a law office in Perth to one in Edinburgh. He had little knowledge of their contents, but judged them to be fifteenth-century documents. It seemed worthwhile that I secure the address of the firm and make an investigation, when my research should come to an end in Perthshire.

For three weeks I sallied forth each day, visiting small libraries and interviewing citizens suggested by John Keay.

His first move was to take me to call upon Isabella Miller, the elderly granddaughter of Sir William's fisherman, living alone in a cozy stone house built by the Laird on the bank of the Tay. She was to prove a splendid help. From her desk emerged news clippings and photographs, and from her lips I learned the story of Sir William's marriage and the birth and death of his son. There were other precious bits passed on by an aunt of hers who, living a hundred and seven years, had been able to tell of her acquaintance with Stewart.

Perth's librarian supplied me with numerous books from

which I culled data on the history of the various Highland clans. The small town of Dunkeld, known to the Romans as early as 138 A.D. and lying across an ancient bridge from still smaller Birnam, provided some twilight exercise after these hours of library sitting.

Having taken along a copy of *Across the Wide Missouri* with its numerous Miller illustrations, I enjoyed showing my various contacts the type of dangerous, primitive life their first citizen had relished during his eight years of absence in the United States.

A friendly rivalry as assistants developed between John Keay and Joseph Sim, the grandson of Stewart's stone mason. When Keay presented the photograph of Sir William it bore the name of a local photographer, A. J. MacKenzie, on its back, and I asked if there might be other examples of his work helpful to my project. His disappointing reply was "On his death many years ago his studio contents were dispersed." I relayed Keay's statement that night to Joseph Sim when I went to pay for car rental at his garage. Sim's reply, "Nothing of the kind. I went to the sale after MacKenzie's death and bought all his photographs and they are somewhere about the garage," delighted my history-hunting soul.

As I sat in the small littered office beside a warm stove, Sim began his search and in time came to me with a broad grin on his round, purple-cheeked face, a battered cardboard box in his arms. It held dozens of glossy prints of prime interest—enough to illustrate the book and to spare. These he gave to me. Need I refer to his pleasure in besting John Keay, and to my own delight in the find?

However, it was good fellow John who became my companion for an exploratory jaunt to Logiealmond, the ancestral seat of Stewart's mother, Catherine Drummond. He eased my way by querying a liveried butler and soon there stood by our car the handsome Earl of Mansfield, whose great-grandfather had purchased Logiealmond of Sir William. Master of Scone Palace, he had taken residence there that Scone might fill a wartime need for schools. I was soon enjoying the sight of flower-filled rooms that had sheltered Drummonds for centuries. With the Earl for guide, a few photographs were taken and we were off. Without John Keay, inherent timidity would have kept me at the outer gate.

In the evenings I hugged the hotel parlor's fire and watched the ladies knit and joined them in small talk. Their florid, grouse-shooting husbands seemed to prefer the bar and from it jolly noises emerged. The tiring activities of my days made early bed desirable.

John Keay brought a caller, the Honorable Esme Graham-Murray, spinster of the House of Atholl and distantly related to the duchess admired by Sir William. Esme's grandfather, Lord Dundeen, had been a friend of his and she recalled several stories, one of them solving the mystery of long standing concerning Stewart's religious life. Another related the town-shocking actions of American Indian visitors at Murthly.

Miss Murray opened the doors of a number of luxuriously appointed homes to me, and their owners were kind enough to be interested in my project. Among them were the Coxes, Ronald and his sister Lucy, and when he mentioned that he had once seen a full-length portrait of a young and elegant Sir William in his regimentals worn at Waterloo, I commissioned him to find it. Last seen on the walls of Taymouth's great dining room, it had disappeared when the castle had been stripped of its furnishings in 1938 to become a hospital for a thousand Polish refugees.

My search in Perthshire at an end, I took train for Edinburgh. Perusal of early books and newspapers consumed three days, and on the fourth I sought the address of the Fothringhams' family solicitor, and by so doing was figuratively to "hit the jackpot."

The law firm occupied a four-story brick house, conveniently across the street from my hotel and, breakfast over, I was soon at its door. The head of the firm was out, but his secretary was kind and listened to my queries. She remembered that there were some Stewart papers but supposed them to be several centuries old, and suggested that I call upon a Mr. Anderson at the Scotch Bureau of Records, since he had once examined them.

Off I went and to my delight that gentleman had a vague memory of some American correspondence along with the ancestral papers. With wings on my heels I returned to the law office and the secretary. Taking along a janitor, we repaired to an old wine cellar being used as a filing room. Presently a green and dusty box came to light, on its lid the notation, *Stewart correspondence between 1832 and 1851.* These years encompassed the period spent by Stewart in America.

The secretary, as she lifted the lid, said, "Mrs. Porter, these are personal papers. I cannot let you see them without permission from the head of the firm and he has gone for the day." She advised me to return to my hotel while she made an effort by telephone to locate him.

Suddenly the solution came. These papers belonged to my friend Steuart Fothringham, who was interested in my search: his permission could open this new find to me. A dash to the office, a telephone call to Murthly, and consent was obtained.

I settled myself in the quiet quarters of the lawyer, and lifted from the box four folders that held 653 letters—to Sir William from fur traders, from his friend Webb, from the artist Miller, from tenants and social friends. There were a few from his wife and young son, and a number from his mother to his father written during Stewart's boyhood, all supplying pieces for the life mosaic of the man.

Since the hour of departure from Scotland was so close, the folios bearing the dates of his years in America, holding three hundred letters, seemed of greatest importance. The gleaning process began, with each letter yielding data worth recording. The clock struck five at the moment the janitor appeared to put me out, when only half of them had been examined. Mounting dismay was interrupted by the appearance of the head of the firm, returning to his office for a paper. I explained my predicament and he laughed when he said, "This is most unethical, but I am going to let you take those letters to your hotel, provided you promise to give them back to our janitor on the dot of eight tomorrow morning." This I did, and by twenty minutes after eight was off for Paris.

Because of nineteen pounds overweight luggage, I had considered taking the Edinburgh Night Express to London for the economical channel crossing by boat but, too weary to face the many changes while so luggage laden, I purchased a plane ticket instead.

Next morning's Paris newspapers headlined the wreck of the Express at Harrow with 235 dead. A week later, boarding the

Liberté, a porter left the case holding my notes and photographs on the pier, to be discovered only after the "all ashore" whistle had been blown. These two incidents convinced me that a book about Sir William Drummond Stewart was really meant to come to print.

Safely at home, I set to work, but soon recognized the fact that the anonymity of Stewart's adopted son was a stumbling block. Did the letters of his later life that I had not had time to study hold the clue? The expense of returning to Scotland did not seem feasible, but when in mid-October of 1953 Ronald Cox sent word that he had located in an abandoned church near Aberfeldy the five-by-eight-foot portrait of Sir William in his Waterloo trappings, all thought of frugality vanished and I set out for a third time to Scotland.

With my daughter Jean for companion, I flew to London and there rented a small car for the 400-mile drive to Birnam. Arriving at night, we settled into the hotel and the next morning hurried off to Aberfeldy with John Keay.

By prearrangement, the owner of the portrait opened the abandoned church, which was filled with furniture, and two helpers extricated the heavy portrait with its foot-wide, hand-carved, gilded frame. There before us stood proud young William, resting a patent-leather boot on a broken cannon wheel while in the distance Napoleon's Frenchmen retreated in disorder from the field of Waterloo.

In spite of the dampness of the long closed church, the condition of the canvas was excellent and its colors amazingly fresh. Its size precluded all hope of ultimate ownership, so we arranged for a professional photographer to prepare a colored transparency for use in the future book.

We pushed on to Edinburgh for a reading of the remaining letters. These had been moved from the lawyer's cellar to the House of Records and there, after four days of constant application, the work was completed, and seventy-three pages having to do with America's fur trade were selected for photostating as additions to the Missouri Historical Society's data on the subject. Although these later files were filled with fascinating material, they held never a word of the adopted Franc. I came then to the con-

clusion that he must have come into Stewart's family later than
1851.

Time now to return to London, and we decided to leave our
direct route to visit a great-grand-niece of Sir William's wife, Mrs.
John Sear, living in Malvern, England. Located through the efforts of faithful John Keay, she had earlier sent to me, through
him, a prized photograph of Lady Stewart.

Mrs. Sear knew so little of Sir William; I, so little of his wife.
With the assistance of the illustrations in *Across the Wide Missouri*, I sketched his years in America and told her what I had
learned of him through the Edinburgh letters. She in turn related
family anecdotes that threw some light on the private life of the
pair. Mrs. Sear's mother had carried a childhood memory of the
opening of a long-stored trunk holding Lady Stewart's wardrobe
and of the odor of musk that rose from the folds of a moss-green
velvet gown heavily banded with sable. I don't know why, but the
mention of sable surprised me. As we were leaving, our hostess
climbed upon a chair to reach the top shelf of her cupboard and
brought down four silver teaspoons, wedding gifts Lady Stewart
had given her grandmother. One of these she generously gave to
me.

Back in London, a brief visit to the office of the Hudson's
Bay Company Archives, where I found mention of Stewart in a
letter from Dr. John McLoughlin, the company's Director at Fort
Vancouver in Oregon.

Again at home in Kansas City, and with gratifying new material, there still remained that one blank, Franc Stewart. How tell
the story of Sir William without the true identity of his supposedly
adopted son? Could there have been a tie of blood?

In the spring of 1955 a letter from the new historical magazine, *American Heritage*, brought the startling news that they were
about to print an article relating to Stewart's trip west in 1843.
They asked to use several Miller sketches for illustrations.

Dashed by the realization that someone else was interested in
Stewart, I wrote to its author, Alvin Josephy, Jr., of *Time Magazine*, telling him we were about to present a book, *Prairie and
Mountain Sketches*, based upon the same subject as his article,
which he had titled, "First Dude Ranch Trip to the Untamed

West." His reply assured me that his primary interest was in the Nez Percé Indians and that the article would most certainly whet the interest of history readers in our coming book.

When his article appeared in February of 1956 I congratulated him upon its excellence. Shortly the long arm of coincidence took a hand.

We moved to California in mid-March and a week later a second letter arrived from Mr. Josephy, containing the solution of my final problem. In it he enclosed a letter received from a Mrs. Cecil Nichols Schelling, of Dickinson, Texas. She said she had seen his article and found special interest in it since her great-uncle, Franc Nichols Stewart, had lived as an adopted son of Stewart's at Murthly Castle, and upon his death in 1913 had willed a large number of his benefactor's personal possessions to members of her family. At long last, the final piece of my puzzle had dropped into place.

At Mrs. Schelling's invitation, I flew to Texas and under her roof, which had once sheltered Stewart himself, I heard Franc's story and saw many of the personal articles that he had carried away from Murthly. During the months following my visit I received from her a continual stream of photographs and anecdotes.

Delving into the past for history bits to make fresh contribution to the field is pure fun and it is like two things: gold mining and jigsaw puzzling. When a bright and shining truth comes to the surface, one knows the thrill of the seeker after nuggets and when a missing piece at last drops into place to complete the history picture, one has the satisfaction that no puzzle addict could possibly experience. He can only scramble his pieces into nothingness again, but those historical bits can be welded into an everlasting record of the wonderful doings of man.

Fearful that my welding might not do the material justice, and having made the acquaintance of a fellow enthusiast well versed in the art of writing books, a collaboration was formed with Odessa Davenport, of Hollywood. For her, the life story; for me, the account of how and where the material for the book was found.

Fortunately, Mrs. Davenport had already developed an interest in early fur-trade history. Finding the Daniel Ellis Conner

manuscript which chronicled happenings in the life of Joseph Reddeford Walker, the mountain man, she had brought it to print in
1956. Assisted by Donald J. Berthrong with its editing, it appeared
through the University of Oklahoma Press under the title of *Joseph
Reddeford Walker and the Arizona Adventure.* The book deals
with his life in the 1860s, but he had been a bourgeois at Fort
Laramie in the 1830s and in 1837 the artist Alfred Miller, sketching for Stewart, had twice depicted him.

Recalling the twelve-year gestation period of this book I find
myself wondering that so vast a number come to birth, and am
gratefully mindful of the assistance accorded me by so many.

My thanks on this side of the Atlantic to Margery Whyte,
who, when she brought the Miller sketches from their museum
storeroom, inadvertently started the whole project and then paved
the way for my acquaintance with various Miller relatives. Their
contribution to the artist's rough notes to the sketches and his letters written from Scotland put me on my path to Sir William's
story.

The Director of the Missouri Historical Society, Mr. Charles
van Ravenswaay, and his expert staff were most helpful in making
fur-trade ledgers and correspondence available.

From across the ocean, Houghton Mifflin's Grace Hogarth
made first approach to Murthly, paved the way for my acquaintance with Donald Steuart Fothringham. John Keay, Joseph Sim,
and Isabella Miller, worthy descendants of Sir William's tenantry,
contributed invaluable information, as did Ronald Cox and Mrs.
John Sear.

My collaborator, Odessa Davenport, wishes to express her
grateful thanks to Alice Wellman Harris for her encouragement,
and help with several knotty problems that presented themselves
in the writing of this book.

An especial benediction upon Alvin Josephy who, instead of
tossing the letter from Texas into his wastebasket, sent it on to
me. The continuing friendship of its writer, Cecil Nichols Schelling, I count as one of my personal blessings.

WHAT I FOUND IN TEXAS

by Mae Reed Porter

ই৵ The two most arresting Stewart items in the Schelling home, Nicholstone, were to me the chronometer that had marked time for his years of wanderings and the silver-crest-etched whisky flask that had supplied warmth for his "innards" and cheer for his spirit on many an occasion. As I rubbed the latter to a lovely sheen between my palms I found myself wishing that it and the time-piece with its chimes might, through some magic power, tell me of what they had seen as they accompanied their Lord.

There were numerous toilette articles of ivory with Stewart's crest and monogram. China in the blue onion pattern, silver cake plates, gold-lidded perfume bottles, heavily embroidered banquet cloths, and towels of hand-woven flax. A gilded bronze bowl on a six-inch pedestal with its grape pattern had been one of six such and was said to have been used on banquet tables in the days of King James.

A mahogany pier-glass and a corner what-not were the only articles of Stewart furniture in the house, but there were other pieces scattered among relatives and purchasers; a prayer-chair, a tall hall clock with chimes, and a four-poster bed of rosewood with head and foot boards of ancient tapestry.

There was an empty jewel box with a top of gold filigree that had once held a fortune in jewels. Among the gems had been an eight-carat sapphire, a pair of coffee-colored diamonds set in studs, and, most intriguing of all, the black diamond Franc had brought to Texas that had belonged to Mary, Queen of Scots, and which, it was said, she had worn to her beheading in 1587. It had been mounted in a ring of black onyx by a later Stewart in 1735 and in time had been inherited by Sir William. Franc had exhibited it at fairs and liked to have people try it on. In his last years, having need of money, he had sold it to a Mr. Alfred D. Smith, a bar-pilot. His wife, finding the clear white stone with its black stripes too gaudy, had placed it in the family bank vault. A newspaper clipping stated that with the settling of the Smith estate many years later, the stone had been sent to Hollywood to be sold. To date, inquiry there has been fruitless.

Among the trinkets there was a platinum-and-gold watch-chain, a topaz-mounted cocks' foot pin and a Cairngorm smoky-yellow stone-studded bracelet. There were medals—the Waterloo hanging from its ribbon of red and gray, with its date of June 18th, 1815: the Nova Scotia Baronetcy of red enamel; and, in a velvet-lined box, two coinlike medals conferred by the Pope.

A travel shawl of Stewart hunting plaid looked to have seen much service. Mrs. Schelling remembered a stags-head platter and Bristol blue vases removed by renters. There had been a Dresden vase three feet high and a mantel ornament of a lion and a snake with jeweled eyes which she had not seen since her childhood. Carpets of turkey-red and of gray, with violets in its pattern, had long since been worn beyond keeping.

Among the treasures was the two-volume *Red Book of Grandtully*, inscribed to "My Dear Adopted Son, Franc Nichols Stewart," and dated August 4, 1869. Of special interest was the account book of Sir William's housekeeper, Mother Dad, kept during the last three years of his life, for it showed that seven women were regularly employed, and four occasional ones to care for the needs of the two men residing in the hunting lodge, Dalpowie. Mother Dad's yearly wage was forty pounds, while the embroidery girl was content with two shillings a day.

A portrait, painted on a porcelain surface, of an aged face

under a bowler hat suggested that time had not been too kind to
Sir William.

Cecil Schelling carried me off to Galveston for getting dates
from Franc's gravestone and to ask at the Rosenberg Library that
we be allowed to see the hand-illuminated *Book of Hours* that,
purchased by Sir William in 1846, had been presented to it by
Franc in 1909.

We called upon ninety-two-year-old Mrs. Tudor Nichols,
whose husband had been executor of Franc's estate. Her water-
front hotel room contained several Stewart items. On her hand
I saw the five-carat diamond Sir William habitually wore upon his
little finger. There was an ivory miniature of a white-wigged Sir
John Drummond, and a very small bust portrait of Sir William in
his Waterloo regalia. Mrs. Nichols had known Franc and volun-
teered the information that he had brought from Murthly four
chests of silver, each as large as a bed.

Especially anxious to learn if there had been any personal
papers and books, I questioned her, but all hopes were dashed
by her reply, "Why, yes, but I kept them in my chicken house
and the flood of 1900 washed them all away."

For punishment, I told her that, had she any copies of Stewart's *Edward Warren*, they could be sold for $1000 apiece. My
visit to her had been made just in time, for a week later she died.

Mrs. Schelling and I visited two Galveston homes in which
there were a few large paintings from Murthly, but none were
Michelangelos, or DaVincis, or Millers. The canvases of supposed
importance had been carried to New York after Franc's death by
Tudor Nichols for sale, but lacking proof of their authenticity they
had, after two years, brought negligible amounts.

In a Nichols family album there were many photographs of
Franc. These, with numerous Stewart articles, were photographed
by a professional and I flew home, satisfied that I had, at long
last, come to the end of my path leading to a book on the life of
a most extraordinary gentleman.

Bibliography

BOOKS

Alter, Cecil. *James Bridger.*

Beckwourth, James P. *James P. Beckwourth, Scout and Pioneer.*

Bonner, T. D. *The Life and Adventures of James P. Beckwourth.*

Burdette, Charles. *The Life of Kit Carson.*

Butler, Captain Lewis. *Wellington's Operations on the Peninsula,* Vol. 2.

Cannon, Miles. *Waiilatpu, Its Rise and Fall.*

Catlin, George. *North American Indians.*

Chardon, Francis B. *Journal at Fort Clark, 1834–1839.*

Chittenden, Hiram M. *The American Fur Trade of the Far West.*

Chittenden, Hiram M. and Richardson, A. T. *The Life, Letters and Travels of Father Pierre Jean de Smet.*

Clark, S. A. *Pioneer Days of Oregon History,* Vol. I.

Coutant, S. A. *History of Wyoming.*

De Smet, Pierre Jean. *Oregon Missions and Travels.* 1847.

DeVoto, Bernard. *Across the Wide Missouri.*

Drury, Clifford M. *Elkanah and Mary Walker.*

D'Urban, Sir Benjamin. *The Peninsular War of Major General Sir Benjamin D'Urban.* Ed. by I. J. Rousseau.

Elliot, T. C. *The Coming of the White Women.*

290

Farnham, Thomas J. *Travels in the Great Western Prairies.*

Ferris, W. A. *Life in the Rocky Mountains.*

Field, Matthew. *Prairie and Mountain Sketches.* Ed. by Kate L. Gregg and John Francis McDermott.

Frémont, John C. *Report of the Exploring Expedition to the Rocky Mountains in the Year 1842, and to Oregon and California in the Years 1843–44.*

Garretson, Martin S. *The American Bison.*

Gray, W. H. *History of Oregon.*

Gregg, Josiah. *Commerce of the Prairies.*

Hafen, LeRoy R. *Broken Hand.*

Irving, Washington. *The Adventures of Captain Bonneville.*

Johnson, William H. *Route Across the Rocky Mountains.*

Journals of Lewis and Clark. Ed. by Bernard DeVoto.

Kennerly, William Clark. *Persimmon Hill.*

Larpenteur, Charles. *Forty Years a Fur Trader on the Upper Missouri.* Ed. by Elliot Coues.

Lavender, David. *Bent's Fort.*

Lennox, Edward Henry. *Overland to Oregon.*

Leonard, Zenas. *The Adventures of Zenas Leonard.*

MacGibbon, David. *Castellated and Domestic Architecture of Scotland,* Vol. I.

Marcus Whitman, Crusader. Ed. by Archer Butler Hulbert and Dorothy Printip Hulbert.

Marshall, William. *Historic Scenes in Perthshire.*

Millais, J. G. *Life and Letters of Sir John Millais.*

Millar, H. A. *Historic Mansions and Castles of Scotland.*

Montgomery, Richard Gill. *White-Headed Eagle.*

Morgan, Dale. *Jedediah Smith.*

Nevins, Allan. *Frémont, Pathmarker of the West.*

Parker, Samuel J. *Journal of an Exploring Tour Beyond the Rocky Mountains.*

Parkman, Francis. *The Oregon Trail.*

Pattie, James Ohio. *The Personal Narrative of James O. Pattie.*

Queen Victoria. *Life in the Highlands.*

Ross, Marvin. *The West of Alfred Jacob Miller.*

Russell, Carl P. *Guns on the Early Frontier.*

Russell, Osborne. *Journal of a Trapper.* Ed. by Aubrey L. Haines.

Ruxton, George. *Life in the Far West.*
———. *Adventures in Mexico and the Rocky Mountains.*
Sunder, John F. *Bill Sublette, Mountain Man.*
Tyrrell, Henry. *History of the War with Russia.*

JOURNALS, NOTES, PERIODICALS

Beidleman, Richard G. "Nathaniel Wyeth's Fort Hall," *Oregon Historical Quarterly,* September, 1937.
Crawford, Medorem. "Journal of Medorem Crawford," *Sources of the History of Oregon, Vol. 1, No. 1.*
Eells, Myra F. *Journal of Myra Eells.*
Journal and Letters of Marcus and Narcissa Whitman. *Oregon Pioneer Association Publications,* 1891.
Miller, Alfred Jacob. Notes on pictures in the Walters Gallery.
New Orleans Daily Picayune. 1843–44.
Scotsman, The. Newspaper files in Edinburgh, 1871.
St. Louis Weekly Reveille. 1843–44.

LETTERS, RECORDS, PRIVATE PAPERS

Anderson, William Clark. Journal, original manuscript. Courtesy of the Huntington Library.
Archives of Scotland. Stewart letters. Logiealmond correspondence.
Geyer, Charles. *Botanical Information, Notes On the Vegetation and General Character of the Missouri and Oregon Territory Made During a Botanical Journey From the State of Missouri Across the South Pass of the Rocky Mountains To the Pacific Coast During the Years 1843–44.* (Original in the Library of Congress, Washington, D.C.)
Hudson's Bay Records, London, England.
Kennerly, William Clark. Unpublished notes.
McLoughlin, Dr. John. Original letters, Fort Vancouver. Permission to use granted by the Hudson's Bay Company Record Society, London, England.
Miller, Alfred Jacob. Original letters to his immediate family while living in Murthly Castle and in London. Courtesy of the owner, L. Vernon Miller, of Baltimore.
Sublette Papers. Missouri Historical Society, St. Louis.

Index